# Forgotten Fleet

# Forgotten Fleet

## The Mothball Navy

Daniel Madsen

Naval Institute Press
Annapolis, Maryland

Naval Institute Press
291 Wood Road
Annapolis, MD 21402

Library of Congress Cataloging-in-Publication Data
Madsen, Daniel, 1960–
    Forgotten fleet : the mothball navy / Daniel Madsen.
      p.   cm.
    Includes bibliographical references and index.
    ISBN 1–55750–543–8 (alk. paper)
      1. United States.   Navy—Reserve fleets.   I. Title.
VA58.4.M34   1999
359.8'32'0973—dc21                              99-30936

Printed in the United States of America on acid-free paper ♾
06 05                          9 8 7 6

*Frontispiece:* The reserve fleet at San Francisco. *U.S. Naval Institute*

*To my wife Lorrinda, without whose love and support and advice this book would not be possible.*

# Contents

# Acknowledgments

Writing a book, especially a first book, is an endeavor not to be taken lightly. Still, it is an enormous amount of fun. One of the benefits is meeting people who are only too happy to help, who are happy for you, who tell you they cannot wait to see the book in print. I only hope their wait will have been worth it.

So very many people have helped along the way. My thanks are many; my fear is that I will leave someone out. To any who I omit, please know it was only a memory lapse on my part and certainly not a reflection of the value I placed on your help. Everyone I met and spoke with about this project was encouraging and helpful, many times in ways they could not fathom.

First, my thanks to Paul Wilderson of the Naval Institute Press, who first saw the merit in this project, encouraged me, and finally gave me the go-ahead to realize a life's ambition. My thanks to Sara Elder of the U.S. Naval Institute, who responded to every request for photographs promptly. No sooner had I requested a new batch of photographs to peruse than they were at my door.

J. Randall Baldini is the managing editor of the Press, and it was he who coordinated the entire process. He assigned Linda Magleby as the copy editor and the manuscript is much the better for it. Her kind words and suggestions were always welcome and immensely helpful. Kimberley A. VanDerveer was the production editor. To all who guided this novice, my most sincere thank you.

My thanks also to Jeff Bockert of the Battleship *North Carolina,* who was enthusiastic, helpful, and a pleasure to correspond with; and, to Aaron Schmidt of the Boston Public Library, who helped locate some photographs. A special thanks to Kathy O'Connor of the National Archives, Pacific Sierra Branch, who, oftentimes on short notice, pulled box after heavy box of documents and photographs out of a cavernous vault. A heartfelt thank you is due Randy Beasley, who kindly took me in his boat on a trip to the reserve fleet at Suisun Bay, a trip that spawned the idea for this book.

My very special thanks to my friends who constantly encouraged me; their support meant more than they could know. My family, of course, was the foundation upon which I was able to rely time and time again: my mother and father, sister, and brother; my two young sons whose dad was not able to play with them as often as he wanted to; and my wife, Lorrinda, who shouldered more than her share of the burden of running the household while I was off doing research or bent over the keyboard for hours on end, who endured my frustrations with patience, and who shared my joy. The book would not have been possible without her.

*Forgotten Fleet*

# Introduction

IN Boston harbor, swaying gently at her moorings, is the oldest commissioned warship in the United States Navy. Indeed, she is the oldest known warship afloat anywhere in the world. When she was built, George Washington was serving as the nation's first president. Her ship's bell, copper bolts, and spikes were supplied by none other than silversmith and midnight rider Paul Revere. Who among her original crew possibly could have imagined that sailors of the United States Navy would still be aboard her more than two centuries into the future? Eight times she was placed out of commission, "in ordinary" as it was called, the term deriving from the sixteenth-century English practice of paying for the cost of the ship's upkeep while she was out of service in the dockyard, out of the "ordinary" naval budget. Funds to keep the ship at sea, as well as the expense of building new ships, were raised by "extraordinary" taxes and levies (Rodgers, *Safeguard of the Sea,* 232). Eight times she was recommissioned, the last in 1940 at the order of President Washington's thirty-first successor, Franklin D. Roosevelt.

She has been berthed at Boston for more than sixty years now. She continues to draw huge crowds of visitors each year, much as she did at Charlestown in the 1930s (fig. 1). She has no hull number, no official designation or classification in the navy of the late twentieth century, but she is a source of inestimable pride to her countrymen and a tangible link with the nation's past. On Independence Day it is her guns, not those of a steel-hulled, computerized warship, that fire the national birthday salute. Her name, of course, is the USS *Constitution,* "Old

*Fig. 1. The*
Constitution *at*
*Charlestown Navy*
*Yard in 1933.*
National Archives,
Pacific Sierra Region

Ironsides" herself. That she has survived for over two hundred years is a tribute to many factors: her sturdy design and construction; the fame she earned in victories over the Royal Navy in the War of 1812; her numerous rebuilds; and the years she spent in ordinary, laid up in reserve, awaiting the next call to duty as more than two centuries passed.

The *Constitution* is, of course, a special case. She is a ceremonial ship, not a functional one, and has not been a viable warship for over 150 years. She was not held in reserve these many years in the hope she could serve again as a frigate in the United States Navy, but rather because the navy and the country could not bear to part with her. However, in modern times other ships would serve again as frontline warships many decades after they were laid down primarily because, when there was no longer an immediate need for them in the fleet, they were stored—"mothballed" rather than scrapped—in the event they should be needed again.

The most familiar concept of a fleet in hibernation, the long rows of silent, gray warships with igloos sprouting from their decks and paint peeling from their hulls, did not begin with the demobilization of the United States Navy after World War II, although the practice was refined then to a degree unequaled before. Great Britain, during its series of conflicts with France, Spain, Holland, and her former colonies in North America in the late eighteenth and early nineteenth centuries, routinely kept a huge fleet of ships in ordinary to be brought back into active service when the need arose, as it frequently did until the downfall of Napoleon in the muddy fields of Belgium in 1815. Moored in rivers, estuaries, and dockyards, these vessels were stripped of guns, upper masts, and supplies, and were maintained by a few officers and crewmen whose main job was to ensure that routine repairs were carried out and the ships did not spring leaks and sink outright where they rose and fell on the tide. Back into commission they went as hostilities broke out. Back into reserve they would go when peace again was declared. When the American Revolution ended, the Royal Navy placed 243 of its over four hundred ships into reserve. By the 1790s, when Britain and France went to war yet again, many of these ships would be taken from ordinary and recommissioned, allowing a far more rapid expansion of the fleet than if the ships had to be built from the keel up, though many needed extensive repairs. After the Peace of Amiens in 1802 ended hostilities (for a time) between Great Britain and France, the Royal Navy again went from 101 active ships of the line to thirty-two in just twelve months.

In its infancy, the United States had neither the resources nor the willingness to maintain an active or reserve fleet, and the navy ceased to exist, briefly, when independence was won in 1783. But the necessity for a maritime nation like the United States to maintain a navy became apparent within a decade. The British and French both sought to throttle the trade of the other with the resource-rich and militarily weak new nation across the Atlantic. Their vessels preyed incessantly on American shipping. In addition, there were pirates sailing off the North African coast demanding ransom and tribute in exchange for allowing American merchant ships to sail unmolested in the Mediterranean. In 1794 the Washington administration signed an act to provide for six frigates, ships that would be named the *Constitution, United States, President, Congress, Constellation,* and *Chesapeake,* and that would become the basis for a new United States Navy.

Time and again the navy was built up for war, the ships either broken up or taken out of commission when hostilities ended. All the original frigates were soon laid up in reserve only to be reactivated within a few years to deal with the Barbary pirates preying on American shipping. Then back they went to reserve. The *Constellation* was returned to ordinary from 1805 to 1812, the *Chesapeake* from 1803 to 1807. By the 1820s veterans of the War of 1812 were being laid up. The *Constitution* went into reserve. So did the *Independence,* the Navy's first seventy-four gun battleship of the line. The first time she decommissioned she spent fifteen years in ordinary and was destined to serve nearly a century in the United States Navy. Fighting ships of the Civil War spent their time in reserve, too. The *Hartford,* flagship of Admiral David Farragut at the battle of Mobile Bay, was laid up from 1868 to 1872 and again from 1890 to 1899. The *Kearsarge,* which sank the Confederate raider *Alabama* off Cherbourg, France in June 1864, was decommissioned and recommissioned many times after the war ended in 1865 before running aground off Central America nearly thirty years later. Throughout the years no specific, organized effort was made to preserve the ships laid up in reserve. They were simply docked or moored and left alone with possibly a caretaker crew aboard. Occasionally they were inspected. If they were still in good material shape and of use, so much the better; they stayed in the fleet and possibly hoisted a commissioning pennant again. If unfit or obsolete, they were stricken and broken up.

With the antiwar, antimilitary sentiment of the 1920s came shrinking military budgets, a reaction to the enormous expense of the arms race that had led to World War I and revulsion at the carnage that had ensued. Though the United States was spared destruction to its cities and farmlands, suffering far less grievously on the battlefield than the other major combatants, the people and Congress demanded a reduction in the size of the fleet in the aftermath of the "war to end all wars." Capital ships like the fifteen-thousand-ton battleship *Rhode Island* went into reserve.

Launched in 1904, she joined fifteen other battleships four years later as President Theodore Roosevelt's Great White Fleet made an unprecedented fourteen-month, forty-six-thousand-mile cruise around the world in a dramatic display of American naval reach and might. The *Rhode Island* saw duty in home waters in the Atlantic during World

*Fig. 2. The hospital ship* Comfort *and battleship* Rhode Island *in reserve at Mare Island in 1923.* National Archives, Pacific Sierra Region

War I before joining other ships such as the hospital ship *Comfort* in the reserve fleet at Mare Island in 1923 (fig. 2).

Many of the destroyers built during and shortly after World War I were decommissioned and laid up as part of the Washington Naval Treaty of 1922 that dictated fleet reductions and limited the size of capital ships. By 1926 there were eighty-five of these flush deckers at the Philadelphia Naval Shipyard reserve fleet basin and another seventy-six at San Diego (Friedman, *U.S. Destroyers*, 48). Side by side in long rows they lay, either tied to piers or moored to buoys offshore. They were referred to as the "Red Lead Fleet" because of the red, rust-preventing paint slapped on each ship when decommissioned (fig. 3). Their machinery was protected against corrosion (it was hoped) by thick layers of grease. Some of these destroyers stayed in reserve nearly twenty years; many returned to service and others were scrapped, having never again rejoined the fleet. In 1929 the navy decided sixty of its destroyers,

*Fig. 3. "Red Lead Row": decommissioned destroyers at the San Diego Naval Base in 1922. U.S. Naval Institute*

built with unsatisfactory boilers, would be scrapped. Their replacements would come from the Red Lead Fleet. Three active squadrons would be replaced by three reserve ones. The ships in ordinary were inspected; those in the best material condition after six or seven idle years at anchor were selected and towed from their berths by the ship they were to replace. They were moored to buoys or to a tender, and the work of fitting out commenced. Usable machinery such as torpedo tubes and even entire bridge structures was removed from these ships leaving the fleet and shifted to those coming out of reserve. Between January and June 1930, all sixty destroyers were replaced from the stocks of the reserve fleet. The cost of retaining them had proved to be a good bargain.

When another world war erupted in Europe in September 1939, less than a quarter of a century after the end of the last, a number of old flush deck destroyers were brought out of reserve to serve again. On 8 September 1939, President Roosevelt declared a state of limited national emergency and six days later the navy announced that forty of its 110 reserve destroyers would be recommissioned. Fifty others were later traded to the British, badly in need of convoy escort ships, in exchange for bases in the Caribbean. Many saw duty in what was called the Neutrality Patrol, safeguarding American and British convoys across the Atlantic against the menace of the German U-boat fleet. One of these was the USS *Greer*. Anonymous in the rows of identical warships anchored in the San Diego reserve fleet of the 1920s, the *Greer* saw new life when she recommissioned in 1930. The twenty-three-year-old destroyer, obsolete but still useful, found herself patrolling between Iceland and Newfoundland in September 1941, on the lookout for U-boats in the undeclared naval war between America and Nazi Germany. Trailing a submarine under attack by British aircraft, the *Greer* was in turn fired on by the U-boat. The torpedo missed and the old destroyer retaliated with depth charges. Pearl Harbor was still two and a half months away, but the *Greer* was already at war, becoming the first American warship to fire a shot in anger at a German vessel.

The navy's experience in activating reserve ships in 1940 and 1941 was an unhappy one. Ideally, the ships had been put away in three states of readiness, permitting reactivation in thirty, sixty, or ninety days. Some had been at anchor for twenty years and when it came time to actually bring these vessels back to life, it was often discovered that the time needed to place them back into service had tripled. Little money had been spent on the reserve fleet between the wars, and little energy had been expended in maintaining it. In many cases the condition of the ships was a direct result of the care taken when they were decommissioned. A thorough job of overhaul and machinery preservation invariably meant the ships were in better shape than those put away "wet." Over time, mildew, rust, and general deterioration had taken hold. Machinery was frozen or corroded, and exposed, rusted metal merely had been painted over. Obsolete equipment needed to be removed or replaced.

The British listed for their American allies and benefactors some of the deficiencies of the destroyers given to them: leaks in the hulls and bulkheads; rusted superstructures; electrical and plumbing systems corroded; a large number of machinery defects (Goodhart, *Fifty Ships*, 202). Most of the fifty destroyers traded to Britain served only a few years in escort duty before being relegated to training duties or even retirement. In May 1940, in the midst of the reactivations, the American secretary of the navy wrote that no one had fully realized the importance of maintaining these ships in a state of readiness so as to actually permit a timely reactivation. In short, the ships had not been cared for in their years tucked away in reserve. Inspections were infrequent and inadequate, concealing the true condition of the ships from the Navy Department as well as distorting the time needed for reactivation. Underlying these problems was the simple fact that funds had not been allocated to either study or carry out the proper inactivation and preservation of naval vessels.

In the midst of World War II, while the outcome was still in some doubt, the Navy Department was already making plans for an orderly transition of the fleet from war to peace, hoping to learn from bitter experience. The Bureau of Ships was advised by the office of the chief of naval operations in May 1944 to begin acquisition of enough material and equipment to place about one thousand ships, at a rate of approximately one hundred ships per month, in an inactive status. A year later, the expectation of the number of ships that would eventually be taken out of service had grown, and the Bureau of Ships was again advised to procure all that would be necessary to preserve what would be an ever-growing reserve fleet, a fleet of veteran warships eventually numbering in the thousands (Letters, RG 181).

The inactive ships in mothballs were a fleet held in readiness, composed of ships that were not merely obscure shapes in a bay, a river, or a quiet section of a bustling shipyard, but the very ships one could read about in books and newspapers—the ships that had made the history of the United States Navy. These fine ships had, in reality, two careers: one of action and service with the fleet, of endless patrols and cruises in war and peace, and another of retirement, of being maintained in the remote chance they would be used again in the nation's defense. These include famous ships and those known only by their crews, the ones still preserved for the appreciation and enjoyment of successive generations and the vast majority of those that are only a memory.

In the quiet, often-overlooked sections of the naval shipyards at Bremerton, Philadelphia, Mare Island, Boston, Charleston, and a handful of other locations such as Bayonne and Green Cove Springs, row upon row of bleak, gray vessels would lie at their moorings for years. The warships were quiet, still, lifeless, like an old house that had been boarded up and abandoned. Few passersby knew their names or cared to. No crewmen walked their decks or passageways. Hatches were sealed shut. Boilers were lifeless and cold. The wind whistled through masts and superstructures stripped of sensitive radar and communication equipment. Electrodes hung suspended over the rust-streaked sides into the oily waters, emitting a protective current of electricity to protect the steel hulls from the salt water. Belowdecks there was only the sound of the dehumidifiers, removing moisture from the air, retarding the buildup of rust and deterioration. Berthing areas, mess spaces, repair shops and radio rooms were frozen in time, looking exactly as they did when sealed years or decades before.

Standing on the deck of one of these warriors on a warm summer day with eyes closed, one could hear the long-forgotten voices of their crews. The names on the sterns were well known: *Enterprise* and *Missouri*. They were little known: *Fall River* and *Abner Read*. They belonged to ships with long distinguished careers in the active fleet: *Midway* and *St. Paul*. They belonged to ships decommissioned and put away almost as soon as they were completed: *Oregon City* and *Amsterdam*. These were and are the ships of the reserve fleet. The mothball fleet. The forgotten fleet.

# ONE  *From War to Peace*

O N 5 August 1945 the United States possessed the largest navy the world had ever known. The next day, as the city of Hiroshima disintegrated under an atomic bomb, the ships of America's fleet were suddenly too numerous, too old, too war-weary, or were just no longer needed for the peace to follow. In numbers, fighting power, and the logistical capability to deliver that power to any ocean on the globe, the navy had no equal. A month later, on 2 September, as the Japanese surrendered aboard the battleship *Missouri,* the navy also had no enemy to fight, no threat to justify its existence in such awe-inspiring numbers. The number of U.S. vessels flying a commissioning pennant in September 1945 was staggering: 20 fleet carriers (with another five near completion, including the huge new *Midway* and *Franklin D. Roosevelt*), 8 light carriers, 70 escort carriers, 23 battleships, 2 battle cruisers, 22 heavy cruisers, 48 light cruisers, 373 destroyers, 365 destroyer escorts, 240 submarines, as well as a vast number of auxiliary ships such as destroyer and submarine tenders, oilers, mine craft, repair ships, and amphibious craft of every description (*Pictorial History,* 374). Now the war was over and it was time for the country to decide what to do with this massive fleet. It was time for the fleet to come home from Japan, the Philippines, the Mediterranean and the South Atlantic, time for most of it to go into storage against the day when it might again be needed.

Plans for the fleet in the immediate postwar years were ambitious in terms of the numbers of ships the navy wanted to retain. There would in fact be three fleets, according to the new Chief of Naval Operations, the former commander in chief of the Pacific Fleet and of the Pacific Ocean Areas, Fleet Admiral Chester W. Nimitz. The first would be the active fleet: 4 battleships (the *Iowa* class), 13 carriers, 13 escort carriers, 8 heavy cruisers, 20 light cruisers, 139 destroyers, 40 destroyer escorts, 90 submarines, as well as all the auxiliary vessels needed to support them. There would also be a semiactive (and less expensive) reserve fleet: not a fleet in storage, but ships "in commission, in reserve," manned by partial crews, fully provisioned and supplied, ready to join the active forces as soon as additional personnel reported aboard. This reserve fleet would be made up of six battleships (the two *North Carolina*s and the four *South Dakota*s), five carriers, nine heavy cruisers, nine light cruisers, thirty-six destroyers, and a number of mine and patrol craft. The remainder of the two-ocean navy—ships that were not too old, too damaged in action to be repaired or obviously obsolete— were to be kept inactive, according to the admiral, with caretaker crews, "but in such excellent shape that they can be put back into full fighting condition within a few days or weeks at most" (*Pictorial History,* 374). These ships were to be out of commission and preserved. They were to be the mothball fleet.

As a result of the problems experienced before World War II with reactivating and recommissioning ships improperly or inadequately laid up in reserve, a careful plan called Operation Zipper was developed during the World War II years to adequately preserve selected ships (per- haps thousands of them), with an eye toward an eventual and speedy reactivation if necessary. The procedures for this were actually already in place, but were not adhered to in the 1920s and 1930s. The plan was that as each ship was ordered to be placed "out of commission, in reserve," it was to receive a careful overhaul so that its machinery, espe- cially its propulsion plant, was in good working order. Stores and spare parts would be inventoried, material and machine deficiencies logged so that a complete record would exist of each ship. Peeling camouflage war paint would be chipped and scraped away and a new coat of peacetime gray would be applied. The ship would be sealed against the weather, with any exposed equipment on deck either removed or covered and waterproofed. Dehumidifying equipment would be installed to circulate dry air throughout the interior. Then the vessel would be towed to a nest of similar ships in one of fifteen locations on both coasts and in the Gulf of Mexico and carefully monitored and tended by the specially trained sailors assigned to the reserve fleet.

The reality of the postwar years was far different from this vision of a three-tiered navy and the orderly reduction of a wartime fleet to a peacetime one. The sudden and unexpected end of the war had an unfortunate impact on these plans. Once the euphoria over the end of the fighting had died down, the American public quickly reverted to its peacetime life. "Remember Pearl Harbor!" was the wartime rallying cry, but, "Bring the boys home NOW!" became the peacetime chant. Congress and their voters demanded a hasty demobilization, and the navy reluctantly acquiesced. Sailors left the fleet by the tens of thousands, slowing the process of deactivating the ships. There were more vessels waiting to decommission than there were piers and dry docks to accommodate them. The most senior and trained personnel had acquired the most demobilization points and left the fleet in droves to return to their families and former lives. More and more work had to be contracted out to civilian shipyards, with a resulting loss in the quality of both the overhaul work and the recordkeeping. The civilians simply did not know the ships as well as the crews did, and the crews were abandoning ship as fast as the required points added up to the magic discharge number. Chipping and scraping gave way to sandblasting to speed the process of repainting and rustproofing the ships, but still they backed up in the stream, waiting to stand down. At the core of the matter, of course, was a paucity of funds. Neither Congress nor the public would pay for a large peacetime navy, which meant both men and machines had to leave the active fleet. There would be no active reserve and inactive fleet as the navy had envisioned. Instead, there would be an active fleet—far smaller than anticipated when the war ended—and a fleet of ships in hibernation, preserved and maintained as well as meager peacetime budgets would allow.

Uniform deactivation procedures and recordkeeping meant that whenever possible the navy tried to keep similar types and even classes of ships together as they were sealed, preserved, and towed to their reserve fleet berths. By the end of the 1940s most of the backbone of the Pacific Fleet's striking power, the *Essex*-class carriers, had been put in storage. Four went to the San Francisco Naval Shipyard, six to Bremerton; others went to Philadelphia and Norfolk and a pair to Bayonne. The light carriers came home to Philadelphia and Alameda. A few of the escort carriers, the "jeeps," went to San Francisco and San Diego, but most were divided up between the Boston Navy Yard and Tacoma. Five of the older battleships, as well as nine modern ones, survived the postwar scrapper's torch and were placed in mothballs. By the end of the decade only the *Missouri* remained in the fleet. The decommissioned *Baltimore*-class heavy cruisers all stayed on the West Coast, most in Bremerton, and a pair in San Francisco. The prewar cruisers all went to Philadelphia. Both of the large battle cruisers went to Bayonne. The *Brooklyn*-class light cruisers and about half of the *Cleveland*s went to the increasingly crowded reserve fleet basin at the Philadelphia Navy Yard. Eleven other *Cleveland*s tied up at San Francisco, a few more at Bremerton, and one at Boston, nestled among the escort carriers. There were almost four hundred destroyers in the fleet at the end of the war and most of the older ones went for scrap or were sunk as atomic bomb targets. Forty-six *Benson*s were decommissioned at the Charleston Navy Yard in 1946; the rest joined them there in mothballs in 1947. Over a hundred *Fletcher*s left the fleet in 1946, and another twenty the following year. Most went to San Diego, Long Beach, and Charleston. The destroyer escorts, too, left the fleet in droves. Many that were not scrapped en masse were stored with hundreds of amphibious craft at Green Cove Springs, Florida, tied four or five abreast to twelve piers that jutted out over a quarter mile into the warm waters of the St. John's River. Others went to San Diego, and ninety-six were in storage there by 1950. The submarines that had severed Japan's economic lifelines returned to New London and to Mare Island. The auxiliaries, tenders, oilers, repair ships, transports, cargo ships, and amphibious ships of every size and variety came home to be retired. One by one the ships were pushed and pulled into dry dock and alongside piers to go through the process of becoming mothballed.

As early as the end of World War I, the problems inherent in preserving ships built of steel against the ravages of time were quite well known. Iron corrodes when exposed long enough to moisture in the air. Not only is metal affected, but fabric, wood, and electrical equipment will in time deteriorate from the moisture present in the air. Pans of unslaked lime in various compartments of the old World War I flush deckers had helped remove moisture from the air and retard corrosion between the wars, but the difficult experience of reactivating ships for both World War I and for the period of national emergency before Pearl

Harbor demonstrated the need for a better method of preserving a reserve fleet.

There were three elementary problems associated with ship preservation:

1. Moisture caused corrosion, rust, mildew, and a general deterioration of whatever material was exposed to the air;

2. Removal of the equipment aboard a ship, such as radar, electronics, machinery, and electrical fittings was expensive, time consuming, and there was no guarantee that facilities ashore would provide better protection than the ship itself;

3. Coating machinery with a rust-preventing compound was not an adequate method of preservation, and in any case the thick preservative needed to be removed before the machinery could be made operational (Urdahl and Queer, *Pacific Marine Review,* 409).

The solution was fairly straightforward: use the hull of the ship as a storehouse for sensitive machinery; seal the hull and circulate dry air throughout the ship at a relative humidity of about 30 percent. The problem, both at the end of World War I and between the wars, was that the technology did not exist to adequately remove moisture from a large volume of air over a long period of time, and there was not a great deal of impetus or funding to develop a practical solution. The coming of World War II changed that. During the war, through experimentation, the Bureau of Ships determined that humidity of no greater than 30 percent was necessary to retard deterioration. Experience and observation provided the needed data to determine how much dehumidifying equipment was needed to provide the required level of dry air for a given-sized vessel.

The procedure was simple and effective. Once a ship received orders to begin deactivation, it would be overhauled. Machinery such as boilers, blowers, pumps, fuel lines, reduction gears, and evaporators was thoroughly inspected and cleaned, and a thin film of rust preventative applied. The preventative was a two-part mixture of a solvent such as kerosene and a wax-like solid that was dissolved in the solvent. When the preventative was sprayed on exposed metal or machinery, the solvent evaporated, leaving the protective coating on the metal. This dissolved into the working parts of the equipment once it was reactivated and did not need to be removed. The preventative came in three grades:

Fig. 4. A shipyard worker sprays a liquid plastic solution to seal a gun mount.
National Archives, Pacific Sierra Region

grade one was used on exposed metal, while grades two and three were used on machinery belowdecks as a backup in case the dehumidifiers failed to keep the air dry enough to prevent corrosion. The ship would be fumigated to rid it of any vermin. The hull would then be sealed from the weather, though the seal did not have to be airtight. Hatches were locked shut, portholes closed. On the five-inch mounts tape or a thin netting was stretched from the mount to the barrel, forming a lattice framework. The same covered the antiaircraft weapons and other exposed equipment such as winches on the weather decks. Then a liquid plastic solution, a webbing agent, was sprayed on, making a rubbery casing that dried between the strips of tape (fig. 4). Finally, three layers of a strippable coating were applied, each layer a different color: blue, red, and yellow. When dry these layers sealed the gaps where moisture could leak in and dry air could escape. A small hole was left where heat could be applied to dry the paint. Silica bags were placed inside and then a Lucite window sealed the last hole. This was repeated anywhere above deck where equipment might be corroded and rusted by exposure to the weather. Within the ship, belowdecks, and inside the superstructure, hatches would be opened to facilitate the movement of air. Belowdecks, of course, great care was needed in determining which passageways and watertight doors would remain open, lest a leak below the waterline spread quickly throughout the ship and sink her at her moorings.

The selection of open and closed hatches divided the ship into zones. Dehumidifying units containing two beds of a solid drying agent, or desiccant (either silica gel or activated alumina) were then set up. One bed was used to absorb moisture from the air, while the other was off line being reactivated with electrically heated warm air. The absorbed water was then evaporated into the warm air and pumped outside the ship. These units were self-contained and could operate indefinitely. Only one unit was needed for a destroyer; cruisers needed three, while battleships and fleet carriers required eight to handle the huge internal volume of air to be kept dry. The air was pumped throughout the ship using the fire mains that had been drained of water. Initially, portable units and cans of desiccant were used in the ship in a predrying period, which allowed the crew to remove excess moisture from the bilge, piping, and machinery that normally contained water. There was an initial drying period of from four to six weeks, when moisture was removed by the dehumidifiers from clothing, life jackets, fabric, rope, mattresses—anywhere where moisture could have collected. Once the air inside the ship reached an average humidity of 30 percent, the machinery automatically maintained that low humidity, using sensors located throughout the ship to take a reading of the air every twelve hours or so. If needed, the fans were switched on and the humid air cycled through the drying units. Sometimes dry air from other parts of the ship was pumped in as well. Where the fire mains could not effectively maintain a flow of dry air (in tanks and voids for instance), or where the watertight integrity of the ship was compromised by the opening of hatchways, large perforated cans filled with desiccant were used.

Reserve fleet crewmen assigned to monitor each group of vessels in the inactive fleet could check the readouts of the internal atmosphere at any time, analyzing the performance of the units. The dehumidifiers proved quite economical. Since the ships were sealed from the effects of outside air, and 70 percent of the moisture had been removed from the atmosphere inside the ship, the machinery needed only to operate when the ambient humidity became too great. The power cost for a unit maintaining a $7 million destroyer came to about one hundred dollars a year. A battleship, with a price tag of nearly $100 million, would have an electrical bill of a little over one hundred dollars a month (Urdahl and Queer, *Pacific Marine Review,* 456). This was quite an inexpensive insurance policy. Dehumidification was not the only means of preserving these ships for the future, but was certainly a major factor in husbanding valuable and relatively new ships against the day they might be used again. Less than five years after the end of the Pacific war, this foresight would pay off.

Pictured is the New York Group of the Atlantic Reserve Fleet at Bayonne, New Jersey in the 1950s (fig. 5). Bayonne was one of the smaller reserve fleet units, but contained some of the more famous World War II fighting ships. At the top of the annex are a pair of *Cleveland*-class cruisers and a *Juneau*-class antiaircraft cruiser. Along the wall at the left are the large battle cruisers *Guam* and *Alaska* with another *Juneau*. Astern of the large cruisers are the battleships *Washington* and *North Carolina*. Outboard of the trio astern of the battleships is the cruiser *Fargo*. The carrier to the right is the *Franklin* and behind her is the bow of the *Enterprise*.

The first of a new generation of United States battleships, the *North Carolina* was commissioned eight months before Pearl Harbor. Eighteen years had passed since the last battleship, the *West Virginia*, had entered the fleet. In appearance, the new battleship was radically different from

Fig. 5. *Aerial view of the Bayonne reserve fleet in the 1950s. Courtesy of* Battleship *North Carolina*

her predecessors. She was a hundred feet longer than the older warships, yet displaced only about another three thousand tons. Her boilers and geared turbines produced almost four times the horsepower of the turboelectric-driven *West Virginia*.

On 11 July 1942 the *North Carolina* sailed down the narrow channel leading into Pearl Harbor, the first of the reinforcements for the battle line crippled seven months before. Reminders of that terrible defeat were still plainly visible. The upturned hull of the capsized *Oklahoma* still lay in the water off Ford Island, a tomb to four hundred of her crew. The emasculated hulk of the proud *Arizona*—her toppled foremast now cut away by salvage crews and almost one thousand of her crew still buried in her submerged hull—leaked oil a few hundred yards away. Ashore and aboard the ships of the Pacific Fleet in the harbor cheers rang out from the sailors as the *North Carolina* moved slowly into the harbor. The cheers were for this huge new battlewagon that would help them exact revenge on the Japanese.

Two months later, a Japanese sub put a halt to the *North Carolina*'s war. Submarine *I-19* slammed a torpedo into the port side of the new battlewagon. It blew an almost six-hundred-square-foot hole in her hull below number one turret and the flash from the warhead's explosion penetrated the handling room beneath the turret. Had one of the magazines caught fire, the resulting explosion would have been fatal. The *North Carolina* nearly became the third American battleship sunk in the war. She was repaired, however, at Pearl Harbor and soon rejoined the fleet.

Both the *North Carolina* and her sister ship were placed in reserve after the war at Bayonne. Like the *South Dakota*s, the pair were considered for modernization while in mothballs to increase their speed and allow them to keep up with carrier task forces, but this process was far too expensive and the project was abandoned. From 1947 to 1960 they lay idle. The *Iowa*s returned to service, but neither the *North Carolina* nor the *Washington* was called back to duty. The *Washington* was towed from her longtime berth at Bayonne and scrapped. The fate of the *North Carolina* was a happier one. Interest in her preservation by the citizens of her home state was such that the "Showboat" was donated to that state; she was dedicated as a war memorial at Wilmington on 3 October 1961. She still resides there, in excellent condition, looking as ready for sea as when first commissioned more than fifty-five years ago.

Shown in front of the pair of battleships along the long wall are two unique warships built for the navy during the war (fig. 6). From the air they distinctly resemble the battleships in size and tower superstructure. Longer than the *North Carolinas*, much longer than the *South Dakotas*, though displacing less than either, they were the large cruisers *Alaska* and *Guam*, sometimes referred to as battle cruisers. They were a cross between the conventional eight-inch-gunned heavy cruiser and the battleship, less heavily armed and armored than a battleship, more so than a cruiser. Their main armament was the twelve-inch gun and, in fact, the *Alaska* class had been designed partly as a kind of supercruiser to effectively counter the Japanese eight-inch heavy cruisers. Six were authorized, all named for territories of the United States: *Alaska, Guam, Hawaii, Philippines, Puerto Rico, Samoa*. Only two were completed, though the third, the *Hawaii*, was very nearly finished when construction was suspended on her in the late 1940s.

The lead ship of the class, the *Alaska*, was laid down ten days after Pearl Harbor and commissioned two and a half years later. The *Guam* entered the fleet about the same time, and both joined the Fast Carrier

Fig. 6. *The moth-balled carrier* Franklin *as seen from the stern of the* North Carolina. *Courtesy of Battleship* North Carolina

Task Force in the early months of 1945. When the *Franklin* was bombed and nearly sunk, both the *Guam* and the *Alaska* were part of a small task force assigned to protect and escort the carrier out of danger. They would meet again when all three were quietly towed into New York harbor and moored at Bayonne a few years later.

The *Franklin* was the fourth *Essex*-class carrier commissioned, serving only three years before being laid up for good but seeing more of the war than many ships that served much longer. She is astern of the two *North Carolina*s (fig. 6). While in mothballs she bore none of the scars from wounds suffered only a few years before. She joined the Pacific Fleet in June 1944 and her air group began hitting the Marianas in preparation for the assault there. She was hit by a suicide plane, then took a bomb hit, then was again crashed by kamikazes, all in October of that year. The last onslaught was the worst and sent her back to Puget Sound for repairs. She returned to the war in early 1945.

Shortly after 0700 on 19 March 1945, while the *Franklin* was launching aircraft for strikes against Japanese shipping in the home islands, a lone enemy aircraft evaded detection by the task group's escorting battleships, cruisers, and destroyers, screamed in low over the carrier's flight deck, and dropped a pair of bombs. One exploded on the flight deck, the second in the hangar. Both sites were jammed with fully fueled and heavily armed aircraft. The result was a catastrophic series of fires and explosions as gasoline burned and bombs, rockets, and ammunition exploded. Casualties aboard the 872-foot carrier were horrific: 724 men died in the smoke and flames, another 265 were wounded, and 1,700 more sailors were fished out of the water after abandoning ship or being blown overboard. The list of dead would have rivaled that of the *Arizona* at Pearl Harbor had not Lieutenant Donald Gary discovered three hundred sailors trapped in a mess compartment below the hangar and, in a series of daring trips through smoke-filled passageways, led all of them to safety. Intense training in damage control, learned from the bitter experiences of ships damaged earlier in the war, saved "Big Ben," though she took on a dangerous list to starboard from the weight of firefighting water flooding her upper decks (fig. 7). After nearly being sunk only fifty miles off the enemy coast, she limped slowly and painfully to New York via Pearl Harbor and the Panama Canal, a voyage of over twelve thousand miles. Her burned flight deck and shattered hangar were graphic reminders of the war most believed had another year or two to go.

The *Franklin* was repaired, for at the time no one knew the war would last but five more months. Plans were under way for the invasion of Japan (of the island of Kyushu in November and Honshu the following March), and every vessel, especially the carriers, would be needed. Then came the mushroom clouds over Hiroshima and Nagasaki and in 1947 the *Franklin* went into reserve in New York harbor, repaired and rebuilt. She was in good condition, but was not selected with other veteran *Essex* carriers after the war for upgrading to operate the new jet aircraft under development. She lay in reserve at Bayonne throughout the rest of the 1940s, 1950s, and the early 1960s, never again to be called to service.

Pictured is the *Enterprise* (fig. 8). Prior to 1938 six other vessels of the United States Navy had carried the name: two served in the Revolution; another in the War of 1812; a fourth was commissioned before the Civil War, a fifth after; the sixth was a nondescript motorboat that served during World War I. But none ingrained themselves in the public's imagination or naval lore like the seventh. She gave her name to

*Fig. 7. The* Franklin *on fire and listing after being bombed fifty miles off Japan in 1945. U.S. Naval Institute*

another aircraft carrier, a space shuttle test vehicle, and a series of fictional spaceships in two of the most popular television and movie series of all time. But it was CV-6, the "Big E" of World War II, that captured the imagination.

She very nearly became another casualty at Pearl Harbor and her war career might possibly have been finished before it began. She was on her way back to Pearl from Wake after delivering a deckload of marine fighters and was due in on the morning of the seventh; heavy seas delayed the refueling of her escorting destroyers and slowed down the task force, so she arrived after the attack.

In June, her planes, along with those of the recently arrived *Yorktown,* surprised and sank four enemy carriers at Midway, and in one afternoon changed the course of the Pacific war. Then it was on to the South Pacific where she was hit three times by bombs that killed sev-

*Fig. 8. The* Enterprise, *somewhere at sea. U.S. Naval Institute*

enty-four and wounded ninety-five of her crew. Repairs at Pearl Harbor took a month, and then she sailed below the equator to the Santa Cruz Islands where two bombs killed another forty-four of her sailors and wounded seventy-five more. There was no time for extensive repairs, since the *Enterprise* was the sole remaining American carrier in the war: the *Saratoga* was at Pearl Harbor being repaired after a Japanese sub hit her with a torpedo. The Big E was patched up in New Caledonia by the repair ship *Vestal* and then quickly sailed back to the Solomons to help sink sixteen Japanese vessels in the naval battles for Guadalcanal. In early 1943 she steamed to Puget Sound for an overhaul after a stop in Hawaii that saw Admiral Nimitz bestow a Presidential Unit Citation (PUC) on her for work throughout the previous year. From then on she participated in every significant fleet action of the war, winning twenty battle stars in all and a Navy Unit Commendation to go with her PUC, the only carrier to win both awards. She suffered numerous hits and the last, a spectacular kamikaze hit that blew her forward elevator four hundred feet into the air, knocked her out of the Pacific. She was repaired, but by then the war had ended, and so had her days in the fleet.

She was the sole survivor of her class, her sister ships *Yorktown* and *Hornet* going to the bottom in the first year of the war. Thousand of visitors came up her gangway on Navy Day in October 1945 as the navy celebrated its achievements and victory in the war ended only a few weeks before. Then, like so many others, she was stripped of her radar and antennas, her twenty-millimeter guns were removed and her forty-millimeters covered. Her compartments were dried out, she was sealed, given a coat of navy gray paint to cover the rust and bare steel, and then tied to a lonely dock at Bayonne. No longer was she part of the mighty and proud Fast Carrier Task Force. Now she was a member of "the New York Group, Atlantic Reserve Fleet"—just another relic. The Korean War would erupt in 1950 and the *Essex* carriers would be pulled from reserve to join the conflict. But not the *Enterprise*. She was too small, too weary from months and years of near-constant wartime duty. She was only three years old when the United States was drawn into the Pacific war, yet the war years made her old before her time, like the sailors who served aboard her while the bombs and suicide planes tried to sink her.

In 1953 she was reclassified as an antisubmarine support carrier, but it was a change in name only. No work was ever done on her, no modifications made to enable her to hunt down Soviet subs. By 1956 it was obvious that she was surplus. When the navy announced its plans to sell the *Enterprise* for mere scrap metal, a brief effort was made to save her as a war memorial. No finer ship could have been selected for preservation, no finer example found of the dark days of 1942, of holding the thin defensive line against the Japanese, of the turning point at Midway, of the relentless drive of the fleet back across the Pacific. But over a decade had passed since the end of the war, since Secretary of the Navy James Forrestal had recommended to President Truman that "the *Enterprise* should be retired permanently at some proper place as a visible symbol of American valor and tenacity in war" (Stafford, *Big E,* 504). Ike was in his second term in the White House in 1957, and though he signed legislation to have the *Enterprise* towed to Washington, D.C., the public donations to carry this out were not forthcoming. There was little public interest in buying this old ship that had lain forgotten in the mothball fleet in New Jersey for so long, so far

*Fig. 9. The* Enterprise *at the New York Naval Shipyard. The carrier behind her is the new* Independence. *Naval Historical Center*

*Fig. 10. "Battleship X," the USS* South Dakota *under way. U.S. Naval Institute*

removed from her glory days. The fund-raising effort failed, despite a plea from "Bull" Halsey, and the navy had no choice but to consign her to the scrapper's torch for $1,561,333.00 (Pawlowski, *Flat-tops and Fledglings,* 64).

She is pictured at the New York Navy Yard in 1958, awaiting a tow to the breakers (fig. 9). Majestic and imposing during the war, the *Enterprise* looks old and shrunken here. The carrier behind her fitting out is the last of the *Forrestal*-class supercarriers, the *Independence.* Ironically, four decades later the home port of the *Independence* would be in Japan. As the *Independence* took her place in the fleet, and as another, even bigger flattop that would carry the name *Enterprise* was under construction, the old war veteran, CV-6, World War II's most famous aircraft carrier, was torn apart little by little along the Hackensack River.

This is one of the Big E's escorts during the war (fig. 10). She was "Battleship X" in the press and the "Big Bastard" to her crew, but she was commissioned in March 1942 as the USS *South Dakota,* lead ship of a class of four thirty-five-thousand-ton, twenty-seven-knot battleships. Unique among the fast battleships, she carried sixteen five-inch guns as her secondary armament, rather than twenty. The extra space and weight savings were used for flag quarters, since she was built and served as a fleet flagship. On 26 October 1942, while shielding the *Enterprise* during the battle of the Santa Cruz Islands, her sharpshooting antiaircraft gunners destroyed an amazing twenty-six Japanese aircraft. Almost three weeks later off Guadalcanal, the battleship *Kirishima* and cruisers *Takao* and *Atago* pounded her with gunfire at a range of under three and a half miles. She took forty-two hits from large-caliber guns that killed thirty-eight sailors and wounded another sixty, while the battleship *Washington* pummeled the *Kirishima* so badly she had to be scuttled. In the words of naval historian Samuel Eliot Morison, Battleship X had been "lucky to escape alive," in large part because of the excellent gunnery of the *Washington*. After repairs, the *South Dakota* returned to the war, earning thirteen battle stars, and was present in Tokyo Bay flying the flag of Admiral Chester Nimitz when the Japanese surrendered aboard the *Missouri*.

*Fig. 11. The lonely South Dakota after a decade and a half in mothballs. U.S. Naval Institute*

The *South Dakota* was laid up in 1947. Though briefly considered for a major conversion to increase her speed from twenty-seven-and-one-half knots to thirty knots (which would have allowed her to keep formation with the *Iowa*-class battleships and the carriers, but would have necessitated the removal of her aft sixteen-inch turret), she remained mothballed at the Philadelphia Naval Shipyard for fourteen years. Too big to be moored in the reserve fleet basin behind the shipyard, she was tied up at one of the piers along the Delaware River at the south end of the shipyard, along with the *California,* the *Tennessee,* and the old *Olympia.* She is shown in 1962, looking stately yet forlorn and forgotten (fig. 11). Her tall, compact superstructure towers over the tugs pushing her to her gravesite. Some of the young sailors in the foreground were probably in grade school when the *South Dakota*'s now silent main battery lashed out at the Japanese fleet in the Solomon Islands, half a world away and a generation gone by. Despite her exploits in the war, there was no place for the *South Dakota* in the navy of the 1960s, and she was stricken and sold for scrap. She was not forgotten, though. Much of the *South Dakota* was preserved by former crew members and citizens of the state, and today there is a fine memorial to her in Sioux Falls.

Another ship of the once-mighty Pacific fleet, the USS *Birmingham* is anonymous in a photograph of the San Francisco Navy Yard in the late 1940s (fig. 12). From the air, even from the piers, there is nothing visible to distinguish her from her sisters. Paint her hull number on another, and few would be the wiser, for she wears the same peacetime gray paint, the same sleepy, abandoned look as both the others of her class and the lone *Baltimore*-class heavy cruiser lying side by side at the newly built piers south of the dry docks. Some of these cruisers saw hardly any of the war; some saw more than their share, more than any ship and crew should have to. One of them was CL-62: the USS *Birmingham,* the "Mighty B."

The *Birmingham* fought hard and often. Fresh from her shakedown cruise, she headed for the Mediterranean where her six-inch guns poured fire into the German positions near Licata, Sicily as American and British forces invaded the island. She then transferred to the Pacific and was promptly torpedoed and bombed off Empress Augusta Bay. Five thousand miles to Pearl Harbor she steamed with two torpedo holes in her hull. Returning to the fleet in the spring of 1944, she then fired over eighteen thousand rounds of six- and five-inch shells into Japanese-held Saipan, Guam, and Tinian as the islands were retaken by marines. Then came the battle of Leyte Gulf. When the light carrier *Princeton* was mortally damaged and set ablaze by Japanese aircraft on 24 October 1944, the *Birmingham* came alongside to help. Many of the cruiser's crewmen came topside and rigged firefighting gear, their hoses spraying streams of water as Captain Thomas Inglis skillfully brought his cruiser alongside the carrier's port side and, using a line and his engines, kept the *Birmingham* close until all but one of the *Princeton*'s fires were out (fig. 13). The one remaining fire was near her after magazine.

When enemy aircraft approached, Inglis cleared the area to give his ship room to maneuver, then headed back to the *Princeton* a second time. As another line was made secure between the ships, the *Princeton*'s torpedo magazine exploded without warning. Like wheat before a scythe, half of the *Birmingham*'s crew were cut down instantly as fragments from the carrier sprayed across the deck and superstructure. As the *Birmingham*'s captain wrote, "The carnage on the *Birmingham* was too terrible to describe adequately. . . . blood so thick on the decks that

*Fig. 13. The Birmingham comes alongside the Princeton, shortly before the latter exploded. U.S. Naval Institute*

sand had to be spread to prevent slipping." Two hundred sixty-seven sailors died and another 426 were wounded. Yet the Mighty B's crew carried on. Captain Inglis expressed his pride: "Where confusion and hysteria might have been excusable there was nothing but order, coolness, and selfless devotion to duty, ship, and shipmates." (Inglis, *Shipmate*). The *Birmingham*'s wounds, or at any rate her visible and tangible ones, were repaired in San Francisco and she returned to the Pacific, only to be crashed by a kamikaze off Okinawa in May 1945, killing another fifty-one of her crew and wounding eighty-one more. After the war this battered and bloodied ship returned to San Francisco to be deactivated, preserved, and quietly moored among identical warships in the quiet waters of the Bay, nothing distinguishing her from her sister ships, nothing indicating the ordeal she had gone through in the Pacific.

The USS *Intrepid*, moored between the *Birmingham*'s sisters and the battleship *Iowa* (fig. 12), was no stranger to San Francisco. Three times she steamed under the Golden Gate Bridge for repairs during the war, having seen more than her share of combat. The "Fighting I" was torpedoed in February 1944 and was then hit by a kamikaze in October of that year. A month later she was hit twice within twenty minutes by kamikazes. Her ventilation trunk, running most of the length of the ship, spread the dense smoke throughout and fires erupted everywhere. Sixty-nine sailors were dead and thirty-five wounded before the fires were out. Her flight deck and arresting gear were so mangled that the seventy-five aircraft she had in the air were forced to land on other carriers. Badly damaged, she was out of action for months, and when she returned to the Pacific, was hit yet again by another kamikaze in April 1945, knocking her out for most of the rest of the war. Bruised and battered but repaired, the *Intrepid* quickly left the peacetime fleet. In early December 1945 she was in Yokosuka, Japan with the occupation forces and just eight months later she was placed "in commission, in reserve" in San Francisco. For half a year she was overhauled before her commissioning pennant was lowered, her crew marched off, and she was finally left alone save the ships she served with, now moored nearby. One of those was the only battleship ever to be mothballed in San Francisco, the USS *Iowa.*

The *Iowa* was the first of her class, the last battleships to be built by the United States. *Iowa*'s catapults have been removed, as have her twenty-millimeter-antiaircraft guns just aft of number three turret (fig. 12). Cocoons have been placed over her forty-millimeter mounts, and her smokestacks have been sealed tight. The *Iowa,* for now, is a sleeping giant.

Task Force 38, the fast carrier striking force of the Pacific Fleet, rides serenely at anchor at Ulithi Atoll in a photograph taken in early December 1944 (fig. 14). The *Lexington* is at left, her hull and superstructure painted a dark navy blue. In dazzle camouflage of blue, black and varying shades of gray, from front to back, are the *Wasp, Yorktown, Hornet, Hancock,* and *Ticonderoga.* Also visible are several *Independence*-class light carriers, which were normally teamed with the larger fleet carriers in task groups. Missing from this shot are the *Enterprise* and the *Essex.* The *Franklin, Intrepid,* and *Bunker Hill* were all undergoing repair or alteration. The *Saratoga* was at Pearl Harbor training night fighters with the *Ranger.* The *Randolph* and the *Shangri-La* had just been commissioned but were not yet ready to join the fleet. The might of American naval aviation is apparent in this photo taken by a plane from the *Ticonderoga.* There were over six hundred aircraft on these carriers alone, not including the smaller air groups aboard the light and escort carriers. The big flattops were supported by six of the light carriers, eight modern battleships, ten cruisers, and approximately

Fig. 14. "Murderers Row": the carriers of Task Force 38 at Ulithi Atoll in December of 1944. U.S. Naval Institute

fifty destroyers. It was this force that was tasked with locating and destroying the Japanese fleet. The *Essex*, lead ship of the new twenty-seven-thousand-ton carriers, arrived in the Pacific in the spring of 1943. Within a year nine more had been commissioned. By the end of the war there would be seventeen in the fleet, and the class would eventually number twenty-four.

Shortly after the photograph was taken in the peaceful waters of Ulithi, the Third Fleet under Admiral William "Bull" Halsey, flying his flag on the *New Jersey,* sortied to cover General Douglas MacArthur's army landings at Lingayen Gulf in the Philippines. A week later it was Mother Nature, not the Japanese, who was the enemy as the fleet was battered by typhoon Cobra. Violent winds whipped up the sea and rain poured out of the sky. From the bridge of the *New Jersey* Halsey was unable to make out the bow of the battleship, so blinding were the rain and spray. The *Hancock* rolled violently enough that she took water over her flight deck, and the log of the *Wasp* recorded mountainous seas and wind gusts over one hundred knots. Though the big carriers rode out the storm well, some smaller vessels did not. The light carrier *Langley* rolled seventy degrees to starboard—almost on her side—and the cups on her anemometer blew off when the gale reached 105 knots. On the *Monterey* the planes lashed down in the hangar broke loose, smashed into each other, and caught fire. The flames spread below the hangar deck level, but within forty minutes were brought under control. The escort carrier *Altamaha* carried sixty-five replacement planes for the fleet carriers, but when the typhoon was over only twenty-two were left, the rest having being blown overboard or damaged beyond repair. Three destroyers—the *Spence,* the *Hull,* and the *Monaghan*—low on fuel and thus poorly ballasted, rolled over and sank in the storm, drowning over eight hundred sailors. But for the survivors the biggest threat still lay ahead, despite the fact that the Japanese Navy had ceased to exist as a potent offensive weapon. The menace was one they had tasted in October and would feel the full effects of in the new year. It was the threat they feared most and understood least: the kamikaze.

Some of those same carriers are photographed in mothballs at Bremerton in 1948 (fig. 15). The vessels look identical, but they are unique. Each name evokes images of separate scenes of the war. Each awaits a different fate. They are lonely, yet peaceful, not majestic as when photographed in their war paint, yet noble in retirement. Each was populated by over thirty-five hundred men, each a small town but probably bigger than many of the hometowns of the men aboard, with barbershops, diners, ice cream stands, small stores, and movies if they were lucky. These ships had what small towns do not have: bombs, torpedoes, huge tanks of gasoline and fuel oil, and rows of guns lining the flight deck.

Now, only maintenance sailors stand watch over the carriers. "Vulture's Row," the platform along the island where crewmen could watch the aircraft take off and land, is empty. So are the gun tubs. The twenty-millimeter machine guns, more noisemakers than killers of aircraft, are gone. The aircraft are gone. Most of the crewmen who were not among the hundreds lost in the last seven months of combat off the Philippines, Iwo Jima, and Okinawa have gone home to San Francisco, California; Cornersville, Kentucky; Brooklyn, New York; and Elk

Rapids, Michigan, to resume interrupted lives. Some of the former crewmen go to school, some find jobs and begin families. Some would be changed profoundly by their war experience. Others would think it the adventure of their lives. For some it was a horror best forgotten, but many would have to cope with debilitating injuries or disfiguring burns.

The flattops that were once the backbone of the mighty Pacific Fleet are now idle and silent, nestled into piers at the rain-swept shipyard. The rain is gentle compared to the deluge they endured a few years before. Typhoons no longer tear aircraft from their decks. Tracers no longer arc skyward from the guns now sealed under protective cocoons. Radar antenna no longer scan the sky, and sailors no longer keep nerve-wracking vigilance for tiny specks in the sky that mean enemy aircraft, bombs falling into the sea and smashing into flight decks, or torpedoes tearing huge holes beneath the waterline to let in the sea. A carrier at sea is a floating bomb. Her most valuable asset, her aircraft, is also her biggest liability. The gasoline they burn, the bombs, rockets, torpedoes, and bullets they carry can mean death to the enemy, but also can mean death to their own ship.

In Puget Sound in 1948 suicide pilots no longer dive their bomb-laden aircraft into the flight decks, hangar decks, berthing, and mess areas. Fires no longer rage out of control. Smoke, thick, black, and choking no longer fills escape paths belowdecks, nor does it climb skyward announcing to all that another carrier has been hit, that more men are dying. The camouflage paint has been covered over in peacetime gray. Dehumidifying units pump dry air into the hangar decks, the superstructure, repair shops, pilot ready rooms, boiler, and engine rooms, preserving the valuable carriers for a day they may be needed again. The enemies now are rust, mildew, and water in the bilge.

From front to back the carriers are the *Essex, Ticonderoga, Yorktown, Lexington, Bunker Hill,* and *Bon Homme Richard* (fig. 15). All but the last, the "Bonnie Dick," and the *Princeton,* which would soon join this group, saw plenty of the war. All but the last knew combat in the far Pacific.

For example, the *Bunker Hill* was badly damaged by two suicide planes off Okinawa on 11 May 1945 (fig. 16). One plane hit abaft the number three elevator, another at the base of the superstructure; both carried bombs that exploded as well. Gasoline caught fire on the flight deck, but a sharp turn by the carrier spilled the blazing fuel over the side. As the *Birmingham* had closed with the *Princeton* and the *Sante Fe* with the *Franklin,* the light cruiser *Wilkes-Barre* came alongside the *Bunker Hill* to fight fires. Three hundred forty-six of the carrier's crew were killed, 264 wounded and 43 others were never seen again. The *Bunker Hill*'s war record was one of the finest: from the time she entered the fray in November 1943 until she was knocked out of the war, she was in action eleven times, earning a battle star for each and a Presidential Unit Citation for her eighteen months of combat. Though repaired before being laid up, she never left the mothball fleet, was never again given the chance to serve. For nearly twenty years she was moored at Bremerton while her sisters left their berths to be towed to a shipyard, given new life, and rejoin the fleet.

Nosed into piers beyond the flattops are some of the other famous ships of the Pacific war (fig. 15). Five battleships were put to sleep here—the *Indiana,* the *Alabama,* and three of the prewar "Big Five": the *West Virginia, Colorado,* and *Maryland*—as well as seven heavy cruisers (five veterans of the war): the *Baltimore, Boston, Canberra, Quincy,* and the *Pittsburgh.* Another, the *Chicago,* arrived in the last months and the last, the *Fall River,* missed the war entirely, serving for a couple of years off the West Coast and as the flagship of the ships at the Bikini atomic tests. After a six-month tour in the Far East she was mothballed.

*Fig. 16. The* Bunker Hill *burns after a kamikaze hit. U.S. Naval Institute*

Less well known than the carriers and battleships at Bremerton, the *Vincennes* and the *Miami* are mentioned in few but the most detailed naval history books. The *Vincennes* was commissioned in 1944, the *Miami* a year earlier. The *Vincennes* was decommissioned in 1946, the *Miami* a year later. Both stayed in reserve until the 1960s. The *Vincennes* was sunk as a target; the *Miami* went for scrap. Neither was famous. Their antiaircraft guns did not shoot down untold numbers of Japanese aircraft, though the *Vincennes* did knock down more than a few. They did not sink any Japanese ships in a desperate surface engagement, though both joined the cruiser *Biloxi* in pounding the destroyer *Nowaki* beneath the waves. The *Vincennes* and the *Miami* never won notoriety going to the aid of a blazing aircraft carrier, though their crews would have had they been in the wrong place at the right time. Day in and day out, year in and year out, the men of the *Vincennes* and the *Miami* simply served. They took their places in the formations surrounding the carriers, took the same risks as did every other ship in the fleet, suffered the same monotony, the same boredom, and the same terror as the kamikazes rained down. The men aboard them were John Q. Public from Main Street USA. They endured the same separation from their families and suffered the same fear about getting home. They served no less gallantly than those aboard the more well-known ships, those that won Navy Unit Commendations or Presidential Unit Citations.

One photograph shows the USS *Vincennes* returning to San Francisco Bay on 28 March 1946, bringing home three hundred servicemen from New Zealand. This is her final voyage (fig. 17). Her paint is peeling from long months at sea. Perhaps a small crowd of family members, shipyard workers, and local government officials await her. Many, many vessels have returned from the war and the return of yet another light cruiser, almost seven months after war's end, is not an especially noteworthy event. Possibly there is a "Welcome Home!" or "Well Done!" painted on the roof of a warehouse visible from the deck of the ship. Perhaps it is handwritten on a banner fluttering in the breeze that always seems to be blowing in the Bay. Maybe the ship's namesake city kept track of her during the war. The *Vincennes* was originally named *Flint* but she was renamed during construction to commemorate the heavy cruiser lost off Savo Island one very bad night in 1942. Certainly the hometowns of the crewmen kept track of the ships when they could, but the *Vincennes* and the *Miami* did not appear in many headlines. The

*Fig. 17. The*
Vincennes *returns*
*home to San*
*Francisco in 1946.*
*National Archives,*
*Pacific Sierra Region*

news came mainly from letters home, or in telegrams from the War Department.

Another photo shows the *Miami* tied to a Mare Island pier in October 1961 (fig. 18). There is no evidence in this photograph of the damage she suffered in the famous typhoon of December 1944 when her bow was buckled, catapults torn loose, and her nose wrenched half a foot off center. With the *Vincennes* and other *Cleveland*s she was retired to the San Francisco reserve group after the war. When the yard closed in 1958, many of the ships were towed up the bay to Mare Island to finish out their lonely time in the reserve fleet until a board of inspection and survey pronounced a death sentence on them. She had been surrounded by ships at San Francisco, but here at this shipyard at the north end of the Bay she is alone. The dock is deserted. The *Miami* has been forgotten. Soon, she will exist no more.

When the Japanese struck Pearl Harbor two decades before the *Miami* lay abandoned at Mare Island, their focus was on the battleships and (they hoped) the aircraft carriers that were a threat to their south-

*Fig. 18. The moth-balled* Miami *at Mare Island in 1961. National Archives, Pacific Sierra Region*

ward expansion for raw materials. But the small ships that would bring Japanese industry and war-making capability to its knees were over-looked by the planners of the attack. Across from the Navy Yard where the *St. Louis* and the *New Orleans* fired at the diving and strafing air-craft, lay the submarines *Dolphin, Narwhal,* and *Tautog.* A fourth, the *Cachalot,* was at the Navy Yard. The boats quickly got into the fight as torpedo planes sped down Southeast Loch, straight for the battleships moored along Ford Island a little to the west. The antiaircraft armament on the subs was minimal, a few fifty-caliber machine guns, but the *Tautog* made the most of hers and knocked down a Japanese plane. She was the first United States submarine to claim a kill against the enemy in World War II. By the end of the war no submarine would have more Japanese ships to her credit.

In December 1941 the navy had 111 submarines in commission and another seventy-three under construction; fifty-one were assigned to the Pacific, twenty-nine to the Asiatic Fleet in the Philippines, the other twenty-two to Pearl Harbor. Sixteen were modern fleet boats, the remainder were older S-boats, suitable only for local patrolling and training. As the smoke billowed up from the harbor, the order went out that day from the chief of naval operations to all submarine commands: "Execute unrestricted submarine and air warfare against Japan."

Execute they did, but with mixed results in the first years of the war. The United States, the mightiest industrial nation on earth, possessed hopelessly inferior torpedoes. They simply would not work. The magnetic exploder that was to detonate the warhead when it passed beneath the metal keel of a ship, thus breaking its back, did not work well. Neither did the depth-setting mechanism, causing many torpedoes to either run too deep or to broach and then steer an erratic course. When a torpedo did strike the side of a merchantman or warship, the firing pin was found to be too brittle and often broke rather than detonating the warhead. In time, the submarine service overcame all of these deficiencies to slowly, but inexorably, strangle the Japanese empire.

Some of the most colorful naval personalities to come out of the war were sub skippers. Perhaps the most famous was Lieutenant Commander Dudley W. Morton. His nickname at the Academy was "Mush," short for "Mushmouth," but he was never called anything but Dudley or Captain on his boat, the *Wahoo*. Morton took command of the *Wahoo* on New Year's Eve, 1942. His executive officer was to win a name for himself and a Medal of Honor in another submarine named the *Tang*. He was Richard O'Kane, and together they formed a close team. Morton had complete confidence in O'Kane, preferring that his executive officer man the periscope and fire the torpedoes, leaving him free to conn the submarine to the most advantageous position. This confidence was unusual for a submarine commander and was returned by both the exec and crew toward their friendly, aggressive captain who wanted nothing more than to come to grips with the enemy. Morton's theory on submarine warfare was expressed on cards he had placed in each of the compartments aboard the *Wahoo:* "Shoot the Sons of Bitches." He was what the submarine fleet had been looking for.

The *Wahoo*'s first patrol, out of Brisbane, Australia, was a memorable one. Morton's orders were to investigate Wewak harbor on the northeast coast of New Guinea. However, there was one problem: Wewak could not be found on any chart. A school atlas from one of the crewman was examined, the harbor located, traced, and enlarged, and with this crude map Morton took the *Wahoo* on a daring cruise into the Japanese-held harbor. Farther and farther into the harbor they went, the sonar searching for reefs and shallow water. For seven miles they crept along until O'Kane had a destroyer in his sights. She was under way, and the *Wahoo* hurriedly fired four torpedoes. All missed, and the destroyer turned, heading down the wakes left by the fish straight for the *Wahoo*. "That's all right," said Morton coolly. "Keep your scope up and we'll shoot that SOB down the throat" (O'Kane, *Wahoo,* 138). The *Wahoo* had half a minute—and two remaining torpedoes—to put a killing shot into the narrow beam of the approaching warship. The destroyer churned on, headed for the *Wahoo*'s periscope. One torpedo was fired, and before it reached its target the second and last torpedo left its tube. The destroyer was now only 750 yards away. The first shot missed; the second did not. The destroyer was stopped dead in its tracks and went down by the bow. The *Wahoo* turned away and made her escape, threading her way back up the bay to the open sea.

Two days later the *Wahoo* went after a convoy of two freighters, a troop transport and a tanker. Morton torpedoed the first freighter and put a torpedo into the transport, all with his stern tubes. When the *Wahoo* turned to bring her bow tubes to bear, a third ship was sighted as one of the torpedoed ships steamed for the *Wahoo*'s periscope. The third ship was now hit, then the approaching freighter hit again with down-the-throat shots. The *Wahoo* surfaced and the crew found themselves in the middle of thousands of Japanese troops who had been aboard the transport, some floating, some in small boats. Morton, with an order controversial then among submariners (and almost forgotten now), ordered deck guns and machine guns turned on the troops and slaughtered them. He then set off in pursuit of the remaining freighter and tanker and sank both. His message to Pearl Harbor read, in part, "In ten hour running gun and torpedo battle destroyed entire convoy of two freighters, one transport, one tanker . . . all torpedoes expended." Morton and the *Wahoo* headed for home. Another convoy was sighted and though the *Wahoo* lacked torpedoes, she still had her deck gun. She used it on a freighter until she was forced to submerge by a pursuing destroyer. A new message went off to Pearl Harbor: "Another running gun battle today. *Wahoo* running. Destroyer gunning." The *Wahoo* returned to Pearl Harbor with a broom lashed to her periscope, indicating a clean sweep: fired all the torpedoes, sank everything in sight. And so the legend of the *Wahoo* and Mush Morton was born. He was an instant hero, badly needed in January 1943. But the most famous American submariner of World War II did not live to see it end. The

*Wahoo* was lost with all hands in October of that same year when Japanese aircraft and subchasers sent her to the bottom. Morton had showed, however, that the submarine could be a truly offensive weapon, that in the right hands, with a confident, well-trained crew and an aggressive skipper, the submarine could take the war to the Japanese and defeat them.

There were other captains who achieved fame during the war, such as Lawson "Red" Ramage, who took the *Parche* surfaced on a high-speed, forty-six minute, wild ride into the middle of a Japanese convoy, dodging everything and shooting everyone. As bullets flew at him from the escorts, he ordered everyone below except a volunteer quartermaster. The pair conned the sub and tried to avoid being rammed, with Ramage firing all the while with forward and stern tubes. He missed a freighter with two bow shots and then, turning to line up on a pair of tankers, nailed the freighter with a stern tube. The first tanker caught four torpedoes and went down; the second caught two and kept going. The torpedomen in the forward and aft torpedo rooms kept loading, and Ramage kept firing, nineteen fish in all. Twisting and turning, *Parche* was nearly rammed by another freighter. They missed by a scant fifty feet and the *Parche* found herself staring down the bow of yet another merchantman intent on ramming. With nowhere to go, Ramage fired three torpedoes down the throat. Two hit and the freighter stopped dead in the water. The *Parche* passed her, swung left, and finished her off with a stern shot. Then Ramage decided enough was enough and made his escape. For that action on 31 July 1944, Red Ramage received the Medal of Honor.

After the war the *Parche* went to Bikini as a target ship (she survived), but hundreds of others went into mothballs looking much the same as the pictured fleet subs tied up together at Mare Island shortly after the war (fig. 19). They are among the 106 boats that went into reserve here. From front to back, the names are those of the well known and the little known: *Plaice* (SS-390), *Trepang* (SS-412), *Stickleback* (SS-415), *Spadefish* (SS-411), *Roncador* (SS-301), *Loggerhead* (SS-374), *Scabbardfish* (SS-397), *Sterlet* (SS-392), *Lizardfish* (SS-373), *Hawkbill* (SS-366), and *Kraken* (SS-370). The *Stickleback*, *Spadefish*, and *Trepang* were built at Mare Island, the others at Portsmouth, Manitowoc, and Cramp Shipbuilding in Philadelphia.

The *Trepang* was skippered by Commander Roy Davenport, who had won three Navy Crosses before taking command of SS-412 and would win a fourth aboard her. She torpedoed three marus off Luzon in December 1944, and sank eleven ships in all. Of all the boats pictured, none save the *Trepang* had a career to match the USS *Spadefish*. One of her skippers, Gordon Underwood, ranked seventh among sub commanders in numbers of ships sunk, fourteen over the course of three war patrols. Five times the *Spadefish* departed Pearl Harbor, Majuro, and Guam for patrol and all five times she returned successful. She was one of the most deadly American submarines of the war, although she did join an exclusive and unfortunate group of submarines that accidentally sank Russian ships during the war. She returned home to be decommissioned on 3 May 1946. She was mothballed and moored at the reserve fleet anchorage just a little north of the Mare Island Naval Shipyard. Except for the hull number identifying her and the cocoon covering her forward- rather than aft-mounted deck gun, she is nearly identical to those boats whose participation and success in the war could not match hers. Yet the mothball fleet was, outwardly, the great equalizer. One ship or sub looked like another. All were treated the

*Fig. 19. Decommissioned submarines of the Mare Island Group, Pacific Reserve Fleet. National Archives, Pacific Sierra Region*

*Fig. 20. The Sandlance decommissions in early 1946. National Archives, Pacific Sierra Region*

same. There was no place of honor for the ship that sank thousands of tons of enemy vessels, no second-class berth for the ships that arrived on the scene too late, or were not fortunate enough or good enough to receive a Presidential Unit Citation, a Navy Unit Commendation, or a few pages in a book about the undersea war against Japan.

The flag comes down and the national anthem is played as the USS *Sandlance* decommissions on 14 February 1946 (fig. 20). She, too, will join the rows of mothballed subs at Mare Island after an eventful career under the Pacific. She once had the uncomfortable and unfortunate experience of hearing a depth charge attack on another unknown submarine miles away. The boat that may have been underneath those charges was the *Gudgeon*, and she did not get away. The *Gudgeon* was the thirtieth boat lost out of the fifty-two that would never return home. Admiral Husband Kimmel, commander of the U.S. Fleet at the time of the Pearl Harbor disaster, lost his son Manning who captained the *Robalo* when she struck a mine and went down. The first submarine lost, the *Sealion,* was bombed at Cavite in the Philippines three days after the war began. The last, the *Bullhead,* was sunk by Japanese aircraft on the very day Hiroshima was bombed.

The decommissioning of so many ships in the months after the end of the war was news. The following release from the Mare Island Naval Shipyard to Paramount and the Pathe News Pictures is newsreel copy, dated 25 January 1946. It details the inactivation and mothballing process that submarines like the *Sandlance, Trepang,* and *Sterlet* underwent after the war:

U.S. Fleet submarines, the gray gaunt ships whose deadly torpedoes sank two-thirds of Hirohito's merchant ships and one-third of his Navy, come home to "no red-lead row" of rust and corrosion at Mare Island Naval Shipyard. The fifty-nine submarines of the 19th (Inactive Pacific) Fleet will arrive at Mare Island to undergo a comprehensive overhaul, refitting and preservation process planned to keep them in complete readiness to fight again in ten to thirty days.

Some twenty-five submarines are now at the Shipyard or at Tiburon Bay alongside tenders, waiting their turn in the decommissioning and preservation procedure, and more are expected. The subs range in age from the four-year old *Tinosa,* a battle-wise veteran of eleven war patrols, her conning tower bright with painted flags of 22 Jap vessels sunk, totaling 108,000 tons, to the "virgin" *Mapiro,* for whom the Japs quit too soon—as she was on her way to Kyushu to fire her first torpedoes in anger. For some of Uncle Sam's newest subs are going into the Inactive Fleet as insurance against his again having to fight a first-line war with outmoded weapons.

At Tiburon, alongside the submarine tenders *Griffin, Pelias,* and *Aegir,* the preservation process begins. With assistance from the tender force, the sub's crew cleans, overhauls, and puts in perfect operating condition the main engines and motors, the pumps, air compressors, steering and diving motors, and all the other complicated equipment of a modern fleet-type submarine. "RPC", a thin rust-preventative compound, is flushed through the engines, sprayed or brushed on all uncoated metal surfaces; then each piece of equipment is tagged with a card stating what treatment has been given, the date, and detailed instructions as to what must be done before the equipment is used again. Each of the boat's four Diesel engine's [sic], for instance, requires only to have its lube oil, fuel oil and cooling water systems filled before it is ready to put out its full horsepower.

Periscopes are lifted from the shears, and the hull openings plugged; the periscopes themselves are stored aboard the submarine's tender after cleaning and inspection. Electronic gear, radios, radar, and sonar sets, are carefully cleaned and blown out to remove all dust; tubes are replaced and the gear put in perfect operating condition.

Each of the thousand and one spare parts and tools is checked against the ship's allowance list, tagged, wrapped in paper or stowed away in chests. Files in the ship's office show the location and number on board of each item.

The actual preservation process then begins, in drydock at the Mare Island Naval Shipyard [fig. 21]. The propellers are removed and secured on deck, painted with a preservative coating, and the finely machined blade edges protected from nicks with metal guards.

*Fig. 21. Sailors work on the deck of the mothballed Icefish. National Archives, Pacific Sierra Region*

All hull openings, except those which will later be used for the dehumidification process, are covered with welded patches, and all connections from various tanks to sea are closed and sealed. The outer hull is sandblasted clean of paint, then coated with anticorrosive paint and hot plastic preservative.

The boat's huge storage batteries are removed, the electrolyte drained, and the cells cribbed and wedged back in place bone dry.

The deck guns and 20 m.m. guns—star performers of many a "battle surface" against Jap picket boats—are "packaged" in airtight cocoons which will keep them dry and ready for immediate use once the package is stripped off. Over a wooden padded frame, a rubbery net is blown from spray guns, as a spider spins his web. Several coats of special formula paint finish the job. A small clear "window" is left in the cocoon, and a package of desiccant, silica gel, is placed inside after the cocoon is dehumidified. A glance through the window at the color of the desiccant indicates whether the desired dryness is being maintained.

In her final berth near the Mare Island causeway, along with twenty-odd of her sister ships, the submarine receives the finishing touches. The dehumidifying machine is set up on her after main deck, with piping led down the conning tower hatch into the ship's trim manifold, and thence through connections to reach all compartments. The machine, a sensitive, electrically operated, recirculating device, literally makes the sub "breathe," exhaling damp air and inhaling dry air continuously. Its operation is automatically controlled by humidistats in each compartment, and by a master recorder-controller, to maintain the air inside the ship constantly at 25–30% relative humidity, a point which is reached after about two weeks of operation.

The decommissioning ceremony is the submarine's final "performance". Her officers and men, lined at attention on deck, hear the bugler blow retreat, and make their last salute to the vessel's ensign as it is slowly lowered from the staff on the after gun platform. Decommissioning orders are read, and the prized colors are presented to "the oldest man on board"—not the oldest in age, for he may be a twenty-four-year old Chief Torpedoman's Mate—but with the longest service on board—perhaps a "plank owner" who put the vessel in commission and served with her throughout her fighting career.

With Captain Leo L. Pace, USN, Commander Pacific Reserve Fleet, Mare Island Group, the Commanding Officer goes below to make his final inspection. Everything is in order. From the ship's plans, machinery instructions, and watch bills, to the allowance sheets listing the thousand items of equipment down to towels and sheets for the crew, everything is on board—tagged, identified, and shipshape. As the Commanding Officer walks down the passageways through the compartments now aromatic with the smell of clean lube oil and preservatives, he remembers his instructions from "ComSubsPac".

"It is the Commanding Officer's responsibility that his ship is laid up properly. Commander, Submarines, Pacific Fleet is depending on you to do as good a job on this as you did on sinking Japs. He has assured the Commander, Reserve Fleet, that you will turn over a good boat."

The skipper knows he has done so. He knows that his ship, which slipped across Togo's lifelines and choked his Empire to surrender, can, almost overnight, be made fit and ready to fight again. (General Correspondence, RG 181)

Not all of the ships placed in mothballs after the war were combat ships. Many were auxiliary ships and among the most important were the submarine tenders. Admiral Lockwood, Commander, Submarine Force, Pacific Fleet (ComSubPac), called them "the heart and soul of all submarine squadrons." They belonged to the supporting fleet behind the fighting fleet. Pictured is one of them, the submarine tender *Fulton*, mothballed and under way via tug at Mare Island in 1947 (fig. 22). She was launched in 1940, commissioned in 1941, and her days appear numbered in the photograph. Sprayed-on coatings cover her cranes and other topside gear. She will be moored near the submarines she cared for during the war. The *Fulton* was given second life a few years later, however, and did not retire from naval service until fifty years after she entered the fleet, with all but a few of those years spent in active service.

Fewer submarines in the fleet meant fewer tenders, and many besides the *Fulton* went into reserve, though a few were maintained in service after the war at San Diego, Key West, and Norfolk. Glamorous they

were not. Headline makers they were not. Well known they were not. Vital to the war effort against the Japanese, they most certainly were. Sixteen of them served during the war, all but one in the Pacific. All had one purpose: to service, repair, resupply, and make ready for war the submarines of the fleet.

The counteroffensive against Japan by the submarine force operated out of two Australian bases and Pearl Harbor. Wherever the subs were, their tenders were, as well. They served at those three bases and established new ones when the Allied advance pushed back the Japanese defensive perimeter. These forward bases cut down on transit time when the subs headed for their hunting grounds, usually the shipping lanes between Japan and her far-flung empire. Submarines from Fremantle patrolled the South China Sea to cut off Japan from the oil in the Dutch East Indies. From Brisbane the subs ventured into the waters off New Guinea and the Solomons and to the huge naval base at Truk in the Carolines. From Pearl Harbor and later Midway, they ranged far across the Pacific to attack shipping off the China coast in the Formosa Strait and East China Sea, and then into the Sea of Japan. As soldiers and marines pushed back the Japanese island by island, advance submarine bases, centered around the tenders, were set up closer to these patrol areas. No longer would submarines be forced all the way back to Pearl Harbor to have a broken periscope repaired or her radios serviced. The tenders could do it and they did it at advanced bases they established at Majuro Atoll, Tulagi in the Solomons, Seeadler Harbor in the Admiralties, Milne Bay and Mios Woendi on the New Guinea coast, at Guam, Saipan, Subic Bay when the Philippines were retaken in 1945, and Dutch Harbor and Attu in Alaska.

The tenders were no less a target than warships, and perhaps, to a crafty enemy, they were more so. Each represented an entire squadron of fleet boats now preying on Japanese shipping. Disable or sink a tender and all of the submarines under her care were paralyzed as well. The big ships were floating machine, electrical, and welding shops as well as optical shops for the delicate periscopes, warehouses for spare parts, hotels for resting sub crews, gas stations, grocery stores, ammunition dumps, and hospitals. They were named for mythological figures: *Apollo, Nereus,* and *Pelias;* for inventors: *Sperry, Fulton;* and for early submariners: *Bushnell* and *Holland.* And one was named for the skipper of the submarine *Growler,* Howard Gilmore. Topside and wounded by a collision with a Japanese gunboat, he ordered his submarine down without him rather than risk her being sunk as the enemy sprayed the *Growler* with machine-gun fire.

Less than two years after the submarines and their tenders came home to be mothballed after the war, the reserve fleet basin at the Philadelphia Naval Shipyard was filled with decommissioned ships. All of the surviving prewar cruisers were preserved here. Nosed into piers at the far end of the basin were four *New Orleans*-class cruisers, the *San Francisco, Minneapolis, New Orleans,* and *Tuscaloosa* (fig. 23). To their right, just over the bow of the light carrier, were three *Northampton*s: the *Chester, Louisville,* and *Augusta.* At the near side, to the left, were three *Brooklyn*-class light cruisers, among them the *Honolulu* (CL-48) and the *St. Louis* (CL-49). Two sisters, the *Brooklyn* and the *Phoenix,* were the first two major combatants to be mothballed following the war (*Pictorial History,* 376), and all of the *Brooklyn*s soon followed.

Only one, the *Helena,* was lost during the war, sunk during the battle of Kula Gulf by Japanese destroyer-launched torpedoes. Her partner in that action was the *St. Louis,* the "Lucky Lou." On 7 December

*Fig. 23. The Honolulu, St. Louis, and other prewar cruisers in reserve at the Philadelphia Navy Yard back basin. U.S. Naval Institute*

1941 she was tied up in the navy yard at Pearl Harbor between the *San Francisco* and the *Honolulu* in a scene not unlike the one pictured. The *St. Louis* was not ready for sea or combat. She was in the yard for boiler repairs and shipyard workers had cut a four-foot-wide hole in her side. As the Japanese bombed and strafed, workers frantically welded the hole shut while a bomb missed the *Honolulu* by about five yards, exploding underwater and opening her hull to flooding. The crew of the *St. Louis* had seen enough, and at 0931 she backed out of the piers into Southeast Loch toward Battleship Row, the patch on her hull still hot from the welder's torch. A few moments later she was headed down the channel for the open sea. The speed limit in the narrow channel was eight knots; the *St. Louis* was making twenty-two. Her ordeal was not over. A Japanese midget sub fired two torpedoes at her, but both struck the coral and exploded as the cruiser raced by to safety.

The *Honolulu* and the *St. Louis* were again in action together in the long naval battle for the Solomon Islands as both sides tried to wrest control of the sea in some of the most bitter and hard-fought surface actions of the war. On the night of 13 July 1943 the Japanese, as they had done so often, sent a force to challenge the Americans in the "Slot," a body of water that ran from the Japanese bases at the northwestern end of the Solomons chain to the American toehold on Guadalcanal at the southeastern end. A light cruiser, five destroyers, and four destroyer transports carrying twelve hundred soldiers to reinforce Kolombangara came on through the darkness. Out to meet them came an Allied force consisting of the *Honolulu,* the *St. Louis,* the New Zealand cruiser *Leander* and ten destroyers. The American force proceeded up the Slot in column, half of the destroyers in front of the three cruisers, half trailing behind. The leading destroyers fired torpedoes at the approaching Japanese ships and then the cruisers opened up with six- and five-inch gunfire. The Japanese cruiser *Jintsu* was smothered by the rapid and accurate fire of thirty American six-inch rifles. In a little over twenty minutes the two *Brooklyn*s, who would sleep so quietly a few yards apart in the friendly confines of a navy yard only four years later, would blast over twenty-four-hundred rounds from their main batteries and help pound the enemy ship under the waves.

But the battle was not over and a common fate lay in store for the two cruisers. The American destroyers were widely scattered and though the *Honolulu*'s radar picked up approaching targets, her officers were uncertain if the radar blips represented friendly or enemy ships. They were enemy—Japanese destroyers, busy launching torpedoes. The *St. Louis* took one in the bow. So did the *Honolulu.* Casualties aboard the cruisers were light, but while the *St. Louis* had a large piece of bow blown away, the frames and bulkheads directly under the deck held (fig. 24). On the *Honolulu* they did not. Her bow was gone, her main deck forward of turret number one led straight down into the sea. Both she and the *St. Louis* were repaired but it was months before they were back in the fleet and by then the nature of the war had changed.

The Solomons campaign was over. The cruisers were assigned fleet escort duties. The main threat now came from the air, and the *St. Louis* would be in the thick of it. Off New Ireland a dive bomber hit the ship in one of her crew living spaces, killing twenty-three and wounding twenty. In Leyte Gulf Japanese kamikazes scored, too. Within fifteen minutes one November day in 1944, four aimed themselves for Lucky Lou and on that day she was not so lucky. Two hit her, starting major

*Fig. 24. Torpedo damage to the* St. Louis. *U.S. Naval Institute*

fires and heeling her to port. Killed or wounded were another fifty-nine sailors: former students, clerks, mailmen, teachers, mechanics, and farmers, who, a few years before, could not possibly have imagined the horror they would have to endure aboard a ship they had never heard of in the middle of the Pacific Ocean.

The *St. Louis* survived this attack and the war and came home. So did the *Brooklyn, Philadelphia,* and the *Savannah,* who spent their war in the Atlantic and the Mediterranean. The Pacific fleet *Brooklyn*s came home, too: the *Boise, Nashville,* and *Phoenix.* All sailed past Cape May and up the Delaware River to the Philadelphia Naval Shipyard. There they were overhauled, their machinery put in good working order, and their battle damage repaired. Their spare parts were inventoried and any problems noted. Turrets that had fired at Japanese cruisers and German shore batteries were sealed shut. Cans of desiccant were placed in the bilges and voids and fuel tanks. Their flags were hauled down for the last time, and the ships were declared out of commission. The last entries were made in logs and they were taken ashore. The crew was dispersed home or to other ships. Tugs pushed the ships past the shipyard, into the Schuylkill River for a short way, then right under the bridge and through the narrow channel into the crowded reserve basin. Not quite a graveyard, but close. No waves. No ship's whistles or bells. No camouflage, just a sea of peacetime gray. Some of these ships fought together, their crews bled together, watching the same bombs fall, firing at the same shadows in the dark in the South Seas, watching the same flaming, plummeting Zeros and Vals and Judys aim at them as the ships twisted and turned, trying desperately not to be next. Across the buildings and workshops of the shipyard the work of the fleet went on at the piers in the Delaware River. New ships joined the fleet. Older ships continued to leave, and the back basin continued to fill with those whose days were at an end.

The successors to the *Brooklyn*s were the *Cleveland*-class light cruisers. Take that shipbuilding program; a rapidly deteriorating relationship with a potential foe strong in naval aviation (Japan in 1941); a huge gap between the completion of the last of the *Yorktown*s and the first of the new *Essex*-class carriers; and a need for carriers that could be built quickly and operate at long range and high speed with carriers already in existence. Add the influence of a commander in chief who was also an advocate of naval aviation and who did not mind in the least letting the military know his ideas, and you had the reasons behind the development of the *Independence*-class light carriers.

One of them, the *Cowpens*, is pictured at Mare Island in the years after World War II, mothballed and nearly abandoned (fig. 25). She is representative of a small number of carriers that filled a very large gap in the United States Navy in the early years of the war. The *Cowpens* derived its name from the battle of Cowpens, fought in South Carolina during the Revolutionary War in an area of open ground where cattle were allowed to graze. It was an American victory and led to the final victory of the war at Yorktown later in the year. But no ship had ever been named for this battle. In fact, the ship that became the *Cowpens* began life as the cruiser *Huntington* and the sleek cruiser hull is very apparent. The carrier part of the ship, hangar, and flight deck are obviously afterthoughts. The effect of the threat from the air during the war is apparent as well, from the number of preserved antiaircraft mounts

*Fig. 25. The* Cowpens *in moth-balls at Mare Island. National Archives, Pacific Sierra Region*

along the flight deck and on the bow. Though the light carriers were designed to augment and operate with the much larger fleet carriers, they worked with the same limitations that the mass-built escort carriers did in terms of aircraft handling capability and generally inadequate armor protection. Nevertheless, as a group they were very successful.

Nine were built, all of them completed in 1943: the *Independence, Princeton, Belleau Wood, Cowpens, Monterey, Langley, Cabot, Bataan,* and *San Jacinto.* They earned seventy-nine battle stars in all, three Presidential Unit Citations (the *Belleau Wood, Cabot,* and *San Jacinto*), and two Navy Unit Commendations (the *Langley* and the *Cowpens*). One, the *Princeton,* was sunk. The magazines that would have been used to store six-inch shells for the never-completed cruisers instead became bomb storage, but the torpedoes were stowed aft of the hangar, relatively unprotected, and when the *Princeton* caught fire after being hit in the battle of Leyte Gulf, her torpedoes exploded and destroyed her.

No other light carrier received more battle stars than the *Cowpens,*

*Fig. 26. Task Group 38.3 steams into Ulithi Atoll.*
*U.S. Naval Institute*

twelve in all. When she joined the Pacific Fleet in the latter half of 1943, her planes first saw combat flying strikes against the Marshall Islands, which were to be invaded early in 1944. When she and the others of her class joined Task Force 58 it was to continue to batter the Marshalls while U.S. troops went ashore at Kwajalein and Eniwetok. When the force hit the Marianas in the summer of that same year and Saipan, Guam, and Tinian were invaded, the *Cowpens* was there. When the Japanese fleet came out to fight, her air group took part in what was called the "Great Marianas Turkey Shoot," which dealt Japanese naval aviation a blow from which it never recovered.

Naval power personified is Task Group 38.3, one of three task groups making up the Fast Carrier Task Force at the heart of the Third Fleet in December 1944 (fig. 26). The light carrier *Langley,* sister to the

*Cowpens,* is in the lead. The fleet carrier *Ticonderoga* follows, then the battleships *Washington* and *South Dakota,* the light cruisers *Sante Fe, Biloxi, Mobile,* and *Oakland* all steam in column as the group heads for Ulithi. Over fourteen thousand sailors are aboard this small slice of the fleet. They have come, volunteers and draftees, reservists and regulars, from all parts of the country to sail these warships into harm's way, into the greatest conflict man has ever known. The *Langley's* war record was typical of the light carriers. From January 1944, when she left Pearl Harbor for the war, to May 1945 when she returned, the *Langley* never left the front lines, never returned to Puget Sound or Mare Island or San Francisco or even Pearl Harbor for overhaul or battle damage repair.

In March 1945, as the fleet sailed from Ulithi to cover the landings at Iwo Jima, the light carrier *Cabot,* another sister of the *Cowpens,* was host to the most famous newspaper correspondent of the war, Ernie Pyle. He had come to the Pacific after covering the army in North Africa, Italy, and France, and had asked to be assigned to one of the navy's smaller carriers because he thought the big fleet carriers would be too impersonal for his style of writing. For three weeks Pyle lived among the crew of the *Cabot.* She had been in every major battle since she had arrived and, the previous November, was struck by a kamikaze that blew holes in her flight deck in two places and killed thirty-six of her sailors. She was known as the "Iron Woman" for her durability. About the hybrid *Cabot* Pyle wrote, "A carrier has no poise. It has no grace. It is top-heavy and lopsided. It has the lines of a well-fed cow." Yet it was, he wrote "a noble thing" (Nichols, *Ernie's War,* 386). Pyle wrote about the crew, but he wrote from the perspective of a man who had lived among the foxholes and mud and squalor of the combat infantryman in the European theater. While acknowledging their lives were dull and painfully monotonous, to him the sailors were living like kings compared to the dogfaces. The *Cabot's* sailors were proud of their ship but could gripe, as any serviceman could, about their conditions. Pyle wrote about it in a way that made it clear that as far as he was concerned, the men of the *Cabot,* and by extension the men aboard the other ships of the fleet, had no idea how good they had it.

In a way Pyle was right. Yet the griping of the men could only come from their own experiences. To them, the war at sea meant endless days and weeks of sailing: drills, battle stations, steel decks, steel bulkheads, steel overheads, steel hatches, day in and day out. Rarely was there dry land to walk on. Rarely was there any alcohol, even beer, to be had.

Rarer still was the sight of a woman. There was only the limitless ocean and the possibility of being broiled alive by ruptured steam lines, trapped belowdecks by rushing seawater from a torpedo hit, asphyxiated by thick, blinding smoke, burned by blazing gasoline, and death by drowning as their ship—their home—slid beneath the waves and left them to the mercy of the water and the sharks. Perhaps if Pyle had spent some time watching helplessly as the bombs and suicide planes rained down on the *West Virginia* or the *Ticonderoga* or the *William D. Porter* or the *Laffey* he would have written from a different perspective. He left the *Cabot* for an attack transport bound for Okinawa, and was soon back among the ground troops he understood and knew so well. He was killed among them on Ie Shima.

The light carriers operated with the bigger flattops, surrounded by the battleships, cruisers, and destroyers. They carried twenty-three or twenty-four F6F Hellcats and eight to twelve Avenger torpedo planes apiece while the air groups among the big carriers varied. Some like the *Bunker Hill* carried an air group built for fleet air defense with large numbers of fighters. The *Enterprise* carried an air group trained for night flying: thirty-two fighters and twenty-one torpedo bombers. Others like the *Yorktown* carried more balanced groups of fighters and bombers.

All of the light carriers survived the Okinawa campaign. The *Cowpens* returned from overhaul to the western Pacific in July 1945 to begin the aerial pounding of the Japanese mainland in preparation for the invasion, scheduled for November. When the *Missouri* hosted the surrender ceremony, the *Cowpens* was anchored nearby. All of these makeshift carriers but the *Independence* joined the *Cowpens* in the mothball fleet after the war. The *Monterey, Langley, Cabot,* and *Bataan* were decommissioned the same day, 11 February 1947, and went to the back basin at Philadelphia. The *Belleau Wood* and the *Cowpens* had left the fleet a month earlier on 13 January at Alameda, and were joined there by the *San Jacinto* in March. In a little over a year the *Cabot* would be back in the fleet, assigned as a naval air reserve training carrier until the early 1950s.

In the beautiful city of San Francisco, across the bay from Alameda and a few years after the end of World War II, life had returned to normal (fig. 28). Another war was being fought, this time on the Asian mainland, but it was too far away and had not touched the American public as did the last. The blackouts in the days after Pearl Harbor were

Fig. 27. The light *carrier* Cowpens *with her air group on deck. U.S. Naval Institute*

a thing of the past, a memory of those dark days when the Japanese fleet was thought to be just off the coast, and when newspaper reports had enemy aircraft over the city nightly. Not many people knew where Pearl Harbor was before the attack. On 8 December 1941, when Americans in the Bay area looked at a map, Hawaii suddenly looked a lot closer to San Francisco than was comfortable. The Japanese had been there, dropped bombs there, killed Americans there. The attack was a shock. Anyone who read a newspaper could see that war was coming. But not on this quiet Sunday morning three weeks before Christmas. Not in Hawaii. Maybe the Philippines. Maybe the Dutch East Indies. Maybe Indochina. But not Hawaii. Not the mighty Pacific Fleet's main anchorage, the same invincible Pacific Fleet that visited San Francisco Bay often in the 1920s and 1930s, its proud battleships sailing majestically through the Golden Gate to anchor in the peaceful waters or tie up along the waterfront.

That Sunday morning, hunters in the Fort Cronkhite hills beyond the bridge were accosted by soldiers who asked what they thought they were doing on government land carrying guns. Hadn't they heard? Pearl Harbor had been bombed. War had indeed come. Homes high in the hills above Sausalito were seized as lookout posts. Citizens took down rifles and shotguns from walls and went out to the coast to stand guard. Windows were blacked out by frightened parents and children felt suffocated by the unfamiliar heavy, dark curtains. Rumors flew. The damage reports from Pearl were still a closely guarded secret as Christmas 1941 came and went, but there was no doubt that the United States had suffered a crippling blow.

And then a Japanese submarine surfaced off the southern California coast and lobbed a few shells into the American mainland. Antisubmarine nets went across the Golden Gate. The guns at Battery Spencer, overlooking the new Golden Gate Bridge on the Marin County side, were removed, lest the Japanese try to bomb them and hit the bridge instead. The West Coast went dark. No lights were supposed to be shown at night; there was to be nothing to guide an approaching Japanese Zero or outline an American ship against the coastline for a submarine to draw a bead on.

The war years dragged on. San Francisco was a hub, a beehive of naval activity. The shipyard south of the city repaired damaged ships, and at other yards around the immense Bay new ships sprang to life. Warships of every description passed beneath midspan of the Golden Gate Bridge, some to war, some home for a respite. Troops left from Fort Mason to assault islands thousands of miles away while Japanese prisoners of war were brought to Angel Island, near Alcatraz. Newspaper headlines, rationing, propaganda posters and telegrams from the War Department dominated life in the city for three and a half years. In the summer of 1945 more ships left the bay bound for the Pacific with troops and supplies for the invasion of Japan, the invasion that some in the army high command predicted would cost one million American casualties. Among those ships departing was an American heavy cruiser that left Hunters Point Naval Shipyard on 16 July. She carried a special cargo, one few in the world knew about. The USS *Indianapolis* car-

Fig. 28. Aerial view of the city of San Francisco and the reserve fleet piers at the
shipyard in 1951. National Archives, Pacific Sierra Region

ried components of the first atomic bomb to the island of Tinian, where they were assembled, placed in the bomb bay of a B-29 nicknamed *Enola Gay,* and dropped on the Japanese city of Hiroshima.

Peace came to San Francisco. Soldiers and sailors came home. Ships came home to be mothballed, to leave the war and active service behind (fig. 28). The piers at the bottom of the photograph are crowded with such veterans. Those three piers did not exist a few years before. They were built in 1947, south of the shipyard dry docks that had repaired some of the very ships that now slept there. They were built as homes for the ships that were no longer needed. To the far left are attack transports and attack cargo ships. These were the core of the amphibious forces that landed on island after island, atoll after atoll, in the relentless, two-pronged sweep eastward that began on the island of Guadalcanal in August 1942 and ended with the Okinawa landing in April 1945. The sweep would have ended with the landings on the Japanese mainland had not the naval blockade, the aerial pounding and finally nuclear weapons forced Japan to her knees.

These amphibious ships are as anonymous in the photo as they seemed to be in service. But down there is the USS *Lubbock* that landed marines on the volcanic sand beaches of Iwo Jima, then put assault forces ashore on Okinawa under the constant threat of air attack. She made four Magic Carpet runs after her war service, each time bringing hundreds of happy servicemen back home. Down there also is the USS *President Adams,* whose crew sweated in the steamy, fetid air off Guadalcanal as the First Marine Division went ashore. Somewhere in that group of forgotten workhorses is the *Oneida,* which carried survivors of the *Franklin* away from the war zone, carried some of the thousands of casualties away from the hell that was Iwo Jima, and transported Japanese prisoners of war from the fighting on Okinawa to a POW camp in Hawaii.

Nearby is the *Charles Carroll,* named for one of the lesser-known signers of the Declaration of Independence. The *Charles Carroll* was seemingly everywhere in the European theater. She landed troops first in French North Africa, then at Sicily, then at Salerno. On 6 June 1944 she could be found off Utah beach, under German fire, landing troops of the Twenty-ninth Infantry Division on D-day. More landings followed in southern France and then, as if five combat landings were not enough for one ship, she was sent to the Pacific theater, to the Okinawa landings.

Eleven *Cleveland*-class cruisers were moored in San Francisco after the war, including the *Amsterdam, Astoria, Atlanta, Birmingham, Duluth, Miami, Oklahoma City, Springfield, Vincennes, Topeka,* and *Vicksburg.* At the middle pier next to the transports are eight of them, and two more are moored side by side to the right beyond the carriers. Twenty-seven were built, and all but one, the *Galveston,* were commissioned. (She would eventually be commissioned as a missile cruiser fourteen years after she was laid down.) Two more, the *Fargo* and the *Huntington,* were built to a modified design, making twenty-nine in all. Eight more hulls were converted to light carriers. Twenty-two of the cruisers saw service in World War II. All but one, the *Manchester,* were mothballed after the war. Some, like the *Amsterdam,* served only a couple of years before being laid up and forgotten. Four of them survived in the fleet until 1949, the *Springfield* until 1950. None of the ships pictured, nor any of the *Clevelands,* ever returned to the fleet in their original configuration, although three of the San Francisco group—the *Oklahoma City, Springfield,* and *Topeka*—were rebuilt as guided missile cruisers.

At the lower right end of the middle pier, ahead of the three *Clevelands*, are the heavy cruisers *Bremerton* and *Los Angeles.* Both were latecomers to the war, and in fact the *Bremerton* did not even arrive in the Pacific until December 1945. She made one cruise to the Far East, trained a few reservists, then left the fleet in 1947. The *Los Angeles,* too, did not arrive in the Pacific until after the shooting had stopped. With the *Bremerton,* she sailed with the Seventh Fleet in the western Pacific, then returned to the United States and was quietly decommissioned.

The two carriers nearest the cruisers are the *Intrepid* on the left, the *Hornet* on the right. One can imagine, seeing the expansive empty flight decks under the California midday sun, the view that the kamikaze pilot must have had of these ships as he hurtled his plane down, through a hail of tracers and bullets racing skyward straight for his windscreen. Down, down, down he would come. If he took time to notice or was conscious of anything but his imminent death, the pilot could see men on the flight deck scrambling frantically for cover, could see flames from the gun barrels fringing the flight deck and from the five-inchers forward and aft of the island as they pointed straight at his face and fired over and over. He could see the tracers converging on that point in the sky where his diving plane would be. Or was. The escorting cruisers, like the sleeping ones now moored near the *Intrepid* and the *Hornet*, would add their fire to the invisible wall trying to halt the plane. There would come a moment when the pilot knew he would hit his target or would miss; a time when the nose of his aircraft was committed to a few square yards on the flight deck or the island or the side of the big carrier, whose wake churned white behind it, or to the ocean. The steel or the water would rise up and fill the windscreen and possibly a hundred men would die. Or maybe just one. And the men on the escort carrier or the destroyer or the transport who were left would shake their heads in horror, amazement, and relief if the plane missed and then turn their eyes skyward to watch for the next one. Until the end of the war there always would be a next one.

The *Hornet*, in contrast to the *Intrepid*, suffered little during the war. She was not hit by kamikazes nor bombed, though she reached the fleet in the thick of the Pacific war in March 1944. Weather did what the Japanese could not: a typhoon collapsed twenty-five feet of the *Hornet*'s bow. Though she went into retirement right after the war, another place in history awaited her. Two decades later, now equipped with helicopters rather than fighters and bombers, the first voyagers to another world would return to the earth on her flight deck. The president of the United States would be there to greet them. They were the astronauts of *Apollo 11*, the first mission to land on the moon. In the days before the space shuttle would glide to earth like an airliner, spaceships landed in the ocean and often as not were plucked from the sea by aircraft carriers like the *Hornet*—ships that had driven the Japanese fleet from the sea, had been placed in mothballs, and then reborn to serve again.

Across the unusually calm, flat waters of the bay from the *Hornet* is the USS *Shangri-La*, surely the most beautifully named warship in the United States Navy. When Jimmy Doolittle led sixteen army B-25 bombers from the deck of the old *Hornet* to strike Japan several months after Pearl Harbor, the raid was a shot in the arm for American morale. The press and public wanted details of the raid, but President Roosevelt, when asked where the planes had taken off from, replied with a smile, "Shangri-La," the mythical and mysterious kingdom high in the Himalayas in James Hilton's novel *Lost Horizons*. The public was captivated by this answer. Obviously the raid had come from a carrier, though just how heavy army bombers had been launched from the small deck of a carrier remained a mystery. Nevertheless, the public wanted one of the carriers being built to be named for this mythical land. On

*Fig. 29. Escort carriers undergoing inactivation at the Boston Naval Shipyard in 1946. Leslie Jones/Courtesy of the Boston Public Library Print Department*

16 August 1942 aircraft carrier number thirty-eight, eight months into her construction, was given the name *Shangri-La*. When she was launched and christened the following February, Mrs. James Doolittle broke the bottle of champagne on her bow. She became the flagship of Task Force 38, and two years later returned to the United States to join the thousands of ships in reserve, like the *Antietam* moored close by, one of the twenty fleet carriers that were swarmed over by shipyard workers, overhauled, dried out, hooked up to the shore for electrical power, and decommissioned. Just across the slip from the *Antietam*, almost hidden by the overhead crane, is the battleship *Iowa*, about to undergo activation for the Korean War.

Aircraft carriers come in different shapes and sizes. Pictured are escort carriers (CVEs) in the process of being overhauled and deactivated at the Boston Navy Yard in 1946 (fig. 29). Like the light carriers they were a makeshift design, a result of the need to get more flight decks into the fleet faster than was thought possible before the war. They were to be used as convoy escorts along with the destroyer escorts, but eventually they served in many capacities. The first of them, the *Bogue* class, were converted from merchant hulls and completed from mid-1942 to early 1943. Some were built for the Royal Navy. At the same time four fleet oilers were converted into the larger and more capable *Sangamon* class. Oilers were badly needed, though, with oiler hulls at a premium, and only those four were converted. The mass-produced *Casablanca*s followed in 1943 and 1944. These were hurriedly designed from the keel up as escort carriers and were also known as the *Kaiser* class after their builder, Henry J. Kaiser. He had approached the president with an idea for building at least one hundred of the carriers using an adapted merchant design, prefabricated sections, and mass production techniques. Fifty of them entered the fleet in exactly one year. The first, the *Casablanca,* was commissioned 8 July 1943; the last, the *Munda,* was commissioned on 8 July 1944. The last class of CVEs, the *Commencement Bay*s, were built upon the lessons learned from all the previous classes. They were modeled after the *Sangamon*s, the largest and best of the escort carriers. Nineteen of the *Commencement Bay*s were built, though two were completed after the war and never commissioned.

The carriers undergoing inactivation in the photograph are the *Hoggatt Bay, Rudyerd Bay, Shamrock Bay, Kalinin Bay, Saginaw Bay,* and the *Kadashan Bay* at the far end nearly hidden by a cloud of smoke from a nearby warehouse fire. *Kalinin Bay,* CVE-68, had a worse time of it than any of the others in the photo. On 25 October 1944 she was part of Vice Admiral Thomas Kinkaid's Seventh Fleet, which was landing and supporting the troops of Lieutenant General Walter Krueger's Sixth Army on the Philippine island of Leyte. Leyte was roughly in the middle of the archipelago and was needed as an air and supply base for the invasion of Luzon, set for early the following year. More specifically, *Kalinin Bay* was part of Task Group 77.4, the escort carrier group under the command of Admiral Thomas Sprague, whose fighters flew cover over the invasion fleet and whose fighter-bombers provided close air support for the troops ashore. Task Force 77.4 was in turn divided into three small units, called Taffys after their radio call signs. Taffy 3 was commanded by Rear Admiral Clifton Sprague (no relation to the commander of Task Group 77.4), and was composed of six CVEs: the

*Fanshaw Bay, St. Lo, White Plains, Kalinin Bay, Kitkun Bay,* and *Gambier Bay;* the destroyers *Hoel, Heermann,* and *Johnston;* and the destroyer escorts *Dennis, John C. Butler, Raymond,* and *Samuel B. Roberts.*

The Japanese had no intention of letting the Leyte landing go unopposed and developed a two-pronged-pincer attack on the lightly armed American transports in Leyte Gulf to the east of the island. One Japanese group, the Southern Force, would try and punch through the Surigao Strait at the south end of Leyte and steam north. A huge second force under the command of Vice Admiral Kurita would sail north of the island of Samar, through the San Bernardino Strait, turn south for Leyte Gulf and squeeze the transports and supporting ships between it and the approaching Southern Force. A key to the whole operation was the Northern Force, the decoy force which, it was hoped, would lure the fleet carriers and fast battleships of Admiral Halsey's Third Fleet from the coming battlefield. The Japanese hoped that by the time the Americans realized they had been duped, their Southern and Center forces would have been able to wipe out the amphibious ships and transports off the landing beaches and deliver a setback to the Americans from which it would take months to recover.

Task Force 38—three groups of carriers and the navy's newest and most modern battleships—took the bait and headed north in pursuit. The Seventh Fleet's back door would lay unprotected, but Kinkaid still packed a punch in Fire Support Unit North and Fire Support Unit South. These were the old battleships that had been shelling the beachheads. Five of the six had been at Pearl Harbor and felt the first blows of the Pacific war. Under the command of Admiral Jesse Oldendorf, the old ships turned east in column so that they could fire full broadsides at the approaching Japanese warships coming up from the south through the narrow Suriago Strait. Destroyers struck first with torpedoes, the cruisers began shooting at long range, and then the battleships opened up. This is what they had been built for when they entered the fleet between 1915 and 1921: surface action, battleship versus battleship. The de-stroyers' torpedoes made a shambles of the Japanese battle line and the remainder of it was torn apart by Oldendorf's old battlewagons.

No sooner had this action been completed than frantic word was received by Kinkaid from the escort carriers to the north. Japanese battleships and cruisers of the Center Force were attacking them just outside the Gulf. Somehow they had managed to slip past the Third Fleet and were steaming straight for the thinly armored carriers. How the Japanese had managed to do it was a tale of misunderstanding and miscommunication, overoptimism, and overconfidence.

The Center Force had been attacked the previous day by submarines and Halsey's carrier planes in the Sibuyan Sea to the northwest of Leyte. The battleship *Musashi,* one of the two largest in the world, went down after being hit with nineteen torpedoes and seventeen bombs. Three other cruisers and battleships were hit or nearly missed. But still they came on. When Halsey received word aboard the *New Jersey* about the discovery of the Northern Force, he assumed that the Center Force had been crippled and was no longer a threat. Rather than combine his fast battleships into a separate task force (Task Force 34) and detaching it from the fleet to watch over the strait, Halsey ordered all of Task Force 38 (three carrier groups with accompanying battleships) to head north after the Japanese carriers. Leaving the battle line at San Bernardino Strait without air cover would have been dangerous; leaving behind one of the three carrier groups to either watch the strait or cover the battleships would have significantly weakened his striking force. So he took everyone and everything in a dash to the north. Admiral Kinkaid, for his part, assumed that Task Force 34 had in fact been formed and left to guard the strait. In a message to Kinkaid advising that he was going north, Halsey spoke of three groups heading after the Japanese fleet. Kinkaid believed this to be three carrier groups and that the fourth, the nonexistent Task Force 34, was not included. Kinkaid was wrong. No one was watching his right flank. Almost no one, that is. During the night, planes from the *Independence* spotted Kurita's force transiting the strait and relayed word to Third Fleet, but for some reason no action was taken and no alert relayed to Seventh Fleet to the south. The result was that Kurita's force broke through San Bernardino Strait with not an American vessel in sight. He proceeded southeast down the coast of Samar and there, on the horizon to the east, were the targets: the northernmost group of baby flattops, the *Kalinin Bay* and the rest of Taffy 3.

The CVEs in all three Taffys had begun their daily launch cycle. Taffy 3 launched fighters on combat air patrol over Leyte Gulf and an antisubmarine patrol as well. These mundane but vital jobs that the escort carriers performed freed the big flattops with Halsey's Third Fleet to hunt down and attack the main body of the Japanese fleet. At least that was the way it was supposed to work. Not that day, though. As the planes rolled down the flight decks and formed up for their patrols, lookouts on the island of the *Kalinin Bay* and on the other carriers began to see unfamiliar masts and superstructures on the horizon to the west. At two minutes before seven in the morning the Japanese Center Force, still potent despite the battering it had taken in the Sibuyan Sea the previous day, opened fire. The next few hours were among the wildest of the Pacific war.

As splashes erupted in the water around the carriers and destroyers, the men on the ships became fully aware of what had happened. The carriers formed a circle, like prairie schooners under assault in a Hollywood western, and raced east into the wind to get the rest of their planes airborne. They raced only in the sense that they were going as fast as they could. Top speed was seventeen and one-half knots, but it was not fast enough. Given enough time, the battleships and cruisers would be able to overtake them. They were trying to do just that, as the flight deck crews aboard the six Kaiser ships struggled to get their aircraft into the air to attack the warships now dropping heavy caliber shells all around them. Once the planes were aloft the carriers turned southwest and headed for the other two Taffys. The pursuing ships would have to be slowed down and Admiral Clifton Sprague ordered his six destroyers and destroyer escorts (DEs) to strike at them with torpedoes. As pitifully underarmed as the destroyers were against the Japanese ships, the destroyer escorts were ridiculously so. Where the *Fletcher*s carried five five-inch mounts, the escorts had but two. They were barely three hundred feet long and could make only about twenty-four knots. Yet on they all came as the Japanese pounded several into smoking, sinking ruins.

The carriers continued to steam southwest in a circular formation, under fire all of the time, as their escorts struck back at the Japanese and slowed them down. Four heavy cruisers tried to overhaul and outflank them to the east, hoping to cut off their retreat. The *Kalinin Bay*, *St. Lo*, and the *Gambier Bay* formed the rear semicircle of ships, the *Fanshaw Bay*, *White Plains*, and *Kitkun Bay* made up its leading edge. The lone five-incher on each of the carriers spat out at the pursuing cruisers, who replied with salvo after salvo of eight-inch shells. At 0750 the *Kalinin Bay* was hit as her fighters roared off her deck. Then she was hit again, but the "K.B." scored, too, defiantly hitting a cruiser with a five-inch shell from ten thousand yards. The *Fanshaw Bay*—the "Fannie B"—was hit, as was the *White Plains* and the *St. Lo*. The Japanese cruisers continued to have a good firing solution on the *Kalinin Bay* and hit her fourteen times. Several shells slammed into her below the waterline and she began to flood. The *Gambier Bay* was under constant fire. The *Johnston,* before she sank, tried to draw fire away from the *Gambier Bay.* Another destroyer opened fire on the heavy cruisers, which then replied with salvoes that landed so close the destroyer was smothered in water from the near-miss splashes. Help also was coming in the form of aircraft launched from the carriers, sinking the cruisers *Chokai* and *Chikuma,* but it was not soon enough to save the *Gambier Bay.* Her men could see the Japanese ships firing at them, the near misses splashing close by, the hits causing the ship to shudder and burn. She was repeatedly straddled, hit and finally went under.

And then, inexplicably, the Japanese turned away. They believed they had run into a force larger than just a few destroyers and mass-produced, thin-skinned "Woolworth" carriers. The Japanese also incorrectly believed they were not gaining on the American ships fleeing before them and were beginning to be worried about fuel after their high-speed pursuit.

For the men of Taffy 3, though, the day was not over. As if being chased and shelled by a force of battleships and cruisers were not enough for these small ships and their exhausted crews, the kamikaze entered the picture. The *Kalinin Bay* was hit again and then again. So was the *St. Lo.* Her bombs and torpedoes exploded and started a fire that could not be controlled. She became the second carrier from Taffy 3 to go down that day.

Sixteen months later, in Boston Harbor in early 1946, shipyard workers go about their business under the bows of these nondescript miniature carriers (fig. 29). The cars along the pier may have been built before the war, before some steel production was diverted from Ford and General Motors plants to the Kaiser yards assembling these ships on the West Coast. Peace has returned to Boston. Possibly these same men (and more than a few women) worked on ships that returned here during the war for repair or overhaul. Possibly they were hired to process the escort carriers that were to be mothballed here. How many of them know what these ships did during the war? One CVE must look like the rest, and these are not having damage repaired from a battle they may have read about. These are here for a checkup, for a few repairs and a tune-up before they are sealed and locked up for a few years. Maybe forever. Do the numbers on the islands mean anything? Do the names on the stern? Are these vessels just a job to be marked off on a checklist? The shipyards and their skilled labor did a magnificent job during the war. The men and women took great pride in their work, felt a deep satisfaction when another ship was returned to the fleet better than ever because of their handiwork. Yet, these ships and others like them were not headed back to the fleet. They would not leave Boston or Norfolk or Tacoma. Some, like the *Kalinin Bay* and the *Kitkun Bay* would be scrapped. Others like the *Tulagi* had seen too much war and would not be retained in the reserve fleet.

These six ships could have been the carriers of Taffy 3. Indeed, one of them was. Their bows are all pointed in the same direction, like the fleeing jeeps of Clifton Sprague, heading east to launch their aircraft into the wind, then southwest to escape the menacing behemoths behind them. A shipyard worker removing one of the radar antennas from the mast of the K. B. might look aft over the empty flight deck and, if he could see the horizon about seventeen miles distant, imagine he could see a low, dark form, with maybe a hint of a tower rising from near the center. Had he been a lookout aboard her in the autumn of 1944, he might have wondered what ship it was. A junior officer or enlisted man, no matter where he served or what he did, had a limited view of the war. Grand strategy and tactics were not something he thought about or had much information about. A sailor was concerned about his next watch, his next batch of mail from home, getting his uniforms back from the ship's laundry and what the galley was serving for breakfast.

He thought about his job. Maybe he was a radioman, yeoman, machinist mate or gunner's mate. He had watch and battle station assignments and he knew his job well. He knew where the ship was and what it was doing, but most likely had little idea what others in his group, much less the fleet, were doing. He might have wondered just which ship that was on the horizon and what the others were that were now coming into view. Maybe, were he particularly observant, interested, or privy to the information, he would have thought it was one of Halsey's ships. After all, those big carriers and battleships were somewhere to the north, weren't they?

And then, as he pondered this and looked at this watch to see that it was nearly eight o'clock in the morning, the sea around his ship would have erupted in fountains of water and foam. The water would have been colored, an odd sight. It was from the dye that the ships on the horizon were using to identify their own shells, to correct their own aim. And the shipyard worker perched high on the mast in Boston in 1946, tool belt dangling from his waist as he struggled to undo some bolts frozen in place by rust, could imagine that he, that sailor on that very real ship now tied up in a bustling shipyard filled with other obscure ships being stripped of their identities, was looking at the silhouette of the battleship *Yamato,* was firing a salvo of nine three-thousand-pound shells at her from almost three hundred football fields away. He could see, in his mind's eye, the activity down on the deck, no longer empty but full of planes, their engines running, propellers spinning, deck crewmen running about in a carefully choreographed, carefully rehearsed act to get the aircraft launched from the tiny deck in the fastest yet safest manner possible.

This workman, imagining himself aboard this small ship off the Philippine coast in late October 1944, might feel the ship's engines going all out, might feel the noticeable vibration that told veterans, without even looking at the water racing by her hull, that she was making turns for flank speed. The aft end of the ship would vibrate wildly below-decks, and up in the stubby superstructure the wind would blow harder as the carrier tried to get enough airflow along her deck to make up for the lack of runway length and get enough lift under the wings of the planes to keep them airborne once the wheels had left the edge of the deck. As the ship raced east into the morning sun, the shells would continue to splash down, and then he would see the escorts, the big *Fletcher*s and the smaller DEs, headed straight for the Japanese fleet. He would watch and pray for them and would not know that the captain of the *Johnston* was only a short time away from winning a Medal of Honor for his gallant and repeated charge into the guns of the enemy. And he would not know that the medal would be awarded to his family, because Commander Ernest E. Evans, a Cherokee Indian, would go down with his ship.

The worker might imagine he could feel the ship heel sharply to starboard as the last plane left the deck, and if he looked at the nearly deserted *Shamrock Bay* to the right and the *Saginaw Bay* to the left, could imagine they were other members of Taffy 3 making the same turn so that the ships could head away from the shells falling uncomfortably close. He might think he could feel the first of the big shells crashing into the *Kalinin Bay*'s hull below him. Some of the shells would pass through with a jar without exploding, others would detonate and shake the ship from stem to stern as she ran. And he could see the *Gambier Bay* staggering under a hail of shells as a cruiser, clearly visible only a few thousand yards away, slammed shell after shell into her until she vanished beneath the waves.

And as this workman freed the last of the stubborn bolts from the bracket holding part of the antenna and began lowering it with a rope to the deck below, he might come out of his daydream, look around him at the quiet modest ships up and down the piers, and breathe deeply. He might look at the six ships here and wonder what would happen to them, now that the war was over and the Japanese defeated. The sailors and GIs were coming home from every corner of the globe—they were the lucky ones, the ones not entombed aboard the *Gambier Bay* or the *St. Lo* or the *Bismarck Sea* that lay broken and twisted in the dark depths of the Pacific, or buried in a hastily laid out cemetery on Iwo Jima or Italy, or lying somewhere in a jungle or forest or on a mountain top where no one has looked or ever will look or even can look. Most of the ships he can see will go to the reserve fleet, where no one hopes they will be needed again. As he climbs down from the mast he may or may not know that the *Kalinin Bay* will not be among them. By this time next year, 1947, she will have been cut up for scrap, her name gone but for the history books.

As East Coast shipyards began the laborious task of mothballing the fleet in early 1946, so, too, did those on the West Coast. Like sailors on liberty lined up at a waterfront bar, these *Fletcher*-class destroyers are nosed bow first into a pier at the San Diego repair base on 11 February 1946 (fig. 30). All are headed for the reserve fleet. A total of 175 *Fletcher*s were built, the first joining the fleet in June 1942, the last in November of 1944. They were built in shipyards on every coast: at Bethlehem yards in Staten Island, San Francisco and San Pedro; at the Seattle-Tacoma Shipyards, at Gulf Shipbuilding in Chickasaw, Alabama; at the navy yards in Boston, Charleston, and Puget Sound. Nineteen were war losses: one, the *Spence,* as the result of a typhoon. Their job now is finished, most of their wartime crews have departed, and they are here as part of the preinactivation routine. There are twenty of them, a mere sampling of the destroyer fleet that served in every theater of the war, in every kind of weather, against each of the Axis enemies, performing a variety of duties.

The four outboard destroyers in this group were all veterans of the Pacific war. From front to back they are the *Picking, Porterfield, Prichett,* and *Stembel.* The *Prichett* was laid down in July 1942, the others in November and December of that year. Though the first of the four

*Fig. 30. A row of Fletcher-class destroyers being prepared for moth- balls at San Diego in 1946. U.S. Naval Institute*

to be laid down, the *Prichett* was the last to join the fleet in January 1944, while the remainder were commissioned in 1943. She shows no sign of the bomb hit she took in the middle of the night less than a year before. It blew a hole in her stern below the waterline and to keep the water from progressively flooding her compartments forward of the hit, she raced through the night at twenty-eight knots until bulkheads could be shored up. She was repaired at Guam, only to be hit by a kamikaze that summer. The *Stembel* was the only one of the four to serve in the Atlantic, albeit briefly, while the other three went straight from post-shakedown training to the Pacific. The *Porterfield* was part of the force that chased and sank a Japanese cruiser retreating through San Bernardino Strait after the battle of Leyte Gulf, and the *Picking* could still be found afloat, rusty but proudly showing her hull number 685 nearly half a century later, tied up at the deserted Mare Island piers that used to hold the mothballed submarines of the Pacific Reserve Fleet.

On the day the Japanese attacked Pearl Harbor the United States Navy had 171 destroyers in commission, seventy-one of which were the flush deckers built during and just after World War I. The rest had been built in the 1930s. By the end of World War II some 514 destroyers as well as 414 destroyer escorts had seen wartime duty. Seventy-one destroyers and destroyer-types (destroyer-minesweepers, fast transports, etc.) and eleven destroyer escorts had been sunk. Another ten destroyers had been mangled so badly by kamikazes that they were not repaired after the war and instead were sold for scrap. More effectively than the Japanese or Germans ever managed to do, the scrappers dismantled much of this destroyer fleet after the war.

It did not take long to remove these ships from service. Over 150 *Fletcher*s and *Benson*s were decommissioned and placed in reserve in the first eighteen months after the war. In 1947 most of the rest went through the process of inactivation and storage. The yearly cost of maintaining this fleet as the decade approached an end was averaging less than 1 percent of the original construction costs of the vessels, a very good bargain indeed. Modifications were made as the process went on and the sailors of the reserve fleet learned the best methods for preserving the ships under their care. At first the exposed mounts and machinery had been preserved with the spray-on plastic coverings. This method was replaced by the use of metal huts or cocoons. Several of these were then connected by pipe to small dehumidifying machines. It was less costly and more effective. A few of the *Fletcher*s underwent their inactivation overhauls at other yards before arriving at San Diego to be mothballed. Some would go into storage at Long Beach, others would remain in San Diego. The *Fletcher*s at the repair base all had their hulls painted below the waterline in an effort to prevent corrosion from seawater, but overhauls and dry docking in subsequent years would show that the hulls were becoming pitted anyway. In the 1950s cathodic protection, in which a small electric current beneath the water surrounding the ship's hull negated the corrosive effects of the salt water, was in widespread use. The biggest problem that would face these veteran destroyers and indeed most of the ships in the postwar years would be the protection of their weather surfaces. The procedure that would be used on these ships and the others being readied for mothballs would be to strip the old paint (and not a little rust) down to the bare metal and then repaint it. The stripping of the old paint proved to be extremely manpower intensive. Tried and true methods like chipping, scraping, and brushing with thick-wire brushes gave way to sand- and grit-blasting. These were ways to effectively yet speedily remove the old paint so that a new, thick, protective coating could be applied to keep the rain, sun, and ocean air away from the metal hull of the ship as she sat idle for who knew how long.

Destroyers escorted the Atlantic convoys to Britain and were in the thick of the fighting long before 7 December 1941. It was a destroyer, the *Greer,* that was the first United States ship to be attacked in the war, three months before Pearl Harbor. Another destroyer, the *Kearny,* was the first American ship to be damaged in the war when a U-boat torpedoed her in mid-October 1941 as she escorted a convoy from Canada. The torpedo blew a hole in the *Kearny*'s starboard side under her forward stack, but she did not sink. The distinction of being the first American warship to be sunk belonged to another destroyer, the old four-piper *Reuben James,* which was sunk by another U-boat on 31 October 1941. Another destroyer, the *Ward,* fired the first shot of the Pacific war when she spotted and attacked a Japanese midget submarine trying to sneak into Pearl Harbor hours before the attack. Her warnings went unheeded ashore.

Once war was declared the destroyer was everywhere. They continued their convoy duties in the Atlantic and sortied with the pitifully thin task forces that ventured out on hit-and-run raids from Pearl Harbor in the first few months of 1942. In August 1942, men of the First Marine Division came ashore on the second biggest island in the Solomons archipelago—Guadalcanal. The Solomons run for about nine hundred miles southeast to northwest and lie astride the sea lanes between the United States and Australia. Their seizure by the Japanese would cut off Australia from American help and leave her open to attack. Possession of Guadalcanal by the Americans meant that the southern Solomons could be used as a base to strike northwest through the island chain toward New Guinea, blunting the Japanese thrust toward Australia and establishing advance bases for the eventual liberation of the Philippines.

Fierce sea engagements were fought in the waters off the southern Solomons, the names of the locations exotic and unknown to most Americans before the war: Cape Esperance, Tassafaronga and Kula Gulf. Light cruisers and destroyers did most of the fighting. Up the Solomon chain pushed the American amphibious forces, to New Georgia and Bougainville, and more battles were fought with destroyers in the thick of it. Additional *Fletcher*s joined the fleet, such as the *Nicholas,* the *Chevalier,* and the *Radford,* and fought in some of the fiercest surface actions of the war as Japanese ships sortied from Rabaul to lash out at the Allied landing forces and their naval support, or to resupply, reinforce, or retrieve troops from the jungles of Florida Island and Rendova and Vella Lavella.

Throughout 1942 and into early 1943, the Solomons were the scene of a string of engagements: not battleship against battleship but destroyer against destroyer and cruiser against cruiser. Torpedoes raced through the waters of "the Slot," the slender body of water between the parallel groups of islands of Guadalcanal, New Georgia, Vella Lavella, and Kolombangara to the south and South Isabela and Choiseul to the north. The destroyers *Benham* and the *Walke,* among others, went down at Guadalcanal, the *Chevalier* at Vella Lavella and the *De Haven* at Tassafaronga. Fifteen in all went down in the Solomons campaign. Some of them were brand new *Fletcher*s, like those at the San Diego repair base in the photograph taken a few years later as America entered the postwar years.

In November 1943 marines stormed ashore on Bougainville, the last stronghold before the huge Japanese base at Rabaul at the northwest end of the Solomon chain. The Japanese struck back hard. On the night of 1–2 November 1943, two heavy cruisers, two light cruisers and six destroyers came down to hit the invasion forces at Torokina on the eastern side of Bougainville. They were intercepted by four cruisers—the *Montpelier, Cleveland, Columbia,* and *Denver*—and eight destroyers, all of them new *Fletcher*s. All of the destroyers belonged to Desron 23, and their commander was Captain Arleigh Burke. Just as the submarine fleet spawned its own colorful characters, so too did the destroyer force. Both the squadron and Burke were soon to have nicknames destined to live on in naval lore.

Another night melee ensued with torpedoes crisscrossing the water and gunfire flashes lighting the evening sky. At this, the battle of Empress Augusta Bay, Burke had a chance to try out the destroyer tactics he had developed and worked on as commander of Desdiv 12. Burke stressed initiative and opportunism on the part of his destroyer skippers and division leaders. Unfettered to the battle line and stationed far out in front of the main body of warships, they could use their radar, speed and torpedoes to strike a sudden unexpected blow before the enemy knew what was happening. Burke's plan was to divide the two divisions of ships in his squadron into two parallel, steaming columns. The first would deliver a torpedo attack and then peel away, while the second column stood ready. As the first wave unmasked their five-inch guns toward the enemy, the second would bore in and deliver another torpedo attack on the stunned enemy as the guns of the original column brought them under an avalanche of five-inch shells. Though his destroyer-launched torpedoes failed to find their mark, the light cruisers smashed a Japanese light cruiser and threw the Japanese column into confusion. The two divisions of Desron 23 became separated, but Burke's flagship, the *Charles Ausburne,* came upon the stricken *Sendai* and riddled her with five-inch gunfire, sending her under.

The confusion of night battle was no less a problem for the American sailors, and at one point one division fired shells at another, nearly hitting the *Spence.* Finally, contact was made and the *Charles Ausburne* joined the other ships of Desdiv 45 and sank the *Hatsukaze,* which had already been crippled in a collision with the heavy cruiser *Myoko.* Though the destroyers had not landed a knockout punch, they had proved the tactics Burke had developed: freedom of action and initiative and always taking the offensive. At a cost of one damaged destroyer, the *Foote,* the destroyers of Arleigh Burke and the light cruisers of Admiral "Tip" Merrill had sunk a light cruiser and a destroyer, damaged another heavy cruiser and two destroyers, and just as important, had beaten back a strong attempt to destroy the vulnerable shipping off the invasion beachhead.

Shortly after the battle Burke adapted an insignia for his squadron, a small American Indian that he had painted on the bridge wings of his flagship, and the squadron adopted the nickname of the figure, Little Beaver. His flagship remained the destroyer *Charles Ausburne,* pictured in a measure-twenty-two-camouflage design (fig. 31). Camouflage schemes were called measures, and number twenty-two consisted of navy blue and haze gray. The border between the two ran parallel to the waterline along the hull and its highest point was the lowest point of the main deck sheer. Thus on the *Charles Ausburne* the navy blue ran from the stern along the main deck to about where number three turret was, at which point the main deck began to climb toward the bow. The navy blue paint continued parallel to the water so as to blend with the blue water of the horizon. Everything above that line was gray, and the deck, turrets tops, and any flat surface were painted navy blue.

The *Charles Ausburne* was a typical *Fletcher*-class destroyer, com-

*Fig. 31. Flagship of "Thirty-one Knot" Burke, the* Charles Ausburne. *U.S. Naval Institute*

missioned in November 1942 after being built at Consolidated Steel in Orange, Texas. After a brief voyage to Casablanca, she joined Desron 23 when it was activated at Boston on 11 May 1943 and two and one-half months later she and the other destroyers of the squadron arrived at Noumea, New Caledonia, prepared to join the fight for the Solomons. Up the Slot she went on patrol, trying to intercept any Japanese headed down. At Empress Augusta Bay she was in the thick of the fight, helping sink a light cruiser and a destroyer before escorting the damaged *Foote* away from the scene.

At the end of the month, the *Charles Ausburne* and the rest of the

Little Beavers were at it again. On 24 November they were at Hathorn Sound on Rendova being refueled when they received orders to steam for the waters between Rabaul and Buka at the northern end of Bougainville. Intelligence reported that a Japanese force was going to come down from Rabaul, past Cape St. George at the southern tip of New Ireland, and evacuate airfield personnel at Buka. Desron 23 was ordered to top off their fuel tanks and intercept.

Burke's preferred nonbattle speed was thirty-one knots (Howarth, *Men of War*, 516), but boiler problems in the *Spence* had restricted his formation's top speed to thirty knots. Halsey's headquarters sent him a message that christened him with his nickname, "Thirty-one Knot Burke get athwart the Buka-Rabaul evacuation line about thirty-five miles west of Buka . . . if enemy contacted you know what to do." This was Burke's type of order: to carry out a mission without micromanagement from his superiors. Independent operation was exactly what he had trained his Little Beavers for. On the night of 23–24 November, "Thirty-one Knot" Burke led into battle off Cape St. George the five *Fletchers* of Desron 23, the flagship *Charles Ausburne* (which also flew the flag of Desdiv 45), the *Claxton, Dyson, Converse* (flagship of Desdiv 46), and *Spence*. At 0141 the *Dyson*'s radar picked up the Japanese force, mere blips on the radar screen but in actuality five destroyers and destroyer-transports in two columns. Burke ordered Desdiv 45, the *Charles Ausburne* in the lead, to attack. At high speed they closed on the lead pair of unsuspecting Japanese ships and let fly with fifteen torpedoes at close range. One destroyer blew up and another was set afire as the torpedoes slammed home. The *Charles Ausburne* and her sisters turned to the right and immediately picked up the second column of three ships now beginning to disperse. The *Converse* and the *Spence* went after the burning destroyer while Burke led the *Charles Ausburne* and the other two ships of Desdiv 45 after the fleeing second column. The range was too great for torpedo fire since the Japanese ships had a long head start, but the Little Beavers opened up with five-inch fire from their two forward mounts. The Japanese ships fired back but the American gunfire stopped one of them. On raced the *Ausburne, Claxton,* and *Dyson,* slamming shells into the wreck as they went by and finally sinking her, while the *Converse* and the *Spence* drove the first cripple under the waves with torpedoes and gunfire. So ended the battle of Cape St. George, a resounding naval victory and quite a contrast with the confused fights earlier in the Solomons campaign that all too often resulted in a draw or worse.

Quite a different war for the destroyer lay in store off Okinawa some eighteen months later: no dashing torpedo attacks, no running gun battles, no midnight patrols in tropical waters between jungle-clad islands deep in the South Pacific. This was a war of waiting, of nerves stretched taut by days and weeks of being under the guns of one of the most fearsome and effective weapons to be thrown at the American Navy before or since: the "Divine Wind"; the kamikaze.

On April Fool's Day 1945, United States Marines and Army infantry waded ashore virtually unopposed on Okinawa and thus began a nightmare for the sailors of the destroyers offshore. Nearly seven hundred aircraft, about half of them suicide planes of the Imperial Navy's Special Attack Corps, had as their target the amphibious ships that were landing and supplying the forces ashore. Kamikazes had struck the American fleet earlier in the war at Lingayen Gulf as well as in the months since, and the fleet had devised a defensive tactic they hoped would provide early warning of the attack. Picket ships would give combat air patrols from the carriers the chance to intercept and destroy the oncoming suicide planes before they ever got near the fleet. Accordingly, sixteen pickets stations were arranged in a circle around Okinawa, anywhere from forty to seventy miles from the transport area, each initially with one destroyer and later with several.

The first large-scale air assault on the fleet, called a "kikusui" (floating chrysanthemum), was launched less than a week after the Americans waded ashore. Some of the destroyers, like the *Newcomb* and the *Leutze*, were not on picket duty but in the usual role of battleship and cruiser escort when the kamikazes fell out of the sky. The *Newcomb* was smashed by four, starting a blaze amidships that became a solid wall of fire. The *Leutze* closed with her to assist and was promptly crashed, too. Both were towed to Kerama Retto, a logistics and repair roadstead to the west of Okinawa, for repairs. But it was the picket destroyers, far away from the main fleet, far away from the protective umbrella of massed antiaircraft fire from battleships and heavy cruisers and squadrons of fighters flying top cover over the carriers, that bore the brunt of this savage assault.

On the same day that the *Newcomb* and the *Leutze* were crippled, Japanese planes singled out for destruction a trio of destroyers on picket duty: the *Bush* at station one to the north of Okinawa, the *Colhoun* at station two to the east, and the *Cassin Young* still farther to the east and a little south. At 1513 the *Bush* was struck by a kamikaze that came at her a few yards above the water and hit her between the stacks. The *Colhoun* came close aboard to assist as more aircraft appeared in the sky, all headed for the lonely ships. One hundred fifty men of the *Bush* jumped overboard at the approach of one airplane, and then clambered back aboard on knotted ropes trailed over sides. The *Colhoun's* guns blazed. Smoke streaked from the aircraft hit and set afire as they plunged to the sea. Smoke billowed upward from the blazing ships. Tracers flew skyward, and down dived the pilots bent on hurtling their bodies and bomb-laden planes into the American warships twisting and turning and shooting and burning below. The *Colhoun* hit one. Then another. But a third hit her. More approached her. She shot down another. Still another. But again the third one got through and blew a huge hole in her hull below the waterline, leaving her dead in the water. More Japanese planes appeared overhead and in every quarter. Another hit on the *Colhoun*. Another on the *Bush*. At dusk the *Bush* cracked in half and sank, while the *Cassin Young* poured gunfire into the stricken and dying *Colhoun* and sank her.

The kamikazes were everywhere. Some of them carried bombs that would explode on impact, while the kinetic energy of the hurtling plane smashed superstructures, stacks, and open gun mounts and sprayed burning gasoline over the decks. They sank the destroyer-minelayer *Emmons* on antisubmarine patrol and dived on shipping at Kerama Retto. They missed the escort carrier *Tulagi*, but exploded two Victory ships loaded with ammunition.

The destroyers on picket duty for Task Force 58 were hit on 11 April. The *Fletcher*-class *Kidd*, named for the admiral killed aboard the *Arizona*, was crashed and thirty-eight of her crew killed. On 12 April there was another big strike against the fleet. The *Cassin Young* was hit, as were the *Purdy* and the *Mannert L. Abele*, one of the new *Allen M. Sumner*-class destroyers that, along with the near identical *Gearings*, were now entering the fleet. The *Abele* was hit first in the starboard side by a kamikaze and then by an Oka, a piloted glider that was released from a twin-engine bomber, had rocket engines for added speed, and carried a ton of high explosives straight into the sides or deck of whatever warship could not shoot it down. The Oka hit the *Abele* and broke her in two. Another Oka hit the *Stanley*, on her way to relieve the strick-

*Fig. 32. The* Cola-han *approaches the damaged* Hazelwood *off Okinawa. U.S. Naval Institute*

en *Cassin Young,* and two kamikazes crushed the destroyer-minelayer *Lindsay,* killing fifty-six of her crew and wounding fifty-one more. To the east of Okinawa they stalked the battleships and cruisers of Task Force 54 and hit the battleship *Tennessee* and the destroyer *Zellars.* Friendly fire in such quarters, with planes coming in at masthead height from all directions, was a constant danger. The *Bennion* had seven wounded by antiaircraft fire from nearby ships and the *McDermut* had five killed and thirty-one wounded by more American shells. On it went.

Another kikusui hit occurred on 27–28 April. The hospital ship *Comfort* was struck by a kamikaze and several nurses killed. The *Ralph Talbot,* a veteran of Pearl Harbor, Savo Island, and Kolombangara, was hit. So was the *Haggard.* The *Hazelwood* came alongside the *Haggard* and she was promptly pounced upon by Zeros. One came at her from astern but the *Hazelwood*'s gunners deflected it away. Another hit her number two stack, cartwheeling forward into her number one stack and onto her main deck, where the plane exploded. Far worse was the bomb the Zero carried, which exploded against the back of the bridge and demolished it, killing her commanding and executive officers and putting her reservist engineering officer in command. She is pictured as she looked from the cruiser *Flint*, smoking and listing to port (fig. 32). The *Colahan* (pictured approaching the stricken *Hazelwood*), as well as the *Melvin* and the *McGowan*, rendered assistance, fighting fires, fishing survivors from the water, and transferring wounded from her decks. The *McGowan* took her under tow and late that night the *Hazelwood* was able to light off one of her boilers, get up enough steam to produce some turns on her screws, and got under way with the *Flint* guarding her. With the *Melvin* and *McGowan* as escorts, the *Hazelwood* made it to Ulithi and eventually to Mare Island for repair.

Yet another kikusui on 3 May saw the *Aaron Ward* all but demolished by four kamikazes and a bomb. Though she survived, she was too badly damaged to be repaired and was scrapped after the war. Nearby the *Little* was hit by four more kamikazes and went down. The next day the *Luce* was sunk. On station number one the *Morrison* evaded five would-be suiciders, only to have numbers six and seven explode into her and sink her. Her casualties were massive. Only 179 of her crew of 331 were rescued and of them, 108 were wounded, six of whom later died.

Destroyers were not the only victims. Battered *Birmingham*, back in the war after her ordeal alongside the *Princeton*, was hit on 4 May and suffered fifty-one killed. The battleship *New Mexico* had fifty-four killed by a kamikaze on 12 May. The *Bunker Hill* caught it on 11 May, the *Enterprise* three days later. The British Pacific Fleet was targeted too, though the steel flight deck of the carrier *Formidable* easily withstood the blow. But it was the American destroyer fleet that continued to feel the full fury of this last-ditch Japanese defense.

What the invasion of Japan would have meant in terms of suicide attacks against the fleet is, fortunately, a question to be answered only by armchair strategists and novelists. A few months after the horrible ordeal off Okinawa, the war was over and most of the ships were coming home. Five thousand sailors died off Okinawa. Twelve destroyers and destroyer escorts were sunk by kamikazes. Fifteen were sunk when losses from all causes were counted. The list of damaged ships off Okinawa was staggering: eighty-eight destroyers and thirty destroyer escorts received damage in one form or another, many from the suicide planes. The lucky ones came home. The luckier still were mothballed.

The *McGowan*, pictured being inactivated behind another *Fletcher* at Mare Island in January 1946, saw much of the fighting off Okinawa but

*Fig. 33. The USS
McGowan is moth-
balled at Mare
Island. National
Archives, Pacific
Sierra Region*

emerged undamaged (fig. 33). The twin, forty-millimeter tubs behind the number two, five-inch mount have been covered with strippable plastic coating, while the guns have been removed from the inboard destroyer, possibly for servicing before storage aboard ship. The ship-yard workers are in the process of sealing the number two mount and will soon be spraying the plastic solution on the number one mount, which already has the netting installed. On the inboard destroyer the gun shield has been removed from the forward five-inch mount to make access for cleaning and preservation easier before the shield is replaced and the mount sealed.

This quiet scene is a contrast to that aboard the *Hazelwood,* under tow by the *McGowan* less than a year before. But for a twist of fate—and an order given at some unfathomable link in the chain of command that sent the *Hazelwood* to one point on the surface of the ocean and the *McGowan* to another—it could very well have been the *Hazelwood* here undergoing a careful overhaul and preservation, and the *McGowan* pierside at Puget Sound or at Mare Island, her bridge shattered. Where the bridge and main battery director now sit on *McGowan* there was only a crumpled mass of smoking, twisted metal on the *Hazelwood*, containing the mangled bodies of her captain—the "old man"—and her executive officer and some of the seventy-five others who were killed. Another thirty-five sailors, men much like these stepping over ropes and air hoses now, were never seen again, having been either blown overboard or burned to ashes by flaming gasoline that sprayed over the forward part of the ship.

In the still waters of Mare Island these two survivors have returned home to be put to rest. No longer does the radar search the waters of the South Pacific for a target that could be another destroyer, a cruiser or even a battleship. No longer does the main battery director of the *McGowan* search the sky for incoming Zeros or Vals or Judys, their pilots bent on driving the propeller of their airplane somewhere into the 376-foot length of the ship. No longer do the two mounts forward and three others aft turn left and right in response to the director's control, searching for the best bearing and elevation for the barrels to put their high explosive shells on target. Maybe the target was a Japanese artillery position on Vella Lavella, or a transport full of soldiers headed for Bougainville or the sixth out of seven planes headed straight for the ship off Kerama Retto or on picket station number eleven.

Perhaps that ship next to the *McGowan* is the *Miller* or the *Stephen Potter* or any one of the hundreds of *Fletcher*s, *Benson*s, and *Sumner*s that served in every corner of the globe and every theater of the war, performing every duty there was to be done before coming home to be mothballed and forgotten. Maybe across the water in Vallejo a civilian walking past looks over at the shipyard with a practiced eye, searching for the distinctive outline of a heavy cruiser come home from the war, or the darkened, distorted form of a damaged "small boy," a destroyer or destroyer escort that caught it in some battle he read about in newspapers many months ago. Last year's news. Now the paper is full of strikes and labor disputes and "help for the veteran" articles. No, he might say to himself as he squints into the glare of the afternoon sun setting into the coastal hills beyond, nothing there but a couple more run-of-the-mill "cans" being mothballed at the shipyard. Saw a million of them there during the war. Maybe, he hopes as he turns and walks away, there'll be a big ship there tomorrow, a ship like a battleship or a carrier. A ship with a real story to tell.

TWO  *New Life, or the Breakers*

THE end of the war was a time of mixed emotions for millions of Americans. It was a time of great joy for servicemen who came home and for families who had been separated from them for so long. It was a time of reunions, of seeing the neighborhood again after the mountains of Italy or jungles of New Guinea. It was a time of driving the family car down Main Street once more after piloting a B-17 bomber in the flak-ridden skies over Berlin. The United States, as it always did when war threatened, had relied on a citizen army, drafted for the duration, anxious to get back home and on with their lives when it ended. For hundreds of thousands of Americans, however, 1946 was not a time for rejoicing. The war had destroyed their lives. Almost three hundred thousand Americans had been killed overseas. For those families who had lost a loved one, the late 1940s would be a time to heal the emotional and mental scars left by the war. Many soldiers and sailors returned home maimed, disfigured, horribly burned. Some of these young men bore no resemblance to the individual who had left home for the war years before.

In 1946 Samuel Goldwyn released the motion picture *The Best Years of Our Lives,* a film that captured the moods, both joyous and sad, of postwar America and the returning veterans. One of the film's most poignant scenes depicted the return of a sailor whose hands had been burned off when his carrier was sunk. The cab drops him at his home and drives away, taking with it two new friends, also returning vets, with whom he has traveled across the country. Without a thought he raises his arm—his hook—to wave good-bye. This is the first time his family has seen the cold metal that has replaced the warm hands he had when he left home. When she sees the hooks, his mother lets out a cry of anguish and turns away to hide her pain. This was the homecoming for a fictional family, but the same scene occurred in many real ones as America made the adjustment from war to peace. These were simple midwestern parents whose little boy had gone off to war, whose little boy had thrown footballs in high school but would never throw another, whose little boy could no longer button his pajamas at night, whose little boy, now a navy veteran of the bloodiest war ever fought, must tell his childhood sweetheart that without his hooks he is as helpless as a baby.

Even for families who were reunited in joy, it was not always an easy adjustment. The euphoria over the victory and the happiness over the speedy demobilization were tempered by harsh postwar facts. The war had cost the United States about $300 billion. Over 16 million men (and tens of thousands of women) had been uprooted from their homes, jobs, and lives, trained to be soldiers, airmen, and sailors, and sent all over the globe. Now it was over. Military contracts were cut because tanks, aircraft, rifles, and a million and one other items were no longer needed for the war effort. Price controls were lifted, and because the money saved during the war was now available to spend on scarce civilian items, inflation took hold and prices began to climb. The cost of living rose but wages did not, as defense plants, factories, and shipyards ended production and closed down. Hours were cut, paychecks got smaller, and then the unions began to go out on strike: the United Auto Workers, coal miners, steel mills, railroads.

The turmoil in the United States was far exceeded by the unrest in a world struggling to rise from the war's devastation. Much of Europe had been ravaged, and Russia wanted all of it under her control. The wartime alliance was over. Russia and international communism were now the enemies of the West. The United States and Britain saw communism as a cancer that threatened the Free World. For now, Europe— particularly the Balkans and Far East—would be the battleground. The Soviet Union wanted control of the Dardanelles, the narrow stretch of water leading from their Black Sea ports to the Mediterranean. Turkey controlled them, and the Soviets made no secret of their desire to have the Turks fall under their sway. Torn apart by civil strife, Greece was ripe for a communist takeover. France had been ruined by the war: overrun by Germany in 1940, her land again became a battlefield as the

Nazis were forced back across the Rhine after the Normandy landings in 1944. Britain was bankrupt.

It was up to the United States, now the world's greatest sea and air power, to respond to the Soviets. America was a nation desperately trying to return to her peacetime ways, yet handed the responsibility to protect the Free World against Soviet aggression. The American response to Soviet pressure was not military, however; it was economic. The Marshall Plan, named for the ex-Army Chief of Staff, General of the Army George C. Marshall, was a massive influx of American aid to Europe, rebuilding shattered economies so that western European nations could withstand communism on their own while under the umbrella of the United States' monopoly on atomic weaponry.

In the Far East, once dominated by the Greater East Asia Co-Prosperity Sphere (a euphemism for an expanded and expanding Japanese empire), Russia had lived up to its agreement at Yalta and had entered the war against the Japanese, the same day that the second atomic bomb wiped out Nagasaki. The occupation of Japan would be undertaken solely by American forces, of that there would be no doubt. But Korea, invaded and occupied by Japan and about to be liberated, was a different matter. Soviet troops were on their way there. A dividing line was established at the thirty-eighth parallel, which cut the Korean peninsula almost in half. Above the thirty-eighth parallel the Soviets would disarm the Japanese troops. Below it, American forces would land and occupy the country. The Soviets had no intention of leaving Korea nor allowing free elections to unify the north and south; as long as they remained, the United States, too, would maintain troops below the line dividing the country. A divided Korea—like a divided Germany, like the partitioned city of Berlin—would be a legacy of the end of World War II, a reminder that the United States and the Soviet Union began another war in Europe the moment Germany laid down her arms at Rheims and as the surrender documents were being signed aboard the *Missouri*.

In 1949 Communist Chinese forces, with Soviet backing, forced Chiang Kai-shek's Nationalist Chinese Army off mainland China and onto the island of Formosa (Taiwan). The United States backed Chiang, and American warships patrolled the straits between the island and the mainland to prevent either a communist invasion of Formosa or an ill-advised attempt by Chiang to attack the victorious forces of Mao Tse Tung now consolidating their control over the world's most populous nation. But the mighty American Fast Carrier Task Force of World War II was long gone. The Far East was the province of the Seventh Fleet now, and the Seventh Fleet was but a shadow of the force that had driven the Imperial Japanese Navy from the sea just five years before.

The Pacific had been *the* naval theater during the war, but that enemy had been defeated. The focus now was on the Atlantic, on the massive Russian Army in Germany and Czechoslovakia and Hungary and Poland. The focus was also on the Mediterranean, where the big new carriers of the *Midway*-class—the *Midway, Franklin D. Roosevelt,* and the *Coral Sea*—steamed with nuclear weapons in their magazines.

As June 1950 approached, the United States Navy was woefully unprepared to fight another major war. Only four *Essex* carriers remained active. The *Valley Forge* was in port in Hong Kong. The *Leyte* joined the three *Midway*s in the Mediterranean. The *Boxer* was due to return to the West Coast on 25 June. The *Philippine Sea,* having just transferred from the Atlantic Fleet, was at her new San Diego home port. A fifth *Essex,* the *Princeton,* had just been decommissioned and mothballed at Bremerton along with six other carriers, all veterans of the Pacific war. A sixth, the *Oriskany,* was nearing completion at the New York Naval Shipyard, her construction begun in 1944 and suspended in 1947 while her design was altered. Two light carriers, the *Saipan* and the *Wright,* were in service training naval aviators on the East Coast. Like the *Independence* class, they were converted from cruisers, but these two were built on the larger *Baltimore,* rather than *Cleveland,* hulls. The huge wartime fleet of escort carriers had been reduced to just a few, all operating antisubmarine aircraft. A handful of others, the *Block Island, Rendova,* and *Bairoko,* had just entered the mothball fleet.

The only active battleship was the *Missouri,* and she had been relegated to training cruises with Naval Academy midshipmen and naval reservists. Nine heavy cruisers remained in the fleet: four in the Pacific, the other five in the Atlantic Fleet. The *Toledo* and the *Helena* were at Long Beach. The *Rochester* was in the Philippines and the *St. Paul,* like the *Missouri,* was on a midshipman training cruise. The *Salem* had just relieved the *Newport News* as the Sixth Fleet flagship, joining the *Columbus* in the Mediterranean. The other pair of heavy cruisers, the *Albany* and the *Des Moines,* rotated periodically between their East Coast bases and the Atlantic and Mediterranean. Just four light cruisers remained, in three different classes. The *Juneau* was in the western

Pacific, alternately patrolling the waters between Taiwan and the mainland and between Japan and Korea in the Tsushima Straits. Her sister ship *Spokane* had just been retired to mothballs at Bayonne, leaving the *Juneau* as the last of the five-inch-gunned light cruisers. The last of the active *Cleveland*s, the USS *Manchester,* was in overhaul at the San Francisco Navy Yard. The new *Roanoke* had just finished a Sixth Fleet deployment, while the *Worcester* was still in the Mediterranean. All of the *Fletcher*-class destroyers were gone except for a handful training naval reservists. The *Benson*s were small but still considered worthy of retention in the inactive fleet and so had been tied up in rows at Charleston. Some of the *Sumner*s, too, had been decommissioned while the rest of the *Sumner*s and all of the slightly larger *Gearing*s made up the postwar destroyer fleet. Most of the submarine fleet were decommissioned, with Mare Island alone caring for forty-seven subs and four tenders by 1950.

These were the active capital ships of the United States Navy in late June 1950: seven fleet carriers, two light carriers used for training, three jeep carriers converted to antisubmarine warfare, a lone battleship, nine heavy and four light cruisers. The strength of the Marine Corps had been slashed and so, too, had the amphibious fleet. Most of it rested in clusters at Columbia River anchorage, at Green Cove Springs, Florida, and Orange, Texas. Others were berthed with attack transports at Stockton, California. The fleet as a whole was not stagnant, however. Beginning in 1947, some of the other *Essex*-class carriers were undergoing conversion to handle the new jet aircraft then coming off production lines and already flying off the *Midway*s.

Some of the destroyer fleet were also undergoing conversion. This was driven not by American advances in jet aircraft but by German advances in undersea warfare. At the end of the war, both the western Allies and the Russians had captured a number of German Type XXI and XXVI U-boats. These were far more advanced than any submarine in any other navy, with greater underwater endurance, stealth, and speed. The Russians, it was feared, might flood the Atlantic with German-designed and Russian-improved submarines, choke off the convoy routes between North America and Europe as the U-boats had failed to do, and prevent any reinforcement of the American Army in Europe. The massive Soviet war machine would roll over the Allied divisions that would be cut off from American reinforcement and resupply and all of Europe would fall under Soviet domination.

Specialized destroyers were developed—antisubmarine destroyers—that would sacrifice antiaircraft armament for ASW (antisubmarine warfare) weaponry. Rather than build an entirely new class of destroyer to counter the Soviet undersea threat, the navy turned to its huge fleet of war-built destroyers now in reserve. The *Benson*s were too small to take the new ASW weapons and lacked the space for command and control centers that wartime experience had shown to be vital in successfully coordinating attacks against a submerged sub. The *Fletcher*s were bigger and more suitable, but only barely so. The *Sumner*s and the *Gearing*s were of optimum size, but they were needed in the active fleet and it was unacceptable to pull large numbers from their deployment schedules while the work of conversion took place. Their bigger size gave them greater endurance and greater antiaircraft firepower, prime requirements for fleet escort duties, and the navy did not want to sacrifice these qualities (Friedman, *U.S. Destroyers,* 264). One answer, then, was to modify a few of the bigger destroyers while converting ships in the reserve fleet, returning them to reserve as ASW destroyers in case they were needed again.

Two of them, the USS *Nicholas* (DD-449) and the USS *O'Bannon* (DD-450) are pictured at Mare Island in February 1951, preparing to recommission (fig. 34). Scaffolding covers their masts. The small wartime hull numbers they wore a few years before have been replaced by large, peacetime ones painted over the haze gray hulls. Air hoses and cables cover their decks. Both ride high in the water as there is yet little in the way of stores, ammunition, and fuel aboard them. It was fitting that they recommission together. These two vessels had been linked since they were first laid down on 3 March 1941 at the Bath Iron Works in Maine. Both were launched on 19 February 1942, were commissioned within a few weeks of each other in June of that year, and after shakedown cruises sailed for the South Pacific. Both fought in the fierce naval battles in the Solomons in 1942 and 1943, battles costly to the United States Navy. The *Nicholas* and the *O'Bannon* were each awarded Presidential Unit Citations for their participation in this series of battles and both awards were for fighting superior numbers of Japanese warships and the rescue of American sailors whose ships had gone down.

The *Nicholas* and the *O'Bannon,* along with the destroyer *Taylor,* escorted the *Missouri* into Tokyo Bay on 27 August 1945 in preparation for the surrender ceremony to be held aboard the battleship six days

*Fig. 34. The O'Bannon and Nicholas prepare to recommission at Mare Island in February 1951. National Archives, Pacific Sierra Region*

later. On the day when the war ended, the *Nicholas* had the honor of conveying the Allied and American representatives to the surrender ceremony on the *Missouri*. Both returned home after the war, thirty-three battle stars between them (sixteen for the *Nicholas,* seventeen for the *O'Bannon*), and were decommissioned within three weeks of each other in June 1946. With other destroyers and destroyer escorts, the pair joined the San Diego Group of the Pacific Reserve Fleet. Within a few years both were selected to undergo conversion to a new class of destroyer, the DDE, an antisubmarine hunter-killer. Three of their five-inch mounts were removed, the number two mount being replaced with a Hedgehog, a cluster of small bombs that could be fired ahead of the destroyer while sonar contact with the submarine was being maintained. The forty-millimeters were sacrificed and one of the amidship five-inch mounts was replaced with a twin, three-inch antiaircraft gun. Back into reserve they went after conversion, squeezed between two similarly modified destroyers, the *Walker* and the *Sproston* at San Diego. Moored there, in two long, silent rows on either side of the pier, were nearly sixty other destroyers and destroyer escorts and a handful of *Benson* destroyer-minesweepers.

Both were ordered to report to Mare Island to be recommissioned during the naval buildup prompted by the Korean War. On 19 February 1951, moored side by side with a new generation of destroyermen in dress blues lined up three deep on her deck, both were placed back into commission almost six years after they had left the fleet. Fate still paired the *Nicholas* and the *O'Bannon*. They sailed for the Far East, providing antisubmarine escort for the carriers of Task Force 77 off the Korean coast and more than a decade later the pair would fight in their third war together in the waters off Vietnam. It was only fitting that both these ships ended their inextricably linked careers in the same year when they were stricken from the Naval Vessel Register in 1970, almost thirty years after the remarkable pair of *Fletcher*s began their service in the waters off the Maine coast.

On 25 June 1950, the semipeace and calm of the Cold War ended and a new era of confrontation with communism began when North Korean tanks rumbled south of the thirty-eighth parallel and within a few days threatened to conquer all of South Korea. The Soviet-built T-34 tanks that had pushed the German panzers away from the gates of Moscow and Stalingrad now sliced through the thinly armored and poorly trained South Korean forces. Three understrength and poorly equipped regiments of the American Twenty-fourth Infantry Division were rushed in from occupation duty in Japan. They tried to make a stand but they, too, were pushed back, while American naval forces were rushed to the scene.

The lone carrier in the western Pacific, the USS *Valley Forge*, hurriedly sailed with her escorts from Hong Kong and the Philippines. Two cruisers, the eight-inch *Rochester* and the five-inch *Juneau*, twelve destroyers, and a handful of amphibious and mine warfare ships made up the entire United States Navy in the western Pacific. They quickly moved to seal off Formosa (as much to keep the Nationalist Chinese in as the Communist Chinese out) before sailing for Korean waters to allow the *Valley Forge* to begin air strikes against North Korean rail and road communications and provide support to the retreating troops headed for the port city of Pusan at the southeast tip of the Korean peninsula. Within a month navy jets and Corsairs were flying close air support over the battlefield while the British carrier *Triumph* flew combat air patrol over the fleet. Reinforcements were on the way. The

*Philippine Sea* had originally been scheduled to rotate to the Far East and relieve the *Valley Forge* in October. Now she was rushed forward from San Diego, her air group still learning about their new jets, and joined the "Happy Valley" in providing close air support over the rapidly shrinking American perimeter in the southeast corner of the Korean peninsula.

The situation was critical. The United Nations forces, mostly American troops from Japan grown soft over the years from occupation duty, were in very real danger of being pushed out of Korea. Was this the prelude to an invasion of Japan? Or a diversion to draw forces and attention away from Europe so that the Russians could go on the offensive there? Was this the start of World War III? No one knew for sure. More naval forces steamed for Korea. The escort carrier *Badoeng Strait* arrived with two marine squadrons of Corsair fighter-bombers. One of these went to the *Sicily* and the pair commenced air strikes on the North Korean forces. More help arrived. The *Helena* raced west from Long Beach. The *Manchester* came from San Francisco. The *Leyte* was ordered to speed from the Mediterranean to Korea. So was the *Worcester.* The *Boxer* had just returned from Korea and was dockside at Alameda. She was ordered to take her air group west toward the fighting. The *Missouri*, the remaining battleship in the active fleet, was ordered to cut short a midshipman training cruise, take on ammunition and another thousand crewmen to get to wartime strength, and head for the Pacific for the first time since World War II ended. A month after leaving Norfolk she was blasting the coastline with her sixteen-inch main battery.

But this force was not enough. For one thing, the ships on the firing line offshore and launching air strikes could not continue indefinitely. They would need to be relieved for overhaul, refit, or to rest their crews. There was the defense of Europe and in particular the Mediterranean to be considered. If more ships of the Atlantic Fleet also were rushed to Korean waters, the very real fear was that the Russians would strike. They had exploded an atomic bomb of their own in 1949 and had repeatedly tried to force the Allies out of Berlin and the western half of Germany. Korea could very well be a diversion. The United States had let its military forces shrink to dangerously low levels in the years between 1945 and 1950, and now it paid the price. It simply did not have the forces to be everywhere, in strength, at once. But it did, fortunately, have a card it could play: the reserve fleet, the mothballed carriers, battleships, cruisers, destroyers, and ships of every description now idling under the watchful eyes of the reserve fleet sailors. The fleet had been put in storage for just this sort of eventuality. Now it paid off.

The cruiser *Macon* just had been decommissioned in April at Philadelphia and now was ordered reactivated. The dehumidification equipment was removed. Her machinery was started up again and the sprayed-on preservative dissolved into the gears as it had been designed to do. In October the *Macon* rejoined the fleet and headed for the Atlantic. In Bremerton the carrier *Princeton* had been decommissioned and mothballed just a year before. She, too, was ordered reactivated and rejoined the fleet just a month after the outbreak of the war. Reservists comprised 75 percent of her crew and it took her three months of workups to get ready, but by the end of the year she had joined the other carriers of Task Force 77 off the Korean coast.

Within a few days of the beginning of the war it was announced that a reserve fleet battleship would reinforce the *Missouri*. At Bayonne two months later, workmen began bringing the *New Jersey* back to life. Naval reservists, comfortably settled in their peacetime lives and jobs, were jolted by telegrams ordering them to report for active duty to man the big ship. Two months later, in November 1950, after the Inchon landing and as United Nations troops approached the Yalu River and the Communist Chinese prepared the counterassault that would change the course of the war, the *New Jersey* was recommissioned at Bayonne, with Fleet Admiral "Bull" Halsey giving the keynote speech. Still, the battleship was a long way from being ready for war and it was not until mid-May of the following year that she arrived in Korean waters and began to shell Kansong, just north of the thirty-eighth parallel. The *Missouri* had left for home two months before. More battleship reinforcements were on the way. In the early months of 1951, the *Wisconsin* was reactivated at the Norfolk Navy Yard and reached Korea in November to relieve the *New Jersey.* On the West Coast, the fourth and last of the battleships to be reactivated, the *Iowa,* received her orders to recommission.

At San Francisco, as they had at Bayonne and Norfolk, workmen swarmed over another battleship to bring her to life. The igloos covering her antiaircraft tubs were disconnected from the pipes feeding dry air into them and then were lifted off by crane. Machinery was reactivated, main and secondary batteries opened up and inspected. Most of her twenty-millimeter guns, barely effective against World War II

*Fig. 35. The battle-ship* Iowa *is taken from the mothball fleet to relieve the* New Jersey *off Korea. National Archives, Pacific Sierra Region*

propeller-driven aircraft and totally useless against jets, were removed. Compartment by compartment, the ship was opened, inspected, and made serviceable. Powder and shell magazines, ammunition hoists, crew berthing space, and fire control stations were all made ready for work and habitation. The steel plates over the three turret faces were removed and bloomers, designed to keep rain and seawater out of the turrets, were put back on. She is shown at the San Francisco Naval shipyard in 1951 while being reactivated (fig. 35). Behind her is a mothballed heavy cruiser, either the *Los Angeles* or the *Bremerton*. Both would follow the *Iowa* back into the fleet.

Once recommissioned, she had a long period of training that lasted throughout the winter of 1951–1952, and it was not until 1 April 1952 that she arrived in Japan. Like all of the battleships preceding her to Korea, she became the flagship of the Seventh Fleet upon arrival and took up station off the east coast of the Korean peninsula. The *Iowa*'s tour was typical. Her high speed enabled her to shuttle between firing missions at the front and harassment and logistic interdiction missions

*Fig. 36. The* Iowa
*back in action.*
U.S. Naval Institute

behind Chinese lines. She would lob high explosives into enemy artillery positions or to break up an infantry attack, then head north up the coastline to Wonsan, Hungnam, or Tanchon to wreak havoc among the railroad stations, rail lines, power plants, factories, and ammunition dumps. Sometimes she worked alone, sometimes with a heavy cruiser like the *Toledo* or the British cruiser *Belfast*. She is shown firing a sixteen-inch shell from her refurbished number two turret on 11 June 1952 (fig. 36). Her forty-millimeter tubs forward of turret one are empty, but not those above her five-inch mounts. The *Iowa*'s single tour during the Korean War lasted until October 1952 when she was replaced by the *Missouri,* back after training cruises in the Atlantic for her second tour on the gun line. She in turn was relieved by the *New Jersey,* back from midshipman training cruises on the East Coast, in the spring of 1953.

The war came to its shaky, uneasy conclusion when an armistice was signed on 27 July 1953, but by that time many more ships than just the four battleships had rejoined the fleet, to be sent to the Seventh Fleet, to replace ships being sent to the war zone or just to reinforce a navy many had come to realize was inadequate if the United States were to maintain a meaningful defense against the spread of communism in the Cold War.

Both of the heavy cruisers mothballed at San Francisco were returned to service. The *Bremerton* recommissioned in November 1951 and made two trips to Korea, her eight-inch guns augmenting those of the battleships in shelling shore installations. The *Los Angeles* also left her reserve fleet berth in San Francisco and returned to duty. Like the *Bremerton*, the *Los Angeles* went to Korea where she embarked Rear Admiral Arleigh "Thirty-one Knot" Burke, who now commanded Cruiser Division Five. The *Los Angeles* is seen rendezvousing with the battleship *Iowa* in the Sea of Japan in June 1951 (fig. 37). The crew of the cruiser has gathered topside to have a look at the big battleship that was fighting her second war. The *Los Angeles* had served only three peacetime years before being laid up, but once she was recommissioned she spent a good deal of her time in the Far East. This was her first of two war cruises to Korea and she would make eight more voyages to the western Pacific before being decommissioned a decade later. Certainly, the cost of laying up this cruiser proved well worth the expense.

Six heavy cruisers, all *Baltimore*s, were taken from reserve and recommissioned during the Korean war. The *Macon*, *Bremerton*, and *Los Angeles* were joined by the *Pittsburgh*, *Quincy*, and *Baltimore*, all laid up at Bremerton following World War II. Upon her return from Korea, the *Rochester* helped train new crews to man these recommissioning ships. The *Baltimore* and the *Pittsburgh* headed east, not west, upon recommissioning to beef up the Atlantic Fleet and in particular the Sixth Fleet in the Mediterranean. The *Quincy* was recommissioned for a Korean War cruise but missed the war by a few days. Of course, the end of the war came by virtue of an uneasy truce, not an unconditional surrender, and hostilities could break out at any time. The *Quincy* stayed on, relieving other ships, until she herself came back in December. That was her one deployment, and the following summer she again was sent into mothballs at Bremerton, having spent just two and a half years back in the fleet.

Fig. 37. *The recently recommissioned cruiser* Los Angeles *at rendezvous off Korea with the recently recommissioned battleship* Iowa. *U.S. Naval Institute*

There are never enough destroyers for all the duties they are needed for, and this was especially true of the Korean War buildup. More carriers, more big-gun ships, more auxiliaries, and more merchantmen carrying supplies meant more destroyers needed for escort duty in all oceans, and many of the destroyers mothballed in 1946 and 1947 got the mobilization call. All of the *Fletcher*s, with the exception of five naval reserve vessels, were in mothballs by 1950. Seventeen *Allen M. Sumner*s had been decommissioned, too, almost half of them in the last months before South Korea was invaded. Now they flocked back into service. Eighty-four *Fletcher*s were recommissioned between 1950 and 1953, over half of those sleeping in the reserve fleets at Long Beach, San Diego, and Charleston. Some of the names were familiar: *Hazelwood, Heermann, McGowan, Picking, Prichett*. All seventeen of the *Sumner*s in reserve were returned to duty. The time spent in the mothball navy had been exceedingly brief for some of these ships. The *Stormes* was in reserve about a month, and a few others that had been decommissioned in March, April, and May 1950 were recommissioned five months later.

The *Waldron* was typical. She had been laid up in reserve at Charleston on 17 May 1950 after six years of service but had been called back to duty 17 August as American and South Korean forces reeled in retreat before the onrushing North Korean tanks. A mostly reservist crew reported aboard, and they assisted the reserve fleet personnel and Charleston Navy Yard in reactivating the *Waldron*'s equipment. The paperwork concerning activating her machinery was two inches thick. She had not had a proper overhaul before inactivation and much of her gear needed a lot of work. Thick, sticky preservative covered much of her topside equipment. Adding to the clutter and confusion, a movie crew came aboard to film a training movie about the reactivation procedure. The widow of the ship's namesake, a pilot killed leading a doomed torpedo attack at the battle of Midway, came to the recommissioning ceremony, spoke a few words, and watched as the ship that proudly carried her husband's name again hoisted the Stars and Stripes and was placed back in commission (Shaw *Proceedings*, 161–167).

More carriers came out of mothballs to join the fighting. The *Bon Homme Richard* was towed from her berth at Bremerton just after the *Princeton* and sent straight to the war. From San Francisco came the *Antietam*. The *Shangri-La* followed her out of mothballs but was ordered to the East Coast. The *Tarawa* recommissioned in 1951 but went to the Mediterranean to replace carriers that had been sent to the western Pacific. Other carriers had already been taken from reserve because the development of jet aircraft meant that a larger aircraft carrier was needed and modifications had to be made to existing ones. So many ships had been taken from active service by the end of the 1940s that the fleet could not afford the loss of one of the few remaining commissioned flattops while she underwent conversion and alteration to support the new jet aircraft then being tested for carrier operation aboard the *Franklin D. Roosevelt*. Carriers in reserve were selected instead. After a little over a year at Bayonne, the *Wasp* was moved to the New York Navy Yard for conversion. Her island was streamlined and made more compact and her deck five-inch mounts were removed, providing more space on the flight deck for the big jets. The flight deck itself was strengthened and jet blast deflectors installed to channel the exhaust up and away from the aircraft and the flight deck crew. To reduce the chance of a catastrophic fire in the hangar, huge fire doors were installed to subdivide it. The *Essex* joined the *Wasp* in this conversion, and when it was completed and the *Essex* recommissioned in 1951, she joined Task Force 77 twice in the next two years. Though the *Wasp* also rejoined the fleet during the Korean War, she, like the *Tarawa* and the *Shangri-La*, went to the Atlantic.

At Reserve Fleet headquarters, a large chart, two by four feet in size, covered one wall and listed the reserve fleet groups assigned to that fleet. In the case of the Pacific Reserve Fleet there were nine: San Diego, Long Beach, Stockton, Alameda, San Francisco, Mare Island, Columbia River, Tacoma, and Bremerton. The chart listed, by month and by group, the schedule of any ships undergoing or about to undergo activation. The chart dated 1 November 1950 listed the USS *Los Angeles* undergoing reactivation at San Francisco and showed her projected completion date, mid-January 1951. The *Princeton* too, was listed, but mostly amphibious ships and destroyers were on the big yellow chart. A weekly report was delivered to the commander of each reserve fleet listing the progress of each activation and the percentages of material, crew, supplies, equipment, fuel, and ammunition that the ship had received as it prepared to rejoin the fleet. There were problems, of course. Balky equipment refused to operate. Spare parts were difficult to locate. Inactivation overhauls had been incomplete or the documentation had been lost. Still, one by one, and then in increasing numbers, the ships were recommissioned. By April 1951, only nine months into the war, 381 ships and craft had been reactivated, including 236 amphibious ships and auxiliaries to support the growing fleet (Isenberg, *Shield of the Fleet,* 223).

As the fleet built up strength for the fighting and to reassert American naval presence in a world that could erupt into war at any time, more carriers were towed from reserve and sent to the shipyard for modernization. They came from the navy's attic, carefully wrapped up and full of preservatives, at a time when the fleet needed just such a reservoir of hulls. Throughout the early 1950s carriers emerged from retirement to take on a new life. The *Oriskany's* construction was held up at the end of World War II and she was completed to the new design before being rushed to Korea. The *Kearsarge, Lake Champlain, Bennington, Yorktown, Randolph,* and *Hornet* came out of the mothball fleets at Bayonne, Philadelphia, San Francisco, Norfolk and Bremerton to be modernized under this program. The development of the more powerful steam catapult to replace the hydraulic system meant more carriers taken from reserve. The *Hancock* and *Ticonderoga* from Bremerton and the *Intrepid* from San Francisco received all of the modifications of the first batch, plus the steam catapults.

As so often happens, the simplest suggestions and ideas have the most far reaching effects. The British had experimented with an angled flight deck, extending the deck out the port side of the ship which created a new landing area offset from the center line of the ship. The American Navy modified the *Antietam* the same way. The result was a safer and more efficient flight deck. Aircraft that missed the arresting wires could safely fly off the end of the new landing strip, or bolter, avoiding the aircraft parked forward. The angled flight deck also permitted simultaneous launching and landing cycles as planes landed aft and were hurled off the forward catapults. Another aspect of this modification was the enclosed hurricane bow, which prevented the kind of bow and flight deck damage suffered by some of the flattops in the Pacific typhoons. The *Shangri-La* and the *Bon Homme Richard* were taken from the active fleet for conversion, while the *Lexington* was taken from reserve, leaving only the *Bunker Hill,* the *Franklin,* and the *Enterprise* in mothballs. Eventually fifteen of the *Essex*-class carriers were modernized to one degree or another; these carriers, which were to be the backbone (once again) of the navy's carrier force until the big supercarriers were built, had come from the mothball fleet.

While these ships and others stirred from reserve, most never moved

*Fig. 38. The "day of infamy," Pearl Harbor under attack. The upturned hull of the* Oklahoma *is next to the* Maryland. *U.S. Naval Institute*

except to have barnacles and seaweed scraped from their hulls and their machinery inspected every few years while in dry dock. One of these was an old battleship, a veteran of many years of keeping the peace and of one terrible day when peace failed and a war began.

It is the "day of infamy," 7 December 1941, and havoc reigns over the Pacific Fleet at anchor in Pearl Harbor (fig. 38). In the middle of it is the battleship *Maryland*. Next to her is the upturned hull of the cap-sized battleship *Oklahoma*. Directly astern of her is the blazing *West Virginia*, and the black column of smoke blowing toward the entrance to Pearl Harbor is from the *Arizona*, which continued to burn for two days. Men can be seen on the hull of the *Oklahoma* and in boats along-side, as sailors dashed from one ship to the next in any small craft they could find, fishing out survivors and bodies.

On that quiet, warm Sunday morning, a large portion of the Pacific Fleet was moored at Pearl Harbor. Since early 1940 the fleet had been based in Hawaii as a deterrent to Japanese aggression. The Japanese saw the fleet not as a deterrent but as a threat to be eliminated. Vice Admiral Isoruku Yamamoto, Commander of the Imperial Japanese Navy Combined Fleet, knew that the only way Japan could successfully move into the Dutch East Indies and secure needed raw materials would be to paralyze the Pacific Fleet at the outset of the fighting. Yamamoto's plan was to strike the fleet at its anchorage in Hawaii, deliver a crippling blow, seize Indochina, Thailand, the Dutch colonies, and the Philippines, then erect a defensive line and wait for the Americans to regroup, reassemble a fleet, and steam west. The United States would have to operate with long lines of communication, and by taking New Guinea, Japan could effectively cut off any potential American line of advance to Australia. American ships would have to be based in Hawaii while they advanced into the Central and South Pacific. They would lack repair and refueling facilities and safe anchorages where ships and men could rest and recover from the strain of wartime sea duty. The Japanese planners hoped to sink both the battleships and the carriers of the Pacific Fleet; they assembled a force of six aircraft carriers to launch a surprise attack at dawn on the American fleet at anchor in Pearl Harbor on 7 December.

Eight of the nine battleships of the fleet were in the harbor that morning. The ninth, the *Colorado*, was at the Bremerton Navy Yard for an overhaul. Alongside Ford Island, running southwest to northeast in the middle of the harbor, seven battleships were moored. The *California*, flagship of Admiral Pye's Battle Force, was alone at the southernmost set of mooring quays. Just north of her was an impressive lineup of 1941 American naval might. The *Maryland* and the *Oklahoma* were moored together, the *Oklahoma* outboard. Astern of this pair were the *Tennessee* and the *West Virginia*, with the "WeeVee" outboard of the *Tennessee*. Just astern of the *Tennessee*, inboard of the repair ship *Vestal*, was the *Arizona*. At the north end of Battleship Row, moored alone like the *California*, was the *Oklahoma*'s sister ship, the *Nevada*. The fleet flagship, the *Pennsylvania*, was in dry dock number one, across the channel from the *California*. The navy yard was full of ships as well: the heavy cruisers *New Orleans* and *San Francisco*, light cruisers *Honolulu* and *St. Louis* and some destroyers. More destroyers and the cruiser *Phoenix* were in East Loch to the north of Ford Island. On the opposite side of the island, across from Battleship Row, were more ships: the old battleship *Utah,* now converted to a target vessel, and the light cruisers *Detroit* and *Raleigh.*

The Japanese planners, led by the brilliant Minoru Genda, had developed two careful plans for the air assault, depending on whether or not they had achieved tactical surprise. They did indeed achieve this surprise that Sunday morning, for numerous warnings had been ignored by the Americans, but the fog of war, as so often happens, intervened. Commander Mitsuo Fuchida, leader of the attack, had arranged a signal, a flare to be fired from the cockpit of his bomber. One flare would signal that the American fleet had been caught unaware. This would order the vulnerable torpedo planes to go in first and inflict the maximum damage possible before American antiaircraft fire became effective. The second plan, to be signaled by two flares, had the dive-bombers going in first to smash resistance at the airfields and on the relatively unprotected antiaircraft batteries on the decks of the ships before the torpedo planes would go in low to rip open the sides of the battleships. Fuchida fired one, but noticed that one group, the fighters, did not begin to climb as they were supposed to. He fired another. The fighters at last began to gain altitude in order to pounce on any intercepting American fighters. The dive-bombers interpreted this last flare as the second one, meaning that surprise had been lost and that they would attack first. In a matter of minutes the plans so carefully rehearsed by the Japanese felt apart. The dive bombers and torpedo planes would attack together.

Just before 0800 the torpedo bombers, the "Kates" as they were called by the Americans, swung out along the western half of Oahu and then split up. Some came in from the west, toward the *Raleigh, Detroit,* and *Utah* anchored on that side of Ford Island and against 1010 dock, normally the home of the *Pennsylvania.* The others swung out beyond the channel entrance to the harbor, around Hickam Field to the southeast of Pearl Harbor, and came in low from the east, over the navy yard and the submarine base, straight down Southeast Loch toward the battleships lined up against Ford Island.

At 0755, as morning colors were being raised on ships throughout the harbor, the Japanese struck. Kates roared down Southeast Loch, past the sterns of the cruisers at the navy yard, and launched their torpedoes. The battleships in front of them, stationary and barely a few hundred yards away, were perfect targets. No torpedo nets protected the big vessels. None were thought to be needed. Pearl Harbor was only forty feet deep in most places and a torpedo needed a depth of at least seventy-five feet before it would level off after plunging into the sea from an aircraft. Or so it was thought. In fact, the Japanese had solved this problem through innovation and constant practice. Most of their torpedoes would level off before hitting the soft mud of Pearl Harbor and run true.

The *Oklahoma* was quickly hit by several torpedoes and began to list. So, too, was the *West Virginia* right behind her and the *California* ahead of her a little farther down the channel. On the *Maryland* men watched as the *Oklahoma* began to roll slowly to port. More torpedoes hit her as she rolled, striking her above the protective armor belt, and the waters of Pearl Harbor rushed into the ship. She rapidly took on a twenty-five- to thirty-five-degree list as the lines securing her to the *Maryland* began to snap under the strain. In surprise and shock, the men of the *Maryland* watched the bottom of the *Oklahoma* rise up out of the water as her tripod masts and fighting tops disappeared below the oily waters of the harbor. The *Oklahoma* did not stop rolling until her masts struck the mud, snapped off, and her superstructure was buried. Only a portion of her keel lay exposed to the sky. Many of the "Okie's" crew climbed over her side, along her hull and into the water, where they swam over to the *Maryland*. Hundreds of her crew were trapped belowdecks when she turned turtle. Thirty-two were pulled out alive through holes cut in the hull, but over four hundred were drowned. Their bodies were not recovered until the ship was raised over a year and a half later.

The *West Virginia* was hit by six torpedoes but rapid counterflooding by her crew prevented her from capsizing like the *Oklahoma* and she settled to the bottom, her decks on fire, on an even keel. One hundred and five men were killed, including her captain, who was mortally wounded by a fragment from a bomb that struck the barrel of one of the *Tennessee*'s fourteen-inch guns. The *Tennessee* was hit but not badly damaged by a pair of bomb hits, and she was protected from torpedoes by the *West Virginia*, just as the *Maryland* was by the *Oklahoma*. The *California* was another perfect target for torpedoes, and the Japanese pilots did not miss. Her port side was opened by several hits and she flooded rapidly. Pumps went to work, but when burning oil from the *West Virginia* and the *Arizona* drifted down the channel and began to engulf the *California*, her crew was ordered to abandon ship. By the time the fires on the water receded and the crew came back aboard, precious time had been lost. The pumps could not keep up with the flooding and over the next few days the old battleship settled to the bottom. The *Pennsylvania* in dry dock suffered one hit, but the destroyers ahead of her were mangled. Fires detonated magazines and torpedoes and started severe fires and as the order came to flood the dock in an effort to put out the fires, the *Cassin* rolled over onto the *Downes*.

The *Arizona*'s war career lasted about fifteen minutes. She was hit again and again by high-level bombers early in the attack and then was hit near her number two turret. Though the exact sequence of events never has been fully determined, a fire that may have been started by this bomb spread to her forward magazines and exploded them. The sides of the *Arizona*'s hull were blown outward and her main deck, turrets and all, collapsed onto her lower decks. Her foremast toppled forward, and photographs of this sight became one of the most dramatic and recognizable symbols of the attack, a portrait of defeat and retribution. Over one thousand men were either killed by the blast or drowned in the rapid flooding as the *Arizona* sank without moving an inch at her berth. The *Nevada*, at the far end of Battleship Row, took a torpedo that tore a huge hole in her port bow, and then she was hit by dive-bombers. Fortunately, she had two boilers lit even before the attack and now had enough steam to get under way. Defiantly, she steamed past the scene of chaos and defeat that was now Battleship Row, past the huge column of thick, black smoke pouring out of the forward half of the sunken *Arizona*, past the *West Virginia*, also on the bottom and blazing amidships, past the upturned hull of the capsized *Oklahoma*. She was headed for the channel and the open sea, but the Japanese dive-bombers saw her and pounced. She nearly disappeared under the spray from near misses and was staggered by several more hits. Tugs pushed her clear of the channel so that she would not block it when and if she sank, and she was run aground. She, too, settled to the bottom.

The least damaged battleship, and the first to return to action, was the *Maryland*. She was hit twice by bombs. One exploded above the main deck, detonated by a rope holding up one of the awnings that many of the battleships had rigged over their forecastles and sterns for church services. Another splashed alongside the *Maryland*, entered the ship below the waterline, and went off in the hold. Four men were killed and another fourteen wounded that terrible day. By 20 December the *Maryland* was repaired by the navy yard.

Salvage on some of the other damaged battleships was not as easy. Though the *Pennsylvania* and the *Tennessee* rejoined the fleet within a few months, others required much more extensive work. The salvage crews took eighteen months to turn the *Oklahoma* upright and refloat her, and by then it was decided she was too old and too badly damaged to justify using critically needed shipyard space and labor to repair her. She was decommissioned and stricken. The *Arizona,* too, was declared a total loss and after some salvage work, which included removing all superstructure above the water and the fourteen-inch guns from three of her four turrets (the fourth, number one turret, came to rest underwater when the forecastle collapsed), she, too, was decommissioned and stricken. The *West Virginia, Nevada,* and *California* were raised from the bottom. The same shallow water that had lulled the American Navy into forgoing the use of torpedo nets ultimately saved most of the ships sunk there. Divers were able to patch the torpedo holes with tremic cement or build cofferdams around any part of the deck that was submerged (as in the case of the *California*). The water was pumped out of the ships until they came afloat and could be guided gingerly into dry dock by tugs. There the yard repaired them enough to be seaworthy, refurbished the engines, and sent them under their own power to the West Coast for complete repair and modernization. The *Nevada* rejoined the fleet in the spring of 1943, the *California* in January 1944 and the *West Virginia* in the summer of that year. Pearl Harbor was not the last of the damage they would see. The *Nevada, California, West Virginia,* and the *Maryland* were all hit by kamikazes later in the war; the *Pennsylvania* and the *Maryland* were torpedoed as well.

When the war ended there was little doubt that the newest of the battleships, the *North Carolina*s, the *South Dakota*s, and the *Iowa*s, would be retained. Nimitz's plan had the *Iowa*s remaining active, the other two modern classes to be held in reserve with reduced crews. The remainder of the battleships, if any, were to be included in the mothball fleet. The *New York, Nevada,* and *Arkansas* all had been built between 1911 and 1914. These old battlewagons were to be used to test the effects of a nuclear blast on a large warship at Bikini Atoll in July 1946 as the United States carried out a series of tests with its new superweapon. They were joined by the *Pennsylvania,* built over thirty years before and still leaking from the torpedo hit she had taken shortly before the war ended. The *Mississippi* was converted to a gunnery training ship, but her sisters *New Mexico* and *Idaho* were stricken in 1947. These beautiful ships had not been modernized during the war to the degree that the battleships damaged at Pearl Harbor had been and were earmarked for the mothball fleet at first. In the end, though, they were declared surplus and scrapped.

That left the "Big Five": the *California, Tennessee, Colorado, Maryland,* and *West Virginia,* the last battleships built before the modern *North Carolina*s were laid down. These five were selected to be placed into reserve. The *West Virginia* was the first major warship (battleship or carrier) to be retired. She was placed in reserve, in commission, at Puget Sound on 18 June 1946, less than a year after the end of the war. The *Maryland* followed a month later. The *Colorado* joined them there while the *Tennessee* and *California* sailed to the Philadelphia Naval Shipyard to be taken out of service. As slow as they were, the old battleships had shown their value in shore bombardment and were to be spared the torches of the scrap yard for a time. By spring of 1948, all had been placed out of commission, in reserve.

There would not be a second life for any of them. Another war came, this time in Korea, and another amphibious landing by the marines was made, this time at the port city of Inchon, but these old veterans of the landings at Saipan, Tinian, Lingayen Gulf, and Iwo Jima were not called out of retirement to show what they could do. Perhaps in a different type of war—an island war where amphibious assault would be the main mode of advance—they would have been summoned from mothballs and inspected by naval officers and marine engineers. Their power plants would have been checked, the wiring, plumbing, bulkheads, and voids carefully examined as the inspectors looked for telltale signs of corrosion, rust, or indications the hull was no longer keeping out the water of Puget Sound or the Delaware River. The inspectors would have walked through the fourteen-inch triple turrets on the *California* and the *Tennessee* in Philadelphia and the sixteen-inch twin turrets on the three *Colorado*s in Bremerton. They would have walked up into the superstructure, maybe higher still into the ancient fighting tops atop the cage masts on the last battleships to still have them, the *Colorado* and *Maryland.* The inspectors could have surveyed a good portion of the shipyard from there. Depending on when they were making this inspection they might have seen one of the *Essex*-class carriers being towed away to reenter the fleet, or possibly the *Baltimore* that had departed Bremerton in 1951 and returned in 1956 after another tour of duty with a navy about to enter the guided-missile age. They would have seen the

*Alabama* and the *Indiana* still sitting quietly at their reserve fleet piers, the former to be a museum and sometime movie star in her home state, the latter destined for scrap.

If these two ships, maybe only a decade old and never seriously wounded during the war, were not to be returned to service, then why would anyone consider an old relic like the *Maryland,* with her twin main battery turrets, cage foremast, twenty-one knot speed, and thick blisters added onto each side for stability as armor increased for protection against bombs and the kamikaze. Those blisters expanded her beam to 108 feet, and she was barely able to squeeze through the Panama Canal. Other old battleships were widened to 114 feet. In their old age some of the Big Five had grown too thick around the middle to go through the Panama Canal. Like ships of the last century (and many built today), they would have to go around the Horn if they were needed in another ocean. The "Mary" was old. She looked old. She looked old on 8 December 1941 when the carrier became the star of future naval warfare and the battleship became a supporting player. The officers conducting the survey may have decided the *Maryland* could be of some use anyway, that her main battery rifles still could keep down the heads of an enemy ashore while marines stormed out of their landing craft.

But no such war happened, no such inspection took place. Inspections did happen, of course. They were supposed to occur periodically while the ships lay moored in silence. Was the vessel still in good material condition? Was the ship still of value to the fleet? Was the cost of preserving her equal to that value? Eventually, the answer to one or more of these questions was no. For the *Maryland,* the rest of the Big Five, and a number of other ships of World War II vintage, that answer came on 1 March 1959. All were stricken from the Naval Vessel Register. They were naval vessels no more. Now they were hulks to be offered up for scrap sale. The Big Five were all sold.

One by one they were disconnected from their dehumidifying equipment and electrical power. Deep inside the hulls and up on the decks there was only silence now. There was silence where three men of the *West Virginia* had been trapped belowdecks when the ship settled to the bottom at Pearl Harbor and where they had stayed hoping for rescue until they died from suffocation over two weeks later. There was silence in the powder handling rooms deep below the turrets in the *Colorado* where men had worked and sweated as the ship lobbed shell after shell at Tarawa and Leyte. There was silence in the after fire control tower of

*Fig. 39. The* Maryland *awaiting scrapping at Alameda in 1959. U.S. Naval Institute*

the *California* where a kamikaze had hit and killed or wounded 203 of the "Prune Barge's" crew in Lingayen Gulf. There was silence in the mess decks of the *Tennessee,* where men had eaten, talking over the events of the day or reading mail from home, during any one of the tens of thousands of meals served aboard her in a quarter century of service to her country.

There was silence in the control and observation structures atop the cage foremast of the *Maryland* as she sat at Alameda in 1959, awaiting the swarms of men who would dismantle her and do what the Japanese could not do: make her vanish from the water (fig. 39). In that same fighting top, sailors had stood on the night of 7 December 1941, watching the sky, hearing the gunfire erupt from shore and from ships in the harbor as the nervous gunners imagined the Japanese returning to finish the job they had begun that morning. The sailors had stood watch or perhaps had gathered in small groups to share the day's experiences, the day they would always remember in infinite detail even as they tried to forget. From up the channel came a flickering light as the *West Virginia* and the *Arizona* still burned in the night. The sailors high above the deck would listen to—and try not to hear, try not to think about— the tapping that came across the water from the hull of the *Oklahoma* only a few yards away, tapping from men trapped belowdecks and whose exact location had not been found by the rescue crews, nor would not be found at all, tapping from some of the four hundred sailors who would drown in total darkness inside a 575-foot-long ship turned upside down on the first day of the war, the ship that had been tied alongside the *Maryland* some eighteen years before coming to San Francisco Bay for the last time. The *Maryland* was a member of an exclusive sorority, a survivor of the attack that catapulted America into World War II.

Four times the USS *New Jersey* was placed in commission: in 1943, 1950, 1968, and 1982. Four times she was placed out of commission, in reserve. Twice she was placed on the Naval Vessel Register, once when she was commissioned, again in 1998 after being stricken in 1995. She served in three shooting wars and was part of the United States military buildup that eventually ended the Cold War. She fired her guns in anger at the islands of the Pacific in the 1940s, off the mountainous coast of Korea in the 1950s, into the jungles of South Vietnam in the 1960s and against Syrian targets in the Mediterranean in the 1980s. Budget cutters, always her biggest nemeses, precluded her participation in the Gulf War in the 1990s. After each war, each tour of duty, she was mothballed: twice on the East Coast, at Bayonne and at Philadelphia; twice on the West Coast, both times at Bremerton. For over thirty of her fifty-five years on the Naval Vessel Register, she has slept in hibernation.

The *New Jersey*'s first commission lasted a little over five years. She was the flagship of Admirals Halsey and Spruance for much of her time in the Pacific, although Spruance later shifted his flag to the doomed heavy cruiser *Indianapolis*. When the war ended the *New Jersey* headed east to San Francisco with over a thousand troops about to be discharged. In 1947 she sailed through the Panama Canal to Bayonne and took aboard midshipmen for a peacetime training cruise to Europe, but budgets and a lack of trained personnel dictated that expensive and manpower-intensive ships like the battleships be decommissioned. She was laid up in 1948 at Bayonne, in her home state. Her twenty-millimeter antiaircraft guns were removed and some of her forties, too. The rest were covered and sealed by cocoons as she lay tied to the seawall near the dry dock at the naval supply depot.

Her second commission was for almost seven years. She was again a flagship, this time of Vice Admiral Harold Martin's Seventh Fleet off

Korea. Seventh Fleet had replaced the wartime Fifth/Third Fleet combination as the navy's forward deployed fleet in the western Pacific. More training missions followed the war in the next few years, but she again was a victim of her own cost and lack of a specific mission. At the Brooklyn Navy Yard her engineering plant was overhauled and then at Bayonne she went through the inactivation and preservation procedures she had gone through a decade earlier. Once again her commissioning pennant was hauled down and the *New Jersey* joined the reserve fleet at Bayonne in 1957.

In 1962, when the New York Group of the Atlantic Reserve Fleet at Bayonne was disbanded, she was towed to the Philadelphia Naval Shipyard along with the *Wisconsin*. There she stayed while the United States become embroiled in another war in Southeast Asia. Aircraft losses mounted as the war intensified, as did the need for more firepower to support the soldiers and marines fighting the Vietcong and North Vietnamese regulars and to interdict the flow of supplies from North Vietnam to enemy forces in the South. The eight-inch guns of the heavy cruisers on the gun line were effective, but a battlewagon's would be able to fire more high explosives farther inland than the cruisers. The pressure to bring a battleship out of retirement for this job mounted.

The Chief of Naval Operations, Admiral David C. McDonald, adamantly opposed the reactivation of a battleship. Other naval leaders believed aircraft could do the job more effectively and that the existing cruisers like the *St. Paul* and the *Canberra* were adequate for the role of naval fire support. But Senator Richard B. Russell of Georgia, a powerful member of both the Armed Services and Appropriations Committees, wanted to use a battleship and lobbied for it in the Senate. Russell was a great supporter of the navy and his word carried weight in determining what Congress would and would not fund. Russell (who would eventually have an attack submarine named after him) and his supporters won out. In early 1967 the navy began studying what would be involved in bringing a battleship out of retirement.

By this time, only the four *Iowa*s were left in reserve, the other, slower battleships having been sold for scrap or donated as museum ships. The Naval Sea System Command estimated it would cost between $20 and $25 million to reactivate an *Iowa*, though that did not include money to be spent for spare gun barrel liners, ammunition, crew training, or other normal ship operating expenses. The Naval Inactive Ship Maintenance Facilities at Philadelphia and Bremerton (where *Missouri*

Fig. 40. The Wisconsin, New Jersey, and Iowa in reserve at Philadelphia. U.S. Naval Institute

was stored) examined each of the ships in their care and determined that *New Jersey* was the best candidate. Too large for the reserve fleet basin, she was moored between her two sisters *Iowa* and *Wisconsin* along the same wall where the *California* and the *Tennessee* had spent their retirement, her bow pointing at the mothballed carrier *Antietam* a little over a hundred yards away (fig. 40). In the basin lay a few old *Clevelands* that had been there nearly two decades, including the *Portsmouth* and *Wilkes-Barre,* and dozens of destroyers that had replaced the old heavy cruisers that had long ago been towed away for scrap. The *New Jersey* was sealed tight, her dehumidifiers slowing her interior decay. Her compartments had been divided into several zones, each divided by watertight doors, and the atmosphere in each was monitored for low humidity. The fuses in her electrical systems had been removed and any needed electricity for internal lighting was drawn from the dock through an umbilical to a master switch on her main deck. Her electronics were either safely tucked inside or stored ashore. She had relatively new barrel liners in her sixteen-inch main battery, which meant they would last longer before regunning became necessary, and had received a fairly comprehensive lay-up overhaul in 1957. Her fuel tanks were three-quarters full.

The shipyard was asked for a detailed plan to reactivate the battleship, to restore her sixteen-inch turrets, her five-inch mounts, the associated fire control systems, and to replace the communications and electronic equipment that had become obsolete in the ten years she had been away. The comfort of the crew was looked at carefully, too. All berthing areas and mess decks were to be air-conditioned with spot air-conditioning units, since the installation of ducts and pipes required for a central air-conditioning plant would be too expensive and time consuming. Tile would replace steel decks in the berthing compartments. Heads (bathrooms) would be modernized with a degree of privacy unknown in the World War II navy for which the *New Jersey* had been built. Eight hundred thousand dollars were budgeted for shipyard personnel to make a detailed inspection of her. Many different departments within the navy were involved in the complex task of bringing back to life a ship built for a war ended over twenty years before. Ordnance specialists looked at what was required to support and repair the main battery weapons. The Bureau of Naval Personnel drew up the crew requirement for a battleship that was to be a far cry from the ship that had fought with Halsey's Third Fleet. The Philadelphia Naval Shipyard was selected to do the work because it was mainly involved at the time with new ship construction rather than overhaul and repair, and the reactivation of the battleship would not significantly affect the readiness of ships already in the fleet.

On 11 June 1967 tugs pushed the sleeping *Wisconsin* into the Delaware River and slid the *New Jersey* out from between her sisters and over to an industrial pier. Her care was now the responsibility of the shipyard, not the reserve fleet personnel who had watched over her so carefully during her two periods in mothballs. Before her interior spaces could be opened, the ship had to be sandblasted, as her topside paint was in poor condition after a decade of exposure to the elements. Then weathertight seals were opened and the shipyard commenced its inspection. In less than a month the verdict was delivered: Philadelphia could reactivate the 888-foot-long battleship for duty off Vietnam for $23 million and would take nine months to do it.

On 1 August 1967, Secretary of Defense Robert McNamara ordered work to proceed. Almost fifteen hundred workers a day swarmed over, under, and inside the *New Jersey,* and were soon working seven days a week, three shifts a day. The dehumidification units were shut down and the *New Jersey*'s own ventilators were started up to bring fresh air deep into the ship so that workers could go below. Her fuel was pumped out; her equipment, supplies, and spare parts were inventoried; her machinery was examined. Her boilers, for instance, were in good shape, but other problems were found in her propulsion plant that needed to be corrected. Numerous bearings needed to be replaced. Her reduction gears had developed cracks, as had her propellers. All four propellers needed to be replaced in dry dock. Another and more persistent problem arose. No battleship had been built in twenty-three years. None had been in commission in ten. There had been no demand for spare parts in that time and so, in 1968, none were to be found. Sometimes equipment from one of the other battleships (reserve ships and museum ships) was used. Sometimes, if a particular spare part was no longer being manufactured, an entirely new system had to replace the existing one, as in the case of the air-conditioning plants deep inside the sixteen-inch turrets.

Press interest in the work was considerable. The *New Jersey* underwent reactivation during the Tet offensive of 1968. The Vietcong and North Vietnamese offensive was a failure, but it was clear that the enemy had much more strength and will to win than had been thought. During the offensive, Walter Cronkite declared on the *CBS Evening News* that the Pentagon's glowing reports on the progress of the war were false and that the United States should negotiate a peace. The effect of the highly respected and usually impartial anchorman expressing the feelings of so many Americans had a distressing effect on the Nixon White House. The debate over the conduct of the war intensified, as did domestic turmoil that began to rock the country throughout 1968. In the midst of this a World War II battleship was being brought out of mothballs to join the fighting, with a resulting image of escalation and renewed commitment (Morse and Bream, *Naval Engineers Journal,* 859–869).

On 6 April 1968, on time and under budget, the USS *New Jersey* rejoined the Pacific Fleet, looking much as she had when commissioned

*Fig. 41. The* New Jersey *opens fire off Vietnam. U.S. Naval Institute*

in 1943 and again in 1951. Gone this time were the forty- and twenty-millimeters. Gone were the aircraft catapults at the stern. Projecting from either side of her tower were large electronic countermeasure antennas, designed to foil the radar-guided antiship missiles that the North Vietnamese could conceivably launch against her. Six months after again hoisting her pennant she was on the gun line off South Vietnam, firing her guns at an enemy for the first time since 1953. Spare barrel liners for her sixteen-inch rifles were stored at Subic Bay in the Philippines in anticipation of the heavy use of her main battery. And there would be heavy use.

On 30 September the *New Jersey* joined the Vietnam War as her main battery lobbed one-ton shells at a North Vietnamese supply dump just a few miles north of the Demilitarized Zone (DMZ) (fig. 41). About a week later the secondary battery got into action as the battleship fired on some North Vietnamese junks creeping along the shoreline. South along the coast she cruised, firing in support of army troops. Several times shore batteries fired back at the battleship, for she was a tempting target. At one point three days before Christmas, the big ship became a stage as Bob Hope came aboard for a show atop number one turret. Alternating fire support missions with stops at Subic Bay and Singapore, the *New Jersey* continued to pound targets into 1969. She fired over thirty-two hundred main battery rounds at Vietcong and North Vietnamese positions and supply dumps, although her area of operations was restricted by the White House to below the nineteenth parallel and then to below the DMZ. There would be no firing at North Vietnam, no shelling of ports and harbors. In April 1969 she left Vietnam for overhaul in the United States so that she could return later in the year. She spent the summer in training and in port visits, including one to San Francisco in late June.

The *New Jersey* was scheduled to return to Vietnam in September, but that was not to be. Word came from the Defense Department that she was included in the list of ships to be sent into retirement. Officially the reason was a monetary one. The unofficial reason seems, in retrospect, to have been in keeping with the sometimes nonsensical conduct of the war by two successive administrations. So effective was the naval artillery of the *New Jersey* against the Vietcong and North Vietnamese during her one deployment that the Nixon administration declined to send her back a second time in a bizarre attempt at reconciliation with the Communists (Muir, *Iowa Class Battleships*, 117). After all that time, all that money, and many reports of her effectiveness on the gun line, she was to be deactivated and placed back into reserve after less than two years. The Vietnam War had over three more years to run for the United States and many thousands of Americans would die, but the *New Jersey* would not be there to support them. Back into mothballs she went, this time at Bremerton. There throughout the 1970s she remained, while various plans were put forth to either scrap, recommission, or convert her to another role.

The *New Jersey* has not been returned yet to mothballs at the reserve fleet basin at the Philadelphia Naval Shipyard in March of 1955 (fig. 42). World War II has been over for a decade, the Korean stalemate for almost two years. The United States exploded a hydrogen bomb several years before, upping the ante in the nuclear standoff with the Russians. Here in the backyard of one of the largest naval shipyards in

*Fig. 42. Heavy and light cruisers in mothballs at the Philadelphia Naval Shipyard in 1955. Naval Historical Center*

the world sat in mothballs much of the prewar and wartime cruiser strength of the United States Navy.

From the bridge across the narrow entrance to this small body of still water a visitor to the shipyard in the spring of 1955 would see an impressive array of silent gray ships of different sizes and shapes tucked into various nooks and crannies of the basin. If he had the time, the inclination, and the security clearance to make a complete circuit on foot around the basin, he would see volumes of naval history lined up in neat rows like dusty, forgotten history books few read, but containing a wealth of information and experience about the nation's recent, traumatic naval heritage.

The sightseer would leave the bridge on the shipyard side, walk past a few small craft, past some of the innumerable buildings and warehouses, past an escort carrier tied up at the first pier, and down the long straight wall leading to the far side of the basin. On he would walk, warehouses, shops, and offices to his right, and ahead of him, nosed into piers jutting out to the left into the basin, six long gray bows would loom, six large superstructures, twelve main battery turrets sitting atop each hull. As he approached, and if he had a careful eye, the visitor could notice that the first ship was slightly different than the next two in the slip alongside it, and that the last three were virtually identical. He would read the large hull numbers on the first three haze-gray hulls—thirty-three, twenty-eight and thirty-one—and if he were a student of naval history or of the last war, or perhaps a person fond of ships, he might know that the first three ships towering over him were the heavy cruisers *Portland, Louisville,* and *Augusta.* Now these three veterans lay together, moored in silence. As the visitor walked a little farther he could note three old, nearly identical cruisers moored at the next slip, bearing three more hull numbers: thirty-eight, thirty-seven, and thirty-six.

Thirty-eight? Isn't that the old *San Francisco?* The cruiser that was shot full of holes at Guadalcanal as the war was just beginning? The one whose riddled bridge windscreen, mast, and bell were now three thousand miles away in her namesake city on Point Lobos overlooking the Pacific Ocean? Yes, indeed it is. The sightseer looks hard for evidence of that desperate fight off Guadalcanal thirteen years before, but the workers at Mare Island, and those in the intervening years, have done their job well. There is no obvious evidence of the battle she fought that cost her so dearly, the battle fought in what became known as Ironbottom Sound between Guadalcanal and the island of Tulagi.

Both the Americans and the Japanese rushed reinforcements to Guadalcanal during November 1942 as the battle for the island dragged into its third month. As the *San Francisco* stood watch over the transports disgorging troops on 12 November, the Japanese struck at them with torpedo planes. Though no torpedoes struck home, a damaged plane crashed into the aft control station, killing or wounding fifty men. This was just the preliminary, however, as a powerful Japanese force of battleships, cruisers, and destroyers sailed into Ironbottom Sound. Two

*Fig. 43. The* San Francisco *returns to the West Coast for repair after Guadalcanal.*
*U.S. Naval Institute*

heavy cruisers, the *San Francisco* and the *Portland,* three light cruisers, and eight destroyers were there to meet them. The American fleet was badly outgunned as the shells and tracers flew across the water at close range in the darkness. Destroyers fired on battleships from such a short range that the battlewagons could not depress their main batteries low enough to fire back.

Mistakenly firing on the light cruiser *Atlanta,* the *San Francisco* ceased fire momentarily, only to then be shredded by shells from the battleship *Kirishima,* a cruiser, and a destroyer. Shrapnel from the exploding shells riddled the superstructure of the heavy cruiser, the steel shards opening holes in her as if she were made of cardboard. Some evidence of the pounding she took is visible in the photo of her returning to her namesake city after the battle (fig. 43). Her captain, Cassin Young, was killed in the barrage, as was the task force commander, Admiral Daniel J. Callaghan, who also happened to be one of the ship's former commanding officers. Most of her bridge crew were cut down as well. The next day, as the ship was headed for the New Hebrides, the crew watched as Japanese submarine *I-26* fired torpedoes that struck and disintegrated the light cruiser *Juneau,* killing over seven hundred sailors, including the five Sullivan brothers, in a tragedy that shocked the nation.

Alongside the *San Francisco* are two more *New Orleans*-class heavy cruisers (fig. 42). The USS *Tuscaloosa,* cruiser hull number thirty-seven, was the fourth of the *New Orleans* heavy cruisers, joining the fleet in 1934. She spent her prewar years as most ships of the fleet did, in training cruises, goodwill visits and fleet training exercises. The peacetime navy then as now was a training navy. Painted a light gray, with her hull number on her turret tops for identification from the air, the *Tuscaloosa* carried out her training duties throughout the 1930s, when most of America tried to forget the rising nationalism and militarism of Imperial Japan and the new Nazi government in Germany. Of course, she did her part once war came. She was off the Normandy beaches with the *Augusta,* keeping the German troops pinned down while American troops came ashore to liberate Western Europe. The *Tuscaloosa* was not even twelve years old when she was decommissioned and laid up, and over seven of those years were spent in peacetime with endless training exercises, visits to exotic ports of call, routine overhaul, and spit-and-polish inspections. While most of America struggled with the Depression and turned away from the gathering war clouds in Europe and the

Pacific, the *Tuscaloosa* and her sisters stood ready to defend them. Now, her duty done in both peace and war, she remained tied up here for years, should another call to serve come.

The *Minneapolis* was one of the four surviving *New Orleans* cruisers to be berthed in the basin following the war, and now she lay here, the large white numerals three and six on each side of her bow, under the appreciative gaze of the visitor (fig. 42). Her three other sisters are not here, but all of them lie together too, in the murky depths off Savo Island in Ironbottom Sound. All were sunk in one inglorious night a few days after the invasion of Guadalcanal, when the Japanese steamed virtually undetected into their front yard, opened fire, and pounded them and an Australian cruiser beneath the waves. One of the American cruisers, the *Quincy,* a near carbon copy of the *Minneapolis,* sits upright on the bottom of the ocean to the northeast of Savo Island. In contrast with the neat appearance of the *Minneapolis,* her bridge is a shambles; her bow is gone; her forward main battery turrets are at maximum elevation; the area between her forward and aft superstructures is barren, with only her aircraft catapult mounts and a few antiaircraft guns remaining; her stern is bent upward (Ballard, *Lost Ships,* 83–85). Though the visitor to the basin cannot know this, he can perhaps imagine what those ships look like as they lie in their graves at the bottom of the South Pacific. Perhaps he can imagine the hell of that night and the shame of the aftermath as three of American's finest ships, sisters of the one he stares at now, were sent to the bottom in a matter of minutes.

On the visitor would walk, leaving the old-fashioned cruisers behind. They certainly looked different than the *Baltimore*-class heavy cruisers reactivated for Korea a few years before. He had seen them in the newspapers. The *Minneapolis,* the *Tuscaloosa,* and the others were less modern looking, less compact, with odd bits and pieces of superstructure and smokestack and airplane hangar and mast stuck here and there. And those old-looking turrets were a little different from those on the newer ships (fig. 42).

A left turn along the wall and a short walk past a couple of big tankers at the end of the dock and there in front of him, across the water streaked with oil and debris, are the six rounded sterns of more cruisers. The first two belong to a couple of *Cleveland*s, and another just beyond looks like the first pair except for a single stack in place of twin stacks. From here, across the water a little over a hundred yards away, the six ships are just a jumble of masts and igloos, sealed turrets, boarded-up bridge windows, and peeling weathered paint. The visitor strolls along, taking in the sights of the ghost fleet as he heads past a pair of mothballed hospital ships, the *Tranquillity* and the *Sanctuary* (fig. 42).

To the right of the sleeping hospital ships is a tree-lined ball field and he turns left, along the seawall, toward another nest of cruisers. These five are identical, and he knows they are *Cleveland*s (fig. 42). Five of them. Their bows point straight toward the pathway he walks along and the sharp prows of the ships loom above him in stony silence. He passes one after another of the ten-thousand-ton ships, their strength and immobility almost palpable. He can feel the ships as much as see them. They are a presence, a living link with the war. They leap out of the pages of newspapers, the *Saturday Evening Post,* and books written since the end of the war. They screened carriers and shot at planes overhead and their guns spat out at enemy beachheads and ships. They lay at anchor in Majuro, at Ulithi and a dozen other unknown Pacific atolls. They were painted in dazzle camouflage of grays, blues, and blacks. Their hulls were battered and dented from the sea. It is quiet back here, away from the main section of the yard. Birds sing in the trees lining the pathway. Some have come to roost high in the masts and superstructure.

Another left turn and the visitor continues his zigzag course along the perimeter of the basin. He is under the stern now and then along the starboard side of a huge ship. A battleship? It looks big enough. It dwarfs the *Cleveland*s next to it. But where are the turrets? The ship has no main battery. Where are the five-inch dual mounts that make up the secondary battery? Where are the igloos covering the now useless forty- and twenty-millimeter antiaircraft guns? It has a battleship superstructure, to be sure, tall and narrow, and a pair of stacks. But it looks stripped. Emasculated. He walks back to the stern where he first turned the corner and looks up at the faintly visible name on the stern: *Hawaii,* the unfinished battle cruiser whose construction was under way when the war ended and was suspended in 1947 when she was 84 percent complete (fig. 42). She had a distinction shared by only a few other ships, that of being mothballed before being completed. Shortly after work on her was halted it was proposed to convert her to a guided-missile ship and her twelve-inch turrets were removed. But that was about as far as the plans got, and now, in 1955, she is still laid up here among her smaller and less-powerful cousins. What will become of her, he wonders? Surely they will not complete her as originally planned. Her sisters *Guam* and *Alaska* are in mothballs in Bayonne. They have not stirred since the late 1940s, the Korean crisis notwithstanding. It is doubtful they ever will. Did the navy have other plans in store for this minibehemoth, laid up before she had the chance to show what she could do?

Another narrow pier juts out into the basin just beyond the bow of the *Hawaii* and separates the two rows of light cruisers. The sightseer walks past a small shack and out onto the pier. To his right the round sterns with the twin igloos are only a few yards away and he can read the name on each as he walks toward the end of the pier. Nearest the shore is the *Wilkes-Barre* (fig. 42). Ten years ago, almost to the day, Captain Robert L. Porter brought her close to the starboard quarter of the blazing carrier *Bunker Hill*, pouring water up into the flames, as forty sailors from the carrier, trapped near her stern by the flames, leapt to safety aboard the cruiser. The memory of the *Birmingham*'s ordeal next to the *Princeton* was still fresh in the minds of many, but the men of the *Wilkes-Barre* were undeterred and brought their ship alongside the *Bunker Hill*. Next to the *Wilkes-Barre* is the *Cleveland*, nameship of her class and commissioned just six months after the war began (fig. 42). At Empress Augusta Bay she took on four Japanese cruisers and six destroyers along with her sisters, the *Montpelier,* the outboard ship in the line, the *Columbia,* and the *Denver,* now a few yards across the water in the other direction near the *Hawaii.*

The visitor walks on, looking at the other ships moored between the hospital ships and the bulk of the *Hawaii:* the *Portsmouth, Providence,* and *Dayton* (that has been towed down from Boston where she had rested among the escort carriers). His gaze shifts back to the ships to his right as he continues his walk out the narrow pier (fig. 42). The name on the stern of the next in line is familiar to anyone who served in the Atlantic Fleet: *Savannah.* She took a German radio-controlled glide bomb through one of her turrets off Italy in 1943 and one out of every five men who had walked her decks that morning was dead by evening. Navy Department telegrams, 197 of them, announced that a son or brother or father was not ever coming home.

Just outboard of the *Savannah* is the *Huntington.* She benefited from the earlier ship's wartime experience. Her superstructure was more compact, her two boiler room uptakes combined into a single stack. This arrangement allowed for a greater firing arc for the antiaircraft weapons. As the war progressed and the threat from the kamikaze grew, ships were given as many antiaircraft weapons as they could safely carry—and sometimes more. The *Huntington* was not commissioned until February 1946, at a time when most ships were going through their inactivation overhauls. She served just over three years in the peacetime navy, all of it in the Mediterranean and the Atlantic, before she was ordered to join the battle-scarred veteran ships in the Sixteenth Fleet, the Atlantic Reserve Fleet.

Between the *Huntington* and the outboard ship, the *Montpelier,* is the *Houston* (fig. 42). The sightseer knows her story and looks carefully at her starboard quarter, right at the stern, where a Japanese torpedo ripped a hole in her and very nearly sent her to the bottom. The steel plates are heavily wrinkled both port and starboard from the blast of the warhead. Had she gone down she would have been famous. Her survival has assured her anonymity, if not in the history books or in the minds of her crew, then at least here in this graveyard of the well known and the little known.

Back down the pier the visitor walks, past the high round sterns all lined up as if on parade, past names that evoke memories of the not-so-distant past, names that conjure up images of the inferno that was the *Bunker Hill,* now silently aging a continent away in Bremerton ten years after one of these now-anonymous ships came to her aid in the last year of a bitter war; images of the *Houston* settling deep in the ocean, the water swirling in her flooded hangar at the stern; images of the crew of the *Savannah* looking for friends in the aftermath of the bombing off Salerno. They are just mountains of dead steel now, their time come and gone long ago.

The *New Orleans,* sister to the *San Francisco,* lies tied up to the wall (fig. 42). Behind her is the *Chester* and behind the *Chester* is one of the most unusual cases in the yard, the USS *Oregon City.* She is a beautiful ship, even in mothballs. Lead ship of a class of three, she is 673 feet long and displaces over seventeen thousand tons. She is a far cry in design from the *New Orleans* and the *Chester.* With her sisters *Albany* and *Rochester,* and the new *Des Moines* class, she was to form the backbone of the postwar cruiser force. With all the glory and fanfare that such a ceremony commands, she was commissioned on 16 February 1946, as the first of the *Brooklyn*s were entering mothballs. Yet just twenty-two months later she was towed into the basin and retired, her machinery barely broken in, her guns never fired in anger. She was practically brand new, but she never sailed again. Should that visitor happen to come again to Philadelphia fifteen years in the future he would see the *Oregon City* still there.

*Fig. 44. The* Wichita *at sea in rough weather.* U.S. Naval Institute

The upper works of another ship are just barely visible past the short-lived *Oregon City* (fig. 42). The stacks and superstructure look surprisingly like the *Savannah*'s in the next row over but the hull number and her main battery, spotted when the visitor was on the other side of the harbor near the *San Francisco,* give her away. She is number forty-five. She does indeed resemble the *Savannah,* excepting she has three instead of five turrets, two forward and one aft, in what would become standard for heavy cruiser design. Her main battery is that of a heavy cruiser, nine eight-inch rifles in triple turrets.

She is the "Witch," the USS *Wichita* (fig. 44). The Witch spent the early months of the war in convoy duty in the foul weather of the North Atlantic. Cloud cover was frequently down to two hundred feet and sometimes closed over the ship completely. Collision while in a convoy in such rough seas was a constant threat and a frequent occurrence. She was assigned to work with the Royal Navy in convoy escort and then was one of the few ships to be ordered to engage French ships in combat when Vichy forces opposed the North African landings. She fired on the French cruiser *Primauguet* and dodged torpedoes from a French submarine. The visitor shakes his head as he walks back toward the bridge, still unable to grasp the complicated politics of the war that had American and French ships firing at each other and American and French troops liberating Paris together.

Down the seawall he walks, his tour almost over, past a trio of escort carriers, including the *Anzio* and the *Prince William* (fig. 42). Walking between them and the warehouses to his right it is as though he is in a canyon, so tall and steep are the sides of the ships and the warehouse walls. And then he is out on the bridge again for a last look back at America's World War II naval might in hibernation. How long, he wonders, will they stay there? The answer, though he could not have known it, was not long in coming. On a day four years later, 1 March 1959, almost all of the vessels he walked past, admired, wondered about, and felt a bit of reverence for were consigned to the scrap heap. Most were sold within a few months. Tugs came and led them away so that torches, pneumatic hammers, cranes, and jackhammers could rip them apart. The *Portland, Louisville,* and the *Augusta* were gone. The battered but proud old *San Francisco,* the *Tuscaloosa,* and the *Minneapolis* were gone. Suddenly those piers were empty.

Along the far wall next to the ball field the *Columbia* and the *Denver* were towed away. The *Dayton* was moved with the *Huntington* to the Delaware River and tied up next to the *South Dakota,* and by 1961 they, too, were gone. The *Hawaii* was finally towed, ever so carefully for she was the biggest ship in the basin, out through the entrance and away to be sliced up. Of the light cruisers just forward of the *Hawaii,* the *Houston,* the *Savannah,* and the *Cleveland* were stricken that day with the rest. Next to them, and also on the list of ships declared surplus, were the *Chester, New Orleans,* and *Wichita.* Out under the raised bridge they went, as well. Twenty-two cruisers were in the basin that day in 1955. Fifteen of them were wiped off the Naval Vessel Register on that March day four years later. Out on the Delaware the two old battleships, the *Tennessee* and the *California,* joined them

They all had done their part, even the *Oregon City* and the *Hawaii,* as they sat ready to return to action if the call ever came. It never did and time caught up with these fine ships, the ghost fleet that would have made an interesting history lesson had someone really walked all around the basin and taken the time not just to read the numbers and identify the ships but to soak up the days, months, and years wrapped

*Fig. 45. Aerial view of the reserve fleet at San Francisco in 1958. U.S. Naval Institute*

up in each ship's hull, to really feel, to understand what these forgotten ships were all about.

At the San Francisco Navy Yard in 1958 most of the rest of the remaining light cruisers are in reserve (fig. 45). The San Francisco Group of the Pacific Reserve Fleet, the Nineteenth Fleet, was disbanded the next year and some of these ships were towed to other reserve berthings soon after the photograph was taken. Many were scrapped. Nine *Cleveland*s are in view in orderly pairs: the *Amsterdam, Astoria, Manchester, Atlanta, Birmingham, Duluth, Miami,* and *Vicksburg.* A pair of antiaircraft cruisers, the *Oakland* and the *Tucson,* have been there nearly a decade. (The nameship of that class was the old *Atlanta,* CL-51, sunk in World War II; the *Atlanta* here at San Francisco, CL-104, is a *Cleveland*-class ship carrying on her name.) In armament they resemble large destroyers since they mounted five-inch guns in twin mounts along the centerline of the ship. One, the *Reno,* was nearly sunk by a Japanese submarine. Her stern was flooded and almost submerged as she was towed seven hundred miles to repair facilities at Ulithi. Two others were sunk. Both the *Oakland* and the *Tucson* had been built in San Francisco, at Bethlehem Steel, and it was back to San Francisco they came after the war. The *Oakland* was ordered to the reserve fleet at Bremerton after the war but this was changed to an overhaul and continued service. After another three years she was again ordered deactivated, this time for good. In other reserve fleet groups sat the remaining antiaircraft cruisers: the *Flint, Fresno, San Juan,* and *San Diego.* The *Oakland,* along with the *Birmingham,* was stricken less than a year after the photo was taken in the mass striking of 1 March 1959, but the *Tucson* stayed on in reserve until 1966. Unlike many of the other light cruisers in the mothball fleet, those at San Francisco lasted a bit longer on the Naval Vessel Register: the *Vincennes* was stricken in 1966, the *Astoria* in 1969, and the *Amsterdam* in 1971, more than a quarter of a century after the end of the war for which she had been built.

As at Philadelphia, a pair of hospital ships are mothballed here too: the *Consolation* outboard of the *Repose.* Both arrived in the Pacific too late for the war, but not too late to transport hundreds of sick and wounded servicemen home. With the outbreak of the Korean War and the lack of a medical infrastructure in Korea, both were summoned to the western Pacific. The *Consolation* was in commission at the time and arrived off Pusan a month before the *Repose,* in reserve at San Francisco, having been mothballed in January 1950. The *Repose* was reactivated quickly at a time when it looked quite possible that the United States Army would be driven out of Korea. When the *Consolation* returned to the theater in early October after a stateside refit, she pioneered the use of helicopters to evacuate wounded from the battlefield directly to a hospital ship. The *Repose* eventually had a helicopter landing pad installed during overhaul and she, too, returned to Korea. When the war ended both the *Consolation* and the *Repose* were decommissioned again and placed in reserve. A few years after the photograph was taken the *Consolation* was charted to the People to People Health Foundation and began sailing to Third World nations bringing medical treatment, training, and education. No such benign fate awaited the *Repose.* She was destined to go to war again after ten more years in mothballs, recommissioning in 1965. Again the battlefield was in Asia, although this time it was Southeast Asia, as the United States began to commit more and more ground troops to the war that would soon appear to have no end. Long before the Paris Peace Accords were signed in 1973, the *Repose* had again been decommissioned and laid up in Suisun Bay.

Five escort carriers are berthed here: the *Cape Esperance, Rendova, Sicily, Bairoko,* and *Cape Gloucester* (fig. 45). Three light carriers ride out the rest of their days here as well: the *Bataan, Cowpens,* and *San Jacinto.* The *Cape Esperance* was recommissioned for Korea as an aircraft transport, ferrying planes to Japan and sometimes making as many as eight voyages a year. The *Rendova, Sicily,* and *Bairoko* all saw action in Korea, carrying marine squadrons for close air support. The *Sicily* covered the Inchon landings, the victorious breakout north across the thirty-eighth parallel, and the disastrous retreat of the First Marine Division from the Chosin Reservoir. Her aircraft were the marine Corsairs of VMF-214, the famous (and infamous) Black Sheep squadron of World War II, commanded for a time by Pappy Boyington. She was relieved in Japan by the *Rendova,* which had recommissioned in January 1951 and sped west across the Pacific with another marine squadron, VMF-212.

The *Bataan,* too, was sent to the war zone, not in the camouflage paint she wears in a World War II photograph, but in peacetime gray, although peacetime had once again come and fled (fig. 46). She had gone to mothballs at Philadelphia after her World War II duty, been recommissioned back into the fleet before the Korean War had started, and was the only *Independence*-class carrier to go to war again. The *Independence* had been gutted in the atomic bomb tests and recently scuttled. The *San Jacinto* and the *Cowpens,* shown with the *Bataan,* never returned to service after being mothballed at Alameda and eventually were towed across the bay to Hunters Point (fig. 45). The *Cabot* was loaned to the Spanish Navy after decommissioning in February 1947 and recommissioning just a year and a half later as a training carrier. The *Belleau Wood* and the *Langley* went to the French as the *Bois De Belleau* and the *Lafayette,* two symbolic and fitting names for the ex-American vessels. The *Bois De Belleau* was French for Belleau Wood, where two battalions of American Marines had made a gallant attack in World War I. The Marquis de Lafayette was the French nobleman who assisted George Washington during the Revolutionary War. The *Monterey* had been towed out of the reserve basin at Philadelphia for Korea as had many others, but her job, along with the *Cabot,* was to train new pilots in the tricky and dangerous business of landing their aircraft on the pitching, rolling deck of a carrier at sea. But the *Bataan*

*Fig. 46. The* Bataan
*at sea in World
War II camouflage.
U.S. Naval Institute*

saw combat again, making a total of three war cruises. When the war
ended, so did her second career and back to mothballs she went, this
time in the city by the Bay.

All was really not quiet and dead at this and the other reserve fleet
groups, though the piers and the ships appear deserted. A "Material
Readiness and Status Report" was prepared periodically by the headquarters of both the Pacific and the Atlantic Reserve Fleets. These typed
sheets (in an age before computers and spreadsheets) listed each of the
vessels in reserve for each fleet, dividing them by group (Long Beach,
San Diego, Columbia River, etc.), and for each vessel in reserve listed
information such as the date of her last overhaul, her last undocking,
her last "Insurv" (inspection and survey) check, her last quinquennial
(five-year) inventory. All of them were listed, from the tugs and landing
craft at Columbia River, to the cruisers at Philadelphia, to the carriers
and battleships at Bremerton. The report noted whether or not requisi-
tions were made for any supply deficiencies noted after each inventory.
It also listed the allowance material and spare parts available for each
ship. It had a column for remarks as well. The Material Readiness
Status for the Pacific Reserve Fleet dated 15 May 1950 listed the following: for the USS *Tinosa* at Mare Island, "Drydocking, remove flood
valve blanks, reinstall propellers"; at Tacoma the escort carriers *Cape*

*Esperance, Saidor, Altamaha, Core,* and *Steamer Bay* all had the remarks, "Relubricate gyro," while the *Nassau* was having ten forty-millimeter mounts installed. In Alameda the *Belleau Wood* was in the middle of her first overhaul, and across the bay the *Hornet* and the *Intrepid* were, too. The 15 May 1950 report for the ships of the Pacific Reserve Fleet was fifty-two pages long.

Each group of mothballed vessels was inspected yearly by a sub-board of Inspection and Survey. They were charged with examining "all vessels belonging to the Navy, not in actual service at sea [to determine] which of said vessels are unfit for further service," and to "recommend disposition of vessels which are considered to be worn beyond economical repair" (Twelfth Naval District, RG 181). By the mid- to late 1950s the reserve ships were being inspected on inactivation, again five years later, and also if watertight or weather integrity failed some time after the quinquennial inspection. The board would select three or four ships in each group and report, in minute detail, the condition of the ships and recommend any needed repairs. In 1956, for example, there were forty-six ships assigned to the SFGruPacResFlt (San Francisco Group, Pacific Reserve Fleet). The inspectors looked at the newly arrived *Manchester,* the *Atlanta,* and the escort carrier *Rendova* in October of that year, and conducted flooding drills aboard the *Tucson* to see how the reserve fleet personnel responded. The Insurv would grade the reserve group as a whole on administration, personnel, training, security and supply, and the individual ships were graded on the condition of the hull, machinery, ordinance, dehumidification equipment, electrical and navigational systems, medical departments and materials on board. They would examine the barracks of the personnel assigned to care for the mothballed ships and look at their recordkeeping procedures. They checked the records of the dehumidifiers; excessive operation could mean that the dehumidifiers were inefficient or that part of the ship was open to the outside air. The ships, though sealed against corrosion and weather, were not pristine. Aboard the *Vicksburg* the Insurv team noted that "the interior of the ship was very untidy," while a similar team in Tacoma noted that the flight decks of the escort carriers there had deteriorated to a great extent in the decade and more they had been exposed to the rain, fog, and salt air of the Pacific Northwest.

Each type of ship in reserve, from a destroyer to a sub tender, had an activation plan in case the navy decided she was needed again. Within each plan were list upon list of activation sheets, depending on the ship,

*Fig. 47. Civilians touring mothballed submarines on Armed Forces Day 1953. National Archives, Pacific Sierra Region*

everything from "Ultra-High Frequency Antenna and Associated Equipment" to "Turrets Eight-Inch, Fourteen-Inch and Sixteen-Inch"; from "Refrigeration Plants," to "Clocks, Watches, Typewriters, Calculating Machines, and Packaged Materials." Each ship was given such an activation plan that outlined, step by step, the process of bringing it out of hibernation and turning it into a living warship again. The plans were very detailed and even such an innocuous vessel as a YTB (large harbor tug) would have a plan that entailed 189 separate steps in five different phases. From the first step, "Make an immediate survey of all incompleted readiness items in all departments," to the last, "Secure all departments for sea," the activation plan listed them all. When a ship was actually reactivated for service, another report, the "Redelivery Condition Survey Report," was prepared. When the oiler *Pecos* was returned to service, this one report added another nineteen pages to the mountain of papers already associated with her career in the active and reserve fleets (Box 1058, RG 181).

Occasionally there were visitors to the reserve fleet, not maintenance sailors or inspectors looking for signs of rust or sloppy paperwork, but civilians who came for a tour of the ships that had won the war and now crowded together in numbers large and small around the country. It is Armed Forces Day in 1953 at the Mare Island Naval Shipyard (fig. 47). For the navy it was good public relations: let the taxpayer see that the money spent on these fine ships is money well spent, that the submarines and ships of the reserve fleet are in good shape, that they are ready to fight again. The Korean War was grinding its way to a negotiated cease-fire. The Berlin airlift was only five years in the past; World War II less than a decade. Perhaps many of these ships will be needed again, will go to sea again. Certainly some of them will.

Crowds of civilians wander the decks of the submarines *Lizardfish, Trepang,* and *Hackleback* (SS-295). In the background is the tender *Pelias* (AS-14) that had been at Pearl Harbor during the attack almost a dozen years before. Another tender is tied up just astern of the *Pelias.* Sailors of the reserve fleet are there to explain the preservation techniques used aboard the subs, to answer the thousand and one questions the civilians have about the navy, the boats, and the forgotten fleet.

These ships, though, are certainly not forgotten, at least not today. The men, women, and children get a firsthand look at the potent fighting force kept in the nation's closet. They can see and touch the big igloos covering the deck guns, trace the piping that leads from the drum-like dehumidifiers on deck down into the boat's interior. They can walk the deck of a real fighting ship, feel the steel and wood under their feet and marvel at the array of sleeping warships surrounding them on this chilly spring day. They can wonder at the small size of the fleet sub, wonder what sort of person was brave enough or foolhardy enough to live aboard that steel tube for months on end, underwater much of the time, while Japanese destroyers dropped high explosives all around, trying to pierce a hole in the side that would send a jet of ice-cold seawater rushing into the boat, drowning the men trapped like rats inside. The submarine would sink slowly into the dark, unknown depths of the ocean while the men inside frantically looked for a way to stop the flooding, to get the boat to the surface, to get out. For fifty-two similar submarines it happened just that way. These at the dock today were the lucky ones, and the civilians walking their decks even luckier that there were men who would go below, take the boat to sea and the risks involved so that civilians could stand on the deck of the preserved subs a few years later and wonder just what it was like to be a submariner.

Some of the cruisers present in the aerial view of the San Francisco reserve fleet taken a few years after the war did indeed go to sea again. Half a dozen, including three that came from the San Francisco Group—the *Oklahoma City, Topeka,* and *Springfield*—were converted in the 1950s to fire the newest weapons in fleet air defense, the surface-to-air missile. Two heavy cruisers, the *Boston* and *Canberra,* were the first to be so converted. Both were pulled from mothballs in Bremerton and fitted with two twin-armed missile launchers in place of their after eight-inch turret. The missile systems were big and required a lot of room for the launchers and missile magazines as well as for the fire control radars, and a big heavy cruiser from the reserve fleet was the perfect choice. Actually, the *Wichita,* rusting in mothballs at the Philadelphia yard, was first suggested, then rejected for conversion; then the battle cruiser *Hawaii* was proposed as the first missile conversion along with the smaller *Macon.* But the plans for the *Hawaii*'s completion were changed to that of a command cruiser and the *Macon* was replaced in the planning by the *Oregon City.* In the end, the pair of *Baltimore*s were substituted instead (Friedman, *U.S. Cruisers,* 378).

Forward of the funnels the ships were little modified from their World War II appearance, but their twin stacks had been combined into one and missile guidance radar dishes installed atop newly built deckhouses. These ships fired the first surface-to-air missiles, nicknamed the Terrier, and soon the search was on for a platform for another system, this one called the Talos. The *Cleveland*s were the practical, if not the ideal, answer, in part because there were twenty-eight of them in reserve. The Talos was a long missile, thirty-six feet, which meant it would have to be stowed horizontally, for there was not enough room in a *Cleveland* hull to stack these missiles vertically in magazines.

The first ship to be converted was the *Galveston,* the only *Cleveland* that had been laid up before being completed (fig. 48). Her superstructure and all main and secondary batteries were removed aft of her second stack. A large deckhouse containing the missile magazine replaced them, atop which sat the massive search and guidance radars, and a single missile launcher was installed. She was photographed in 1958 as she neared completion, across the pier from the mothballed *South Dakota.* The *Galveston* had been reborn from the forgotten fleet; the *South Dakota* was destined to remain there. The *Galveston* is alive, humming with activity as her new equipment is tested and as her rebuild nears completion. The *South Dakota* has spent the past decade in silence, the

*Fig. 48. The Galveston being converted to a missile ship alongside the mothballed South Dakota.*

*U.S. Naval Institute*

only functioning equipment that of the dehumidifiers keeping her from decaying at her pier. The *Galveston* is the future, the *South Dakota* the past. The *Galveston* has demonstrated the worth of keeping her preserved during the past decade. The *South Dakota* was never given the chance to demonstrate her worth, yet worthy she was. The men of the reserve fleet kept her ready, as they had kept the *Galveston* ready, as they had kept over two thousand ships ready.

In all, three Terrier- and three Talos-equipped missile cruisers were converted from the huge reserve fleet. The first *Cleveland* to be converted to fire the Terrier was the *Topeka*, pulled from the San Francisco Reserve Fleet in 1957 and towed all the way to the New York Navy Yard for the three-year conversion. Of the other four, the *Oklahoma City* and the *Springfield* came from San Francisco, the *Little Rock* and the *Providence* from the Atlantic Reserve Fleet. Each was more extensively modified than the *Galveston* and the *Topeka* because each was to be fitted as a fleet flagship (all of the battleships that had served in this role during Korea were back in reserve or about to be). More command and control and berthing spaces for the flag complement were needed and the only place left for such additions was forward. The number two six-inch turret was removed, as were two of the three remaining five-inchers, and a large superstructure built in their place.

The final missile conversions went even further. For these, the big hulls of a heavy cruiser were needed, as these ships were to have all their secondary mounts and main battery turrets removed so they could fit the big Talos systems both forward and aft. Initially these conversions were to be the mothballed *Oregon City*, *Fall River*, and *Chicago*. The *Oregon City* had been at Philadelphia and *Chicago* and *Fall River* at Bremerton since 1947. None had extensive sea time; all had been laid up within a few years of being completed. There were other heavy cruisers still in reserve—the *Pittsburgh*, the *Quincy*, and the *Baltimore*—but all had served two tours with the fleet, some of it in wartime. Once again, the *Oregon City* was passed over, as was the *Fall River*. Each had only about two years of service after being completed and both were destined to spend almost a quarter century in mothballs and then cut apart. Two active ships, the *Albany* and the *Columbus*, were substituted, and a third, the *Chicago*, was taken from reserve. Each ship was stripped down to the main deck and then rebuilt with a long deckhouse running a third of its length, on top of which sat a tall, straight-sided superstructure, windowless except for the bridge that capped it, and two even taller stacks. Once again the ships of the reserve fleet had made a contribution to the nation's defense.

At the Mare Island Naval Shipyard in the early 1960s three light cruisers from three different wars, with two different designs but a common fate, lie in mothballs, a locked gate blocking entry to their berths (fig. 49). From left to right they are the *Vicksburg*, the *Manchester*, and the *Worcester*. The *Vicksburg* participated in World War II; the *Manchester* and the *Worcester* in the Korean and Cold Wars. The *Vicksburg* and *Manchester* were two of the large number of *Cleveland*s built during and just after World War II. The *Vicksburg* was commissioned in 1944, got to the Pacific in 1945, and finished out the war as so many of her sisters did, screening the big task forces that ravaged the Japanese fleet, the island garrisons and finally the enemy's homeland in the closing months of the war. She was the third ship to carry the name of the Confederate city in Mississippi that had surrendered after a long bitter

*Fig. 49. The* Vicksburg, Manchester, *and* Worcester *at Mare Island. National Archives, Pacific Sierra Region*

siege to General Grant on the Fourth of July, 1863, and that for a hundred years afterward refused to celebrate the nation's birthday.

Despite the need for more ships as the American advance picked up steam in the central and southwest Pacific, the *Vicksburg*'s regimen was one of training after she was commissioned. A new ship and crew needed time to weld themselves into a fighting force such that an emergency would be reacted to instantly. A broken steam line, a fire, or a man overboard required the crew of twelve hundred officers and men immediately to know where to go on the ship, how to get there in the fastest and safest manner possible without getting in the way of others, and what to do once they got to their posts. The *Vicksburg* spent the first month of her commission taking on supplies for sea, and her sailors spent their time learning where they were to berth, what watches they were to stand, and how to negotiate the complicated maze of ladders and hatches they would use to get from the engine room to the galley or the bridge. More cruisers were being built and for a time the crew of the *Vicksburg*, themselves just becoming a real team, trained precommissioning crews on the intricacies of manning a large warship. At last the light cruiser left Hampton Roads for the war on New Year's Day 1945, the year everyone hoped (but almost no one believed) would be the last year of war.

A war of unknown duration and much difficulty faced the new crew of the *Vicksburg* when she steamed for Pearl Harbor and still more training. Her guns fired their first shells off Iwo Jima. All of that training—the endless repetitions of hoisting shells and powder and ramming them into the breeches of the six-inchers, the lectures on safety and proper procedure to the former civilians who made up her crew—now paid off. When the first shells whistled their way toward stinking, sulfuric Iwo Jima, the *Vicksburg* and her crew became battle veterans. They could claim a battle star. Her forty-millimeters warded off attacking planes. Once a torpedo dropped by a "Betty" missed the bow of the *Vicksburg* by only thirty-five yards as she made an emergency turn. A half knot difference in the *Vicksburg*'s speed, a half degree shallower or steeper turn, a slight rudder kick by the pilot of the Betty as he made his run at the ship, and the torpedo might have slammed into the side of the cruiser. It is easy to imagine the effects as she sits here deserted in Vallejo. The hull below the waterline would have caved in. Transverse beams would have been bent inward, their attached bulkheads separating and splitting. The sea would have rushed in, filling whatever void had been left by smashed or displaced steel.

Now, at Mare Island, she really is dead. There is no real hope of her being recommissioned. Six of her kind had been converted to fire missiles, but not the *Vicksburg*. All the small details that made her alive to a knowing eye, even at a quick glance, even at a distance, are gone. The items that gave her a look of life while she fought a war are gone: the delicate radar antenna above her foremast crosstree; the black bloomers over the six-inch guns that made them almost look as if they could see their targets; the guns themselves, fixed parallel to the deck rather than in their active, jaunty, slightly elevated position. The dark windows of the bridge are gone, replaced by gray paint that gives her a glassy-eyed, unseeing stare. She has no color. Never mind the lack of camouflage. The *Manchester* next to her did not wear it, neither did the *Worcester*. The trio are numbingly gray. The paint is weather stained and splotchy in some areas, rusted in others, and fairly screams abandonment. She does not have the polished, clean air of youth, only the dull, worn, colorless look of old age.

The *Manchester,* next to her, looks only slightly better, and only because she has spent far fewer years here (fig. 49). Note that her aluminum igloos and that of the *Worcester* are different than those of the *Vicksburg,* with a pair of tubes rising out of each. These are covering the twin three-inch, fifty-caliber antiaircraft battery that replaced the forty-millimeters carried by the *Vicksburg.* The *Manchester* was the last *Cleveland* to be launched, the last to see active service as a gun cruiser. She spent the immediate post–World War II years cruising the Mediterranean before her transfer to the Pacific in 1949. She was in overhaul in San Francisco when the Korean War began and by 15 September was firing her main battery at the retreating North Koreans behind the port city of Inchon. She spent nearly a year shooting at shore targets up and down the Korean coast in company with heavy cruisers and battleships that rotated in and out, and she ultimately made three trips to the war zone.

At one time in her career, though, she performed a very special, very sacred duty. She is shown in Yokosuka harbor in January 1956 (fig. 50). It is her last western Pacific cruise, and in fact her last cruise ever. She is to enter the reserve fleet upon her return to the States, but she has one final duty as she steams slowly near the moored attack transport *Pickaway.* Marine honor guards stand at attention near her number four turret, and at their feet, draped in American flags, are coffins. Every man aboard the *Manchester,* every officer, chief, sailor, and marine had an identity, a name. The men in the coffins had none any longer. They were unknowns. This was Operation Glory, and these unknown dead were coming home to Hawaii, to the National Memorial Cemetery of the Pacific, more commonly known as Punchbowl.

Thousands of American war dead from World War II, Korea, and Vietnam are buried there. Construction of the cemetery began in 1948 and servicemen killed during the war and temporarily held in mausoleums in Hawaii and Guam later were interred in private mass burials. Not even family members were allowed to attend. Long trenches were dug and over two hundreds caskets brought into the extinct volcano for burial each morning. One was selected at random and Catholic, Protestant, and Jewish services were read over the one body representing all others that day. In July 1949 the cemetery and the services were opened to the public. Among the first to be laid to rest was Ernie Pyle, whose body had been brought home from Ie Shima. Fittingly, the man who extolled the virtues of the common man in the

*Fig. 50. The Manchester at Yokosuka with Korean War unknown soldiers aboard. U.S. Naval Institute*

service, and wrote about him to the people back home, was laid to rest between two anonymous servicemen, two unknowns.

Korean War dead were buried there too, and over three-quarters of them were unknowns. Among them were those brought back across the Pacific in the *Manchester.* Four of those Korean War unknowns were selected in 1958 as candidates to represent the Korean War at Arlington National Cemetery. One was chosen by a combat veteran of the conflict and this body was buried alongside unknowns from World War I and World War II (and would in time be joined by an unknown from a future war) at the Tomb of the Unknown Soldier under an inscription that reads, "Here Lies In Honored Glory An American Soldier Known But to God." Perhaps this serviceman, whose family knew only that he was missing and his body would never be returned to them, who would forever remain unknown but forever would be remembered as he represented all of the nameless ones, once sanctified the deck of this lonely ship at Mare Island.

Next to the *Manchester* is one of the last two light cruisers built for the navy, the *Worcester* (her sister was the *Roanoke*) (fig. 49). Two things about her are readily apparent: she is much bigger than the *Cleveland*s next to her—over sixty feet longer and displacing almost five thousand tons more than the *Vicksburg* and *Manchester*—and she carries a main battery that looks like no other in the fleet. Squat and buglike, these were of a revolutionary design when introduced aboard the *Worcester* but ironically they were already obsolete. The *Worcester*, despite being about as long as the battleship *Indiana*, carried six-inch main batteries, but of a different type, and for a different purpose, than the ships that preceded her.

The devastation wrought by the kamikaze and the success of German engineering in developing crude but workable guided missiles (the kind that rained down on London and nearly sank the *Savannah*) had a profound effect on fleet antiaircraft defense. The light machine-gun-type weapons aboard ship—the twenty- and forty-millimeters—were increasingly viewed as ineffective against fast-moving aircraft. The five-inchers were good weapons, but an even harder-hitting, farther-reaching weapon was needed to counter jet aircraft. The six-inchers were good surface weapons but did not fire fast enough to be effective as antiaircraft artillery, that is, until the development of the eight- and six-inch automatic rapid-firing mounts that used ammunition with the brass casings holding both powder and shells. In addition, the new rapid-firing cruiser mounts could load at any elevation so that the barrel need not be laboriously returned parallel to the deck for turret crewman to access and reload the breech. The eight-inchers were looked upon as being more useful for shore bombardment, and these rapid firing versions eventually went to sea in the *Des Moines, Salem,* and *Newport News.* But as advanced as these mounts were on the *Worcester* and *Roanoke,* they had already been made obsolete by jet aircraft. Missiles, not bullets, would be needed to consistently and successfully cope with the high speeds of the new planes now under development.

The *Worcester,* like the *Manchester,* was a Korean War veteran. She was in the Mediterranean, her new dual-purpose main battery shielding the new *Midway*s, when she was ordered to the Far East. She headed south, steered her way carefully down the Suez Canal and into the

Indian Ocean, through the Malacca Straits between Malaya and Sumatra and up the South China Sea in a dash to the war. She joined the *Philippine Sea* and *Valley Forge* in the Yellow Sea west of the Korean peninsula, ready to guard the flattops against the North Korean Air Force. She was off Inchon with the *Manchester* when the First Marine Division went ashore and began the rout of the North Korean Army back across the thirty-eighth parallel. In mid-October the *Worcester* joined an international flotilla off the North Korean city of Wonsan. Arrayed with her were the battleship *Missouri,* the cruisers *Helena* and *Rochester,* the destroyers *Harold J. Thomas* and *Maddox,* the British cruiser *Ceylon* and destroyer *Cockade,* the Canadian destroyer *Athabaskan,* and the Australian *Warramunga.*

Mines were a constant worry. During World War II the Pacific Fleet had under its command well over five hundred minesweepers. In 1950 this force was down to four steel-hulled minesweepers, three of which were inactive in Japan, and six old wooden vessels. Two of the steel ships were recommissioned in August and a makeshift force sailed to Wonsan harbor. Their task was to clear the thousands of mines laid offshore by the Soviets so that Tenth Corps, comprised of the First Marine Division and the army's Seventh Infantry Division, could land at the port of Wonsan on the flank of the retreating Communist troops and cut them off, as the landing at Inchon had a month before on the other side of the peninsula. Two of the mine craft, the *Pirate* and the *Pledge,* struck mines and went down but the rest of the force continued to sweep lanes through the thick fields. On 12 October with the United Nations flag on the foretruck of the flagship *Worcester,* the Allied battleships, cruisers, and destroyers opened fire, pounding Wonsan as the ROK (Republic of Korea) troops took the city before the Tenth Corps had a chance to land and flank the enemy. The *Worcester* sailed for the East Coast in November, her one Korean tour finished, and after overhaul she spent a few years back in the Mediterranean.

In the 1950s fear of the bomb was pervasive. Thousand of American families built fallout shelters. Children in school learned how to protect themselves in the event of an atomic attack by the Russians. Civil defense shelters were erected in cities and towns across the country. Ships were built (and are still built) with huge sprinkler systems to wash themselves after radioactive water and debris had cascaded down, presumably after a nuclear near-miss. The *Worcester* is shown at sea a year after the Korean armistice, raising a water curtain to cleanse herself of

*Fig. 51. The* Worcester *undergoing atomic wash down at sea. U.S. Naval Institute*

any fallout during atomic defense maneuvers (fig. 51). She made a few more western Pacific cruises in 1956 and then was laid up in 1958 at Mare Island with her sister *Roanoke*, the last two light gun cruisers in the fleet. Later they were towed up the coast and moored near the *Missouri* at Bremerton, but the scrappers eventually got both these fine ships in the early 1970s.

Far less imposing than the cruisers, and nestled in a cluster of sister ships at the north end of the Mare Island Naval Shipyard deeply in shadow on this short winter's day in 1966, is the USS *George A. Johnson* (fig. 52). She is a destroyer escort, one of the many examples of wartime mass production that enabled the United States to overwhelm her enemies with merchant shipping and the warships to protect them. The *George A. Johnson* and the other escorts, crowded so close to her that they seem to be one unbroken mass of steel rather than individual ships, were of the *Rudderow* class. The photo shows her forward five-inch mount that set the *Rudderow*s and one other class of escort apart from the four other types. The *George A. Johnson* was completed rather late in the war for a destroyer escort, commissioning in April 1944 at a time when production of these ships was being rapidly curtailed. She is smaller than a destroyer, distinctly less heavily armed, and much less imposing with her low superstructure and rather unassuming profile. The shadows lengthen and contribute to the melancholy air surrounding these abandoned warships as the sun sets in the Pacific; time is running out for the *George A. Johnson* and the others. Soon, very soon, this cluster of World War II veterans will be pulled apart by tugs as each lonely ship heads off to the scrap yard. Yet it was DE-583, and hundreds of others like her, that helped turn the tide of the Battle of the Atlantic two decades before. By taking over convoy protection they relieved bigger, multipurpose destroyers for the vital duty of fleet escort and produced some of the most exciting stories to come out of the two-ocean naval war that was in many ways the United States Navy's finest hour.

*Fig. 52. The* George A. Johnson, *with other DEs, in reserve at Mare Island. National Archives, Pacific Sierra Region*

The Battle of the Atlantic, the struggle between the German submarine fleet and Allied merchant shipping and their escorts, was in some ways a two-part battle. Early in the war the U-boats exacted a heavy toll on American, British, and Canadian shipping as America, both before and after Pearl Harbor, struggled to keep England in the war by supplying her wartime and civilian needs by sea across the dangerous, stormy, and submarine-infested waters of the North Atlantic. Such was the plight of the British, and so great their need for escort vessels to ensure that the lifesaving convoys arrived from American and Canadian ports, that they were willing to trade valuable bases to the United States for fifty obsolete destroyers, many pulled from the reserve fleet.

It was this need of the British for rapidly constructed escorts, used for convoy protection as well as a variety of other duties, that prompted President Roosevelt to urge development of a new type of vessel, the destroyer escort (DE). The problem inherent in its design was that in order to cram a destroyer escort hull with sufficient weapons (main batteries, torpedoes, depth charges, fire control systems), the vessel would have to ultimately displace nearly as much as existing destroyers. The cost savings in mass producing such a ship were thought to be minimal and a compromise design difficult to produce, since either the destroyer escort would be too small, and thus inadequately armed and engined, or too large, and thus too similar to existing destroyer designs. The challenge was to simplify construction, enabling mass production techniques to lower costs and reduce the time between keel laying and commissioning, while providing an antisubmarine and (later) an antiaircraft weapons suite with enough punch to allow the DE to survive.

Once the British ordered fifty of the new escorts, the United States decided that the DE would be of some use after all. They were more lightly armed and powered than a destroyer, yet able to replace the bigger ships in a variety of roles, freeing up the *Benson*s and *Fletcher*s and later the *Sumner*s and *Gearing*s for long-range fleet escort duties with the fast carrier task forces. But four major problems remained, even after a satisfactory design was settled on and construction authorized and begun.

The first was a lack of shipyard space. The government built brand-new yards at Hingham (Massachusetts), Houston, and Newark specifically for the construction of the destroyer escorts. Navy yards at Charleston, Philadelphia, Boston, Mare Island, Norfolk, and Puget Sound built more. Others were built on the Great Lakes by Tampa

Shipbuilding and by Western Pipe and Steel in San Pedro. In short, they were built everywhere a yard could be set up. Of 1,005 ordered, 563 were eventually completed before the submarine threat had been reduced and the remaining orders canceled. The vast majority were commissioned between 1943 and 1944, including those converted to fast transports. Others were transferred to allies under Lend-Lease. A second problem was the lack of a suitable and available power plant. Much experimentation eventually resulted in five different types of plants being used, both diesel and steam powered, and six different classes of escorts. The third difficulty was the competition for scarce building resources and shipyard space between the destroyer escorts and the various types of landing craft urgently needed for the proposed amphibious operations. Landing craft production soon eclipsed that of the escort vessels. The fourth problem was a lack of five-inch mounts for the destroyer escort main batteries. The *Fletcher*s then under construction each took five, the *Benson*s four, and the destroyer escorts, which were not intended for fleet action or to even engage enemy aircraft, had to settle for three-inch guns as the main battery for the first four classes. The last two, the steam-turbine-driven, twenty-four-knot *Rudderow*s and *John C. Butler*s, received two single five-inch mounts as their main battery.

Ultimately, the destroyer escort program was a victim of its own success. By 1943 there were sufficient numbers in commission that the order for the several hundred remaining ships was canceled. After the war the 290-foot-long underpowered *Edsall*s were scrapped. Most of the *Cannon*s went to foreign navies (Brazilian, Chinese, French and Dutch, among others) after a few years in mothballs. The others went quietly into reserve. A handful were recommissioned for Korea, and a few others, diesels selected because of their long endurance, were converted to radar picket destroyer escorts in the 1950s as part of the Continental Air Defense System, providing early warning in the event of an air strike against the United States launched over the ocean. But in general, the war-built destroyer escorts languished in their reserve anchorages, their exploits forgotten.

The USS *George* was named for Eugene George, born in Grand Rapids, Michigan in 1925 and killed seventeen years later at a time when he should have been finishing high school (fig. 53). He refused to abandon his twenty-millimeter gun on the USS *San Francisco* as a Japanese plane dived at the ship and crashed it. Eugene George, who

*Fig. 53. The USS George at sea. National Archives, Pacific Sierra Region*

stayed at his post as the flaming torpedo bomber bore down on him and maintained his fire until the last, died in the attack.

The *George* was part of one of the most famous destroyer escort exploits of the war, indeed one of the most amazing feats by any type of warship, though she was a bystander for much of the time. Teamed with escorts *Raby* and *England,* both *Buckley*-class like the *George,* she was ordered to intercept Japanese supply efforts to Bougainville. Alone among the trio, the *George* was commanded by a naval reservist. In May 1944 this hunter-killer group pounced on and sank six Japanese submarines in just twelve days. In each case, it was the *England* that dealt the death blow.

The *England* got the first sub by herself with a Hedgehog as the three ships cruised line abreast about two miles apart. Three days later the *George*'s searchlight spotted a sub diving in the middle of the night after first having picked up echoes on sonar. The *George* attacked and missed. The *England* attacked and did not, and sub number two took its last dive to the bottom of the Pacific. The next day the *Raby* and the *George* attacked a third submarine, leaving *England* to try and sink it, and another submarine, *RO-104,* plunged to the bottom. On 24 May the *George*'s radar picked up the *RO-116* on the surface in the middle of the night. The boat dived, the *England* pounced on her with a Hedgehog attack, and soon the debris from the torn hull of the Japanese submarine littered the surface of the ocean. After being ordered to New Guinea to refuel and rearm, the trio then made radar contact on a fifth sub. The *Raby* made the first attack but she lost contact with the sub. The *England* picked up the trail and nailed the fleeing submarine with another Hedgehog salvo from her dwindling magazine. A fourth destroyer escort, the *Spangler,* joined them the next day and rearmed them.

The four ships cruised back north and in the middle of the night on 30 May another contact was made. The *George* and the *Raby* hunted it, and when dawn broke, first the *George,* then the *Raby,* and finally the *Spangler* were all given the chance to sink the elusive sub. Finally, the *England* was signaled to attack and wasted little time. The sixth Japanese submarine fell victim to the *England.* The 306-foot-long destroyer escort, built in two and a half months in San Francisco, carrying the name of one of the victims of the battleship *Oklahoma* at Pearl Harbor, had, in company with the other ships, destroyed six Japanese submarines in under two weeks.

Like the majority of the ships in the fleet, the *George* did not make history. Glory was not bestowed upon her or her crew. She was on the periphery of the action most of the time, a supporting player. It was her destiny to sail in the company of one of the most famous of her sisters, the *England,* and her crew watched as that ship sank sub after sub and earned a place in naval lore. Perhaps the *George* merits few words in a history book. But certainly she merits a footnote. Would the *England* have been able to accomplish her amazing feat without the *George?* Might not the Japanese submarine skippers have twisted and turned their boats beneath the waves in an effort to avoid the pursuing *George,* and in doing so placed themselves directly in the path of the *England?* History rarely notes such things. Yet history is full of unsung heroes and stories that are forever untold. Perhaps the *George* was one of them.

Though the *England* was later severely damaged by kamikazes and scrapped after the war, both the *Raby* and the *George* remained in the fleet and sailed into the 1950s. The *George* was attached to the Fleet Sonar School at Pearl Harbor for a time, but by 1958 she was old and

*Fig. 54. Destroyer
escorts in moth-
balls in 1964.
National Archives,
Pacific Sierra Region*

tired, as were most of her kind, and she was decommissioned and laid up in Stockton, California. Like the *George A. Johnson* at nearby Mare Island, she lay nested in a group of worn-out sister ships. Another decade went by before these ships, built originally for the express purpose of convoy escort during World War II, were scrapped.

There were other stories behind many of the anonymous DEs lined up in mothballs along the shore of the St. Johns River in Green Cove Springs, Florida. Like that of the *Buckley*, who, when she forced a U-boat to the surface, fought a running gun battle alongside the sub as it sank, and whose crew believed it was being boarded by the German sailors abandoning ship. The order "Stand by to repel boarders" had sounded on the *Buckley*'s decks as the Germans clambered aboard trying to surrender, and the *Buckley*'s crewmen had cut some of them down in the darkness before they realized what the Germans were doing. Or the *Pillsbury*, whose crew forced another U-boat to the surface, then put a boarding party on the sinking sub and captured her in one of the most daring and exciting episodes of the entire war.

After the war the destroyer escorts languished in reserve, most of them forgotten. For every *Buckley* or *Pillsbury* there were dozens of escorts like the *Thomas F. Nickel* (DE-587) and the *Howard F. Clark* (DE-533), moored in silence at Mare Island two decades later (fig. 54). The *Thomas F. Nickel* sank not a single submarine, shot down not a solitary plane, never fought hand to hand with a U-boat crew, nor captured an enemy ship on the high seas. Like many of her kind, she had a reservist in command. She served as she was intended to serve, in mundane escort duty in the backwater of the war. She patrolled endlessly for Japanese submarines, watched the sky for unfriendly aircraft as the war, for the most part, passed her by. She was part of the vital logistical link that kept the fighting men supplied and armed, and without ships like her the war could not have been won. But she won no fame for herself or her men; she won but a single battle star in her two years of war.

Unlike most of her contemporaries, after the war she was given a second life as a training ship, sailing up and down the coast giving naval reservists an occasional taste of the sea. And then she was retired and for a decade and a half she rusted away at Mare Island, as the *Pillsbury* and the *Buckley* did at Green Cove Springs, as the *John L. Williamson* did at Stockton and the *Hurst* did at Orange among clusters of sister ships. They achieved no glory in service, certainly no glory and little notice in mothballs. Finally, quietly, they disappeared, these mass-produced, war-built ships: the famous like the *Pillsbury;* the unknown like the *Howard F. Clark.*

In the end, they were all the same—rusting bits of metal in California, Florida, and Texas. The sounds of shipboard life echoed in the wind and salt air and slowly died away over the years: the shouts of alarm from the men on the *Buckley* as they imagined themselves about to be boarded by scrambling, swarming Germans in the Atlantic darkness; the anxious comments and calls of encouragement from the railing of the *Pillsbury* as Lieutenant David captured a sinking Nazi submarine about to blow itself up; the quiet professionalism and cocky boasts in the crew's mess of the *England* as one of her sailors painted submarine after submarine on her bridge in the middle of the Pacific. A Japanese submarine had sunk the *Yorktown*, the *Wasp*, and the *Juneau*. One would sink the *Indianapolis.* But six of them would kill no more thanks to the men of the *England.* Though the *England* never made it to the mothball fleet, many of her contemporaries did. Those sounds, and many others, were replaced only by the sounds of the wind or the waves slapping against the hull or the creaking of metal against metal as the ship swayed with the tide. The world remembered the battleships and the carriers and a few flamboyant submarine captains, but forgot, if it ever really knew, what these little, underpowered, undergunned ships had once done to win the war.

The destroyer-escorts may have been all but forgotten by most people after the war, but the battleships always managed to stay in the public eye. Only once (7 June 1954) did all four remaining battleships operate together (fig. 55). The lead ship is the *Iowa;* behind her is the *Wisconsin,* then the *Missouri,* and finally the *New Jersey.* Though it was brief, the cruise in formation brought back images of the great battle fleets of the past: the ships of guns, not airplanes; Nelson's fleet of line-of-battle ships breaking the Spanish and French line in three places off Cape Trafalgar in 1805; the sixteen imposing American battleships of the Great White Fleet wielding the big stick of Teddy Roosevelt around the globe; the British Grand Fleet steaming out to meet the German High Seas Fleet off Jutland in 1916; the six old battleships of Jesse Oldendorf crossing the Japanese *T* in the middle of the night in Surigao Strait in 1944. The scene was an anachronism to be sure, but it was a majestic one nonetheless with the massive clipper bows cleaving the waves, the high superstructures towering over the sleek unbroken lines of their main decks and the implied power from the big guns, a vision that missiles, no matter what their warhead, could never seem to capture. The very name battleship defines exactly what the ship was built for. These four ships, cruising the placid waters of the Atlantic in peacetime, were a throwback, even in 1954, to another era, when a fleet was defined by its number of battleships; when a series of white, concrete mooring quays in a tropical harbor would be named Battleship Row; when the image of a toppled foremast of an obsolete battlewagon would rally a nation at war.

Three of the ships pictured had returned, carefully preserved, from the mothball fleet. The fourth, the *Missouri,* had been kept in reduced commission as a training ship, some would say only because Harry Truman was in the White House and he loved the ship named for his home state and christened by his daughter Margaret. The only other significant battleship fleet in the world in the late 1940s and early 1950s was in the Royal Navy; her dreadnoughts, the *Vanguard, King George V, Howe, Anson,* and *Duke of York* were in much the same state as the American battle fleet. All the *King George V*-class had been laid up after the war, with only the *Vanguard* in commission, partly as a training ship

*Fig. 55. Four* Iowa-*class battleships in column in 1954.* U.S. *Naval Institute*

(as the *Missouri* had been), partly as a royal yacht. None of the British battlewagons had been recommissioned for Korea. In yearly budget battles they had narrowly avoided the breakers in a financially strapped Great Britain that had lost her place as a world sea power and could no longer afford the prestige of the battleship.

The United States could afford it, and in 1950 had fourteen of the huge ships in reserve and another active one ferrying Naval Academy midshipmen and naval ROTC students to Europe and back on training cruises. When war came again the United States had pulled three of the most modern from reserve, though for the missions the ships performed in Korea, any one of the mothballed old warriors, even the old ships built in the 1920s, could have sufficed. They certainly had performed shore bombardment well enough off the islands in the Pacific. The British made what contribution they could to the United Nations fleet in Korea: a couple of carriers rotated in and out, and a few light cruisers and destroyers. But they could not, or actually would not, send the *Vanguard* or one of the reserve ships. The Royal Navy was continually shuttling ships between commission and reserve, shifting budget pounds here and there to maintain some sort of world-class navy. There were barely enough funds to cover an active fleet, never mind the ones in reserve at coastal cities like Portsmouth and Pmarth, Wales that were seen as a steady drain on manpower and money. The Royal Navy battleships had to go. The *Vanguard* went back to the reserve fleet in 1955 and *King George V*s to the scrap yard shortly afterward. By 1960 the Royal Navy had not a battleship left on the books when the breakers cut apart the *Vanguard,* the pride of the British postwar fleet.

In the United States, however, the death knell for the battleship had not yet sounded. But neither did the call to action. The Big Five were stricken in 1958, the *North Carolina*s in 1960, the four *South Dakota*s in 1962. Only the *Iowa*s were left. The *Missouri* was the first to go after Korea. Eisenhower was in the White House, not Truman, and she was sent to Bremerton in 1955 to lie at anchor for the next thirty years. The *New Jersey* was next. The *Wisconsin* and the *Iowa* followed the following winter, decommissioned within a couple of weeks of each other. The *Iowa* went to Philadelphia, the *Wisconsin* to Bayonne.

These ships cruise together in 1954, almost in defiance of time and of a world that has passed them by. A world that has brought three of them out of hibernation for an encore, but in a role that was not decisive. This moment was captured on film, but it was only a staged picture. This was not the battle fleet; such a fleet no longer existed. Proud and dignified, these ships were again about to bow out: hooked up again to life-support systems and tended by sailors whose function was not to fire their fearsome weapons, nor feed their boilers for a thirty-knot dash across the sea, but to make sure they did not spring leaks or develop rust, to slap a coat of navy gray paint on a piece of exposed metal while the real work of the fleet—of the nation's maritime defense—went on around them. The battle line, drawn mostly from mothballs and given one last photographic hurrah, was no more.

Twenty years later six mothballed destroyers, all *Fletcher*s, all contemporaries of the *Iowa*s, were photographed at the Philadelphia Naval

*Fig. 56. Six moth-*
*balled* Fletcher-
*class destroyers at*
*the Philadelphia*
*Naval Shipyard.*
*Paul Stillwell/U.S.*
*Naval Institute*

Shipyard on 30 July 1974. They represent the aging state of not only the mothball fleet but a large portion of the active fleet in the years follow-ing the Vietnam War. The war officially ended with the Paris Peace Accords, signed the year before, ending United States involvement in the conflict that had bitterly divided the nation. The first combat troops had been sent to Vietnam in 1965, their number had peaked at over half a million by the end of the decade, and it had all been for naught. Within two years after the peace treaty the North Vietnamese would violate the agreement and overrun South Vietnam, guessing (correctly) that neither the United States Congress nor the public had any desire to intervene.

The enormous cost of the war and Lyndon Johnson's Great Society crusade to infuse government money into a myriad of social welfare laws had drained the American economy. The nation could not afford both guns and butter, and the American military machine, though still potent, was in disarray. Many of the ships that had been built during World War II had reached the end of their service lives during Vietnam, and the funds for overhaul, modernization or even to keep them in reserve again were simply not there. The money had gone to fleet maintenance, to a large draftee army, and to the monolithic infrastructure that had supported the American buildup in South Vietnam. Many of the antisubmarine conversions of the *Essex* class that had been pulled from mothballs in the late 1940s and early 1950s had left the fleet during the war, some to reserve, some to the breakers. The *Essex, Randolph, Kearsarge, Shangri-La,* and *Yorktown* went back to mothballs, most for a only a few years before being stricken. Korean War veterans *Princeton, Valley Forge,* and *Boxer,* all converted to amphibious assault ships to carry battalions of marines and the helicopters to lift them, were stricken as the new *Iwo Jima*-class of helicopter carriers entered the fleet. Only a year after recovering the astronauts of *Apollo 11* as they returned from the first landing on the moon, the *Hornet* was decommissioned and placed in storage at Bremerton. The *Bennington* joined her there, as did the *Bon Homme Richard* in 1971, one of only three *Essex*-class carriers still operating as an attack carrier. The *Wasp,* one of the first of the modernized *Essex*es, went to the breakers after twenty additional years of service after emerging from the mothball fleet at Bayonne. The *Bunker Hill* and the *Franklin* were the only two *Essex* carriers never to reemerge from mothballs. The *Bunker Hill* was stricken in 1966, the *Franklin* several years earlier. The poignant sight of this noble ship being cut to pieces was captured in an NBC television documentary narrated by actor and dancer Gene Kelly, entitled, "The Ship That Would Not Die."

Of the escort carriers, the thinly armored and lightly armed jeeps that had been built during the mass production days of World War II, only a few were left. All were *Commencement Bay*s, ships like the veterans *Rendova,* the *Siboney,* and the *Badoeng Strait,* and all were stricken during Vietnam. Of the last few on the navy list, two, the *Tinian* and the *Rabaul,* ironically were the only two never commissioned. Upon completion in 1946 they were immediately mothballed at Tacoma. They never left the reserve fleet and were stricken in 1970 and 1971, respectively.

A few of the remaining heavy cruisers went back into mothballs during the war, too. The missile conversions *Boston* and *Canberra,* which had reverted to the heavy cruiser role after their missile batteries were removed, went back briefly into reserve. So did the long-serving *St. Paul,* commissioned as marines fought a hidden and tenacious enemy in the tunnels and caves of Iwo Jima in February 1945, retired as marines fought an equally hidden and tenacious enemy in the jungles of Vietnam in 1971. As these ships left the fleet during the war other heavy cruisers left the Naval Vessel Register for the boneyard. The *Macon* was stricken in 1969 as the battleship *New Jersey* again proved the worth of shore bombardment off the Vietnamese coast. The sad *Oregon City,* after twenty-three years in reserve without ever firing her guns at an enemy, was stricken and left the Philadelphia reserve fleet basin the following year. The even-more-forlorn *Fall River,* placed in mothballs the same year as the *Oregon City,* managed to last another year in reserve, never having had another commissioning pennant hoisted to her mast, without ever having her boilers fired again, without ever having a crew march up her gangway to place her back in the fleet. She was towed from Bremerton and scrapped. In 1973, as American POWs were coming home from captivity in Vietnam and stepping onto the tarmac at Travis Air Force Base, the *Boston, Bremerton, Rochester, Pittsburgh,* and *Quincy,* consigned to the forgotten fleet since shortly after Korea, all went for scrap. All of the *Clevelands*—the *Amsterdam, Pasadena, Portsmouth,* and the last *Cleveland* on the navy list, the *Wilkes-Barre*— had been stricken by the end of 1971. The two *Worcester*s went the following year. So did the *Spokane,* the last of the antiaircraft cruisers bristling with twin, five-inch dual-purpose mounts, nearly a quarter century after time stopped aboard her. A couple of *Cleveland* missile conversions were decommissioned during the war, too: the *Galveston* in 1970, the *Providence* in 1973.

The destroyer escorts and the destroyers, the "cans" like those in the photograph, were discarded wholesale (fig. 56). Over a hundred World War II destroyer escorts were in reserve during Vietnam, as were another twenty-one that had been converted to radar picket ships (DERs). These were all well past their prime and well past any usefulness to the fleet, and were simply a drain of money. Not that much was being expended to maintain them. Within a few years after the end of the war, the last remaining DEs and DERs had been stricken and scrapped. The large number of *Benson*s, none of which had stirred since being mothballed in 1946, were stricken, the majority in 1971. All of those converted to destroyer-minesweepers (DMS), the *Robert H. Smith* class, went to the breakers, too. The *Sumner*s, many of which had served with FRAM (Fleet Rehabilitation And Modernization) upgrades without interruption since their commissioning in the latter half of World War II, now began to be stricken in increasing numbers. Many were sold to allied countries. The *Waldron* went to Colombia, the *Douglas H. Fox* to Chile. A handful, like the *Collett* and the *Lyman K. Swenson,* had gone into reserve a few years before.

For the *Gearing*s it was the same story, though unlike some of the *Sumner*s none of the slightly larger *Gearing*s had been mothballed following World War II. Most had sailed on through the 1950s and 1960s, receiving their FRAM modernizations along the way. The FRAMs had cost anywhere from $4.5 to over $7.5 million per ship and were designed to extend the service life of the destroyers for another five to eight years (Sumrall, *Sumner-Gearing Class,* 70–79). In actuality it extended the lives of many much longer. The *Glenn* underwent modernization in 1963 and served until stricken in 1976. The *Johnston,* named for the heroic *Fletcher* sunk at Leyte Gulf, received her FRAM in 1962 and was not stricken until 1980. The extended commitment of the fleet to the war in Vietnam as well as to the Atlantic and the Mediterranean, combined with lack of funds to replace this aging destroyer fleet on anything close to a one-for-one basis, meant many were retained in the fleet much longer than was thought possible. There were still some *Fletcher*s in reserve, too, though many had been stricken between the antiwar protests in 1968 and the war's end in 1973. "Peace with honor" was declared by the Nixon administration that year, and the peace accord—that in reality was little more than a temporary truce to enable the United States to extricate itself from that fragmented and ruined country—was signed. Some of the *Fletcher*s had been returned to mothballs after brief duty during Korea to rot for another decade and a half. Others, like the forgotten *Benson*s, had not stirred since 1946 except to be inspected and perhaps transferred from Long Beach to Mare Island or from San Diego to Stockton. Some were sold. Arleigh Burke's Desron 23 flagship, the *Charles Ausburne,* went to West Germany. The *Pritchett,* after four years in mothballs and nineteen more with the fleet, went to Italy. The *Heermann,* one of the heroes of Taffy 3, served in the Argentine Navy.

Many went for scrap. The six in Philadelphia in 1974 are among the last of their breed and their days are numbered (fig. 56). From left to right they are the *Cotton, Sigsbee, Sigourney, Abbot, The Sullivans,* and *Healy.* All but the *Sigsbee* had been recommissioned for Korea. The unusual name of the *The Sullivans* commemorated the tragic loss of five brothers aboard the light cruiser *Juneau.* The boys, from Waterloo, Iowa, had enlisted when they received word a friend had been killed in the attack on Pearl Harbor. They had insisted on serving together, and all had been assigned to the *Juneau*. In January 1943 their parents and sister Genevieve received word via special envoy that all were reported missing and presumed dead in the waters of the South Pacific. The tragedy inspired a wartime movie about the boys as they became a symbol of sacrifice, and the navy named DD-537 in their honor. (In 1996 yet another destroyer would carry on the name of Joseph, Francis, Albert, Madison and George Sullivan.) The *Sigsbee* was never recommissioned. She spent nearly thirty years in reserve until she was finally stricken, with the others in the photo, on 1 December 1974, six months after the photograph was taken. Alone of the six, the *Sigsbee* retains her World War II small hull numbers and narrow original bridge structure, and she is the only one with igloos still covering the forty-millimeter-antiaircraft guns on either side of the number two mount that had long since been removed from the others when they had recommissioned.

The Vietnam War was over, the money spent on it, in the end, wasted; the navy no longer had the funds to maintain its aging reserve fleet, or for that matter, its equally aging active fleet, and the last of the *Essex* carriers was decommissioned. The *Ticonderoga* hauled down her pennant in 1973. The *Intrepid,* which had received an ASW conversion but had been pressed into service as an attack carrier on Yankee station, hauled down her colors in 1974. The last two, the attack carriers *Hancock* and *Oriskany,* were decommissioned in 1976. Only the *Lexington,* still plying the waters off Pensacola as a training carrier, continued to steam.

The few remaining *Cleveland* guided-missile cruisers were decommissioned by the end of the 1970s, the *Oklahoma City* being the last in 1979. She went back into reserve at Bremerton where she joined the *Chicago.* Newer cruisers meant that the older conversions were no longer needed and the *Albany* and *Columbus* were retired. The last of the unmodified gun cruisers, the *Newport News,* her number two turret inoperable because of a turret explosion, joined her sisters *Salem* and *Des Moines* in Philadelphia. The back basin had once bristled with gun cruisers. Now there were only these three, as the last of the *Baltimores* had their names added to the list of vessels stricken from the Naval Vessel Register. Three in San Diego went in 1974: the *Helena, Toledo,* and *Los Angeles.* In fact, the *Los Angeles* did not even have the honor of having her name struck from the register. It had been taken from her and given to the lead boat in a new class of submarines, the SSN-688 class of nuclear attack boats. She was the ex-*Los Angeles* now. The last of the *Baltimore*s, the *St. Paul*, spent nine years in reserve at Bremerton before she, too, was sent to the scrap heap. The remaining handful of *Gearing*s went to the naval reserve force, with composite active duty and reserve crews, making weekend voyages to keep their citizen-sailors in training for the day they might be called up again.

But the huge World War II fleet—the thousands of combatants of every size and description that had swept the seas clean of the Imperial Japanese Fleet, had been retired and stored in Operation Zipper, and had been recalled to duty for one Asian war and served through another—was gone. A few remnants were scattered here and there. Some submarine tenders like the *Fulton* carried on. The *Midway* and *Coral Sea* were still frontline aircraft carriers. Three destroyer tenders, the *Prairie*, *Sierra*, and *Yosemite*, still sailed. The *Prairie* had been commissioned in 1940 and was the oldest ship in commission save the *Constitution*. It was her honor to fly the special Revolutionary War "Don't Tread On Me" flag. The battleships, of course, were still laid up, though only a few diehards expected them ever to see the open sea again. The World War II era was over; the ships built for the great conflict had served their assigned time and then some, their lives extended by their time in mothballs. But the years and the scrapper's torch eventually caught up with nearly all of them.

Some ships, though, were saved for future generations to enjoy. Pictured is the USS *Massachusetts* under tow by a commercial tug in Hampton Roads on 8 June 1965 (fig. 57). After eighteen years at Norfolk, fifteen of them in mothballs, she is leaving the shipyard for the last time. Many vessels preceded her out of Norfolk via tug; many more would follow. Most would be taken to the scrap yard. But not the "Mamie." Though she had been stricken from the Naval Vessel Register on 1 June 1962 with her sisters *South Dakota*, *Alabama*, and *Indiana*, she had another life in store. On the day she departed Norfolk she was officially transferred from the navy to the Massachusetts Memorial Committee whose purpose was to enshrine her at Fall River as a floating naval museum and a memorial to all native sons of Massachusetts who had given their lives during the war.

She was the third of the four-ship *South Dakota* class, and her guns fired their first rounds in anger against the Vichy French. On 8 November 1942 while off Casablanca supporting the Allied landings in French North Africa, she came under fire from a French battleship. The

*Fig. 57. The Massachusetts under tow.*
U.S. Naval Institute

*Massachusetts* put a stop to that with a few well-aimed shots that jammed the forward main battery turret of the dreadnought *Jean Bart,* which was brand new, incomplete, and tied to a pier in the harbor. French destroyers came after the *Massachusetts* and she dealt with them more severely, sinking two. To the Pacific she went next, and after five years of duty in war and peace, was retired. Like the other *South Dakota*s, it was initially planned she remain in reduced commission, with a skeleton crew, but in fact she was mothballed. Alone among the battleships she was retired to Norfolk.

For three years after she was stricken in 1962, the citizens of Massachusetts struggled to come up with the funding and a workable plan to exhibit the ship. It was not enough that they wanted the ship; they had to prove to the navy that they could take care of it, that the ship would be self-supporting, that enough money could be found to maintain her on a continuing basis, that she would be cared for in a dignified manner. The navy was all too happy to donate ships if those conditions could be met. Despite the best intentions, far too often they could not.

The efforts to save and display the *Enterprise* had failed in the late 1950s not because the navy did not wish to see her preserved but because the organizers of the rescue effort were unable to secure the necessary funds to ensure that the Big E would not rust and rot at her moorings once she became a museum or memorial. Other efforts did succeed. The children of the state of North Carolina raised over $300,000 by saving their lunch money and spare change to have their namesake battleship brought to Wilmington as a memorial to the war dead of the state. The *Alabama* was also transferred to her home state. So, too, was the ancient *Texas,* launched a little over a month after the immortal *Titanic* struck an iceberg on her maiden voyage in 1912. When the liner was found at the bottom of the North Atlantic seventy-four years later, the *Texas* still rode at her moorings at San Jacinto, a highly successful museum and memorial since her donation to Texas in 1948. The *Missouri* became the fifth battleship to be donated by the navy as a museum when she was towed to Pearl Harbor in 1998. The people of New Jersey have long hoped to tow their battleship (when she again is stricken) to become another memorial, and recently the city of San Francisco, having lost its bid to make a home for the *Missouri,* has expressed interest in the *Iowa.*

Several *Essex*-class carriers were saved from the breakers as well, though none in their original configuration. The *Intrepid* became the centerpiece of the Intrepid Sea, Air, and Space Museum. The *Yorktown* similarly became the flagship of the Patriots Point Naval and Maritime Museum in South Carolina. The *Lexington,* once her long career of combat and training duty ended in 1991, went to Corpus Christi. The *Hornet,* after a prolonged battle by the Aircraft Carrier Hornet Foundation, including persuading the navy to purchase the ship back from the breakers, became one of the few memorials on the West Coast when she began conversion to a museum at Alameda in 1998. Another group fought to preserve the stricken *Midway* and bring her to San Diego for a museum as the century drew to a close. As an example of the conditions the navy demands from groups hoping to receive a donated warship, the San Diego Aircraft Carrier Museum had to show the navy that they had firm financing for the project, a permanent mooring site with an environmental impact report, a maintenance plan, insurance, and a lease for the mooring site.

Artifacts such as bells, anchors, and commissioning plaques from many vessels were preserved when the entire ship could not be. The mast of the *Portland* stands in Portland, Maine. Two twin forty-millimeter mounts from the *Indiana* sit outside the football stadium at the University of Indiana. The altar of the Naval Academy Chapel is built from the deck planking of fifteen different cruisers, among them the *Duluth,* the *Guam,* and the *Montpelier.*

But for the vast majority of ships that plied the oceans in peace and war, the end came when they were sold for breaking up as the government tried to recover a small percentage of their cost through the only collateral the old ships had left: their steel. Many ships were cut up in Kearny, New Jersey, such as the *Washington, Alaska, Essex, Enterprise,* and the light cruiser *Denver.* Others met their end wherever they could be towed and pier space found for them. The *California* and *Tennessee* died across the pier from each other in Baltimore while the *Indiana* was towed down the coast from Bremerton into San Francisco Bay and ripped apart in Richmond. Many of the escort carriers went overseas to be broken up. The *Saginaw Bay* went to Rotterdam. The *Shamrock Bay* and the *Kadashan Bay* were towed across the Pacific to Hong Kong. The Japanese got a few they did not sink during the war: the *Marcus Island,* the *Manila Bay,* and the *Hollandia,* among others, were scrapped in Japanese ports. The famous and the anonymous, the battered and the untouched, they all went. Ships that never served together were sliced up together, tied up side by side like the *Wasp* and the *Oregon City.* The *Manchester* and the *Miami* were towed across the bay from Mare Island to Richmond and broken up. The *Cleveland, Houston,* and *Montpelier* left Philadelphia and went to Baltimore. The *Mobile* went to Portland, Oregon. Thousands of tons of fine warship were turned into thousands of tons of scrap metal.

The *Pittsburgh* went to the breakers at Tacoma in October 1974, where so many of the escort carriers had been preserved (fig. 58). After seventeen years in mothballs at Bremerton, she is a sad sight. Her hull number is gone. Her name, like the names of so many other cruisers, will be carried on in the coming decades by an attack submarine of the *Los Angeles* class. It has been three decades since this *Pittsburgh* sailed with the mighty Fast Carrier Task Force, since she towed the blazing carrier *Franklin* full of dead and dying sailors away from the Japanese coast, since her bow was torn away in a typhoon. It has been two decades since she was recalled to service during the Cold War, operating in the Mediterranean and Atlantic in case the Korean War spread to Europe and resulted in World War III.

*Fig. 58. The*
Pittsburgh *awaiting*
*scrapping at*
*Tacoma in 1973.*
*U.S. Naval Institute*

The original igloos covering her forty-millimeter mounts have been replaced by slightly altered ones that could accommodate her new anti-aircraft battery of twin three-inchers. All usable gear, and there is not much of that left, has been stripped from her hulk, for a hulk is what she is. The ex-*Pittsburgh*. With large cranes, torches, and pneumatic hammers the men of the scrapping company that bought her will soon go to work. The mast will be cut down and lifted off. Then they will start at the top of her superstructure and work their way down, the hammers and the flame of the torches cutting into the steel, gouging out large chunks of a fighting ship and proud member of the forgotten fleet. A hole will be cut into a section of her tower and a hook attached. Then the surrounding steel and armor will be systematically cut away until another few hundred pounds of the USS *Pittsburgh*, CA-72 when she belonged to the exclusive sorority of the navy list, will be hoisted up and clear, diminishing her size and her being by just a little more. Away will go her air defense stations, fire control stations, combat information center, pilot house, radio room, secondary conn, and her funnels. She will be stripped down to her main deck and turrets. The eight-inch barrels will be sliced away. The igloos will be pulled loose and the antiaircraft batteries torn from their circular splinter shields. The five-inch secondary battery will disappear.

And the disease that seems to eat at her hull day by day will not stop there. Down below her main deck the torches will cut into the crew berthing just forward of her number one turret and just aft of her number three main battery. The cots where her crew slept and the lockers where they stored their few shipboard possessions for months on end will be carried aloft and disappear. The hammers will rip into the galley where meals were prepared and into the mess deck where sailors ate and talked, and those places known only to the men who had served aboard her through two wars will vanish and with them some tangible part of the memories her crewmen carried with them the rest of their lives. The stability of the hulk will become a problem as more and more of her is cut away and deposited on the shore into a great heap of twisted, smoking shards of metal that were once a United States warship.

The ship will be dry-docked or run aground and the work of dismantling her will continue. She will only be an outline of a ship by then, but a careful eye would know that the cranes were diving deep amidships and bringing out pieces of her boilers, and turbines, and thick massive pieces of the armor belt that protected her vitals from enemy shell fire but will not protect her from the heat of the torch. And then, one day, a few weeks or months after she has ridden at anchor one last time at this pier in Tacoma, far away from where she first entered the sea at Bethlehem Steel in Quincy, Massachusetts, the USS *Pittsburgh* will exist no more. Some parts of her will remain in very unlikely places. A clock will end up at Point Loma High School in San Diego. An anchor and a propeller will find their way to Springfield, Oregon (Ewing, *Memories and Memorials,* 114). But the essence of the *Pittsburgh,* the sum of her parts that made her a whole, the ship that sailed the Pacific, Atlantic, and Mediterranean in peace and war, yet spent 80 percent of her life in the mothball fleet, will be gone forever.

# THREE    *The End of the Cold War*

WORLD WAR II, 1,364 days of bloodshed, devastation, and genocide that killed more than fifty million human beings, came to an end on 2 September 1945 aboard the battleship *Missouri*. In his radio address to the nation that day, President Harry Truman said, "My fellow Americans, the thoughts and hopes of all America, indeed of all the civilized world, are centered tonight on the battleship *Missouri*. There on that small piece of American soil anchored in Tokyo harbor the Japanese have just officially laid down their arms. They have signed terms of unconditional surrender." (Sheehan, *This is America,* 960) Though the *Missouri* had been in commission less than two years and possessed a rather undistinguished war record, she became one of the most famous warships in history by virtue of this brief ceremony held on her quarterdeck. The *Missouri* remained on the Naval Vessel Register for nearly a half century more, but this was the most significant role of her career.

The *Missouri* had been named for the home state of then Vice President Truman and christened by his only daughter Margaret. The "Mighty Mo" arrived in the war zone in January of what was to be the final year of the war and eight months later two atomic bombs, with equally devastating conventional air raids, a naval blockade, and a belated Russian invasion of Manchuria in August, drove the Japanese to their knees. Shortly after the B-29 *Bock's Car* dropped the second atomic bomb on Nagasaki, the Japanese announced they had accepted the terms of the Potsdam Conference: unconditional surrender. The war was over. But the surrender was not yet signed. Where would that take place? Who would sign? Truman had designated MacArthur as Supreme Commander of the Allied Powers with authority to sign for all the nations that had fought Japan. The Secretary of the Navy, James Forrestal, recommended to the president that a fitting site for the surrender ceremony would be the deck of a battleship anchored right in Tokyo Bay. Not so coincidentally, the battleship was to be the *Missouri.* Admiral Chester Nimitz would sign for the United States, helping preserve the navy's role in the end of what had been in large measure a naval war and victory.

On 2 September the Japanese delegation approached the big battleship, her sides rusty and stained, in the destroyer *Landsdowne.* They were transferred by small boat to the *Missouri,* and came up the ladder to the main deck (fig. 59). Above and surrounding them, perched on every available turret, gun mount, deck, and superstructure outcropping, were hundreds of American sailors in whites. The officers wore khakis, open at the necks. No dress uniforms for the Americans, not even neckties. Halsey had temporarily shifted his four-star flag to the *Iowa,* and from the *Missouri*'s truck flew twin five-star flags for General of the Army Douglas MacArthur and Admiral of the Fleet Chester Nimitz. At the staff flew the national ensign, the same that had flown over the Capitol dome that shocking afternoon of 7 December 1941 when the East Coast had learned that the United States was at war. In a frame on the bulkhead of the starboard quarterdeck, where the surrender documents were laid out on a table borrowed from the chief's mess, hung the thirty-one-star flag flown by Matthew Perry when he first made contact with Japan in 1853. Now, Foreign Minister Mamoru Shigemitsu, representing the Japanese government, and General Yoshijiro Umezu, representing the Japanese Armed Forces, stood quietly with their delegation to surrender to the nation they had attacked more than three and a half years before. Yamamoto, the architect of the attack, was dead. All of the carriers that had launched the strike had been sunk. Nearly all of the ships sunk or damaged at Pearl Harbor had been salvaged and returned to action. One, the battleship *West Virginia,* was anchored nearby.

MacArthur came out onto the quarterdeck and looked over the scene, Nimitz alongside him. The Japanese were instructed to sign the surrender documents and they did so in silence as thousands of eyes watched them. MacArthur then stepped forward to sign. Behind him stood two Allied officers, victims and symbols of the dark, early days of

*Fig. 59. The surrender ceremony aboard the battleship* Missouri, 2 *September* 1945. *U.S. Naval Institute*

the war: General Jonathan Wainwright, who had surrendered Corregidor after MacArthur had been ordered to Australia, and British Lieutenant General Sir Arthur Percival, who had been forced to surrender Singapore. Both had been located in prison camps in China and flown in for the ceremony. MacArthur laid out five pens and began to sign his name. He stopped, and motioned to Wainwright to approach. Wainwright, startled, began to salute automatically, then realized MacArthur was handing him something. It was one of the pens. A few more letters were written and the second pen went to Percival. It was a moving gesture. A third pen went to the National Archives, a fourth to West Point. The fifth and last MacArthur kept for his wife and son. Nimitz then stepped forward and quickly signed for the United States. Then representatives from the other nations at war with Japan signed the document. MacArthur then said, "Let us pray that peace be now restored to the world and that God will preserve it always. These proceedings are now closed." The war was over. The Japanese delegation left the quarterdeck, this time with honors to symbolize that with the signing of the surrender documents they were enemies no longer. The USS *Missouri* was now on every news broadcast and in every newspaper in the United States and throughout much of the world. She was the most famous ship on the planet.

Back home she came, and the vessels that had sailed with her in the Pacific and lay at anchor with her as the war ended in Tokyo Bay were retired. The *Missouri* stayed in commission and wherever she went crowds flocked to see what had become, by 1949, the last American battleship. She was a training ship now, carrying midshipmen on summer cruises; she was in the press again in 1950 when she ran aground for almost a half mile on the sands of Thimble Shoals. Now she was an embarrassment. Already in 1950 the calls had come for the retirement of all of the battleships as outmoded, out-of-date, expensive dinosaurs. It did not help to have her stuck in the sand in full view of the shoreline and the world's press. For two weeks she lay stranded there—the butt of jokes outside the navy and the subject of consternation and concern within the ranks—until a fleet of tugs and salvage ships dragged her off. Then, in the midst of another midshipmen cruise that summer, war erupted again.

She reached Korea, but just too late to support the Inchon landings, her guns opening up in anger for the first time in five years on the east coast in support of South Korean troops. The war dragged on and the

*Missouri* went home. By 1951 the war was a stalemate; by 1952 it was the *Missouri*'s turn to go back; by 1953 the war had come to its shaky conclusion.

Eisenhower was the president now. It was time again to decommission all the battleships. The *Missouri,* the only one to be continuously in commission since the end of World War II, with ten years of duty under her belt, was the first to go. In the fall and winter of 1954 the *Missouri* was overhauled and slowly, methodically deactivated at the Puget Sound Naval Shipyard in Washington. Truman was not happy with her location in the Pacific Northwest, but as an ex-commander in chief there was nothing he could do about it. On 26 February 1955 the *Missouri* was decommissioned and delivered to the Bremerton Group of the Pacific Reserve Fleet.

There she lay at Bremerton for thirty long years. Seven presidents occupied the White House in that time. The easygoing, relaxed White House of Eisenhower gave way to the dynamic Camelot of the Kennedy administration. The *Missouri* slept as Camelot was shattered in one unbelievable day in Dallas just before Thanksgiving 1963, a day that, like Pearl Harbor a generation before, seared its moments into the American consciousness. The social programs of Lyndon Johnson's Great Society followed. So did Vietnam. One battleship briefly made a curtain call, but it was not the *Missouri.* The *New Jersey* was in the best shape of the four *Iowa*s and she went back to the fleet. Still the *Missouri* slept; the only footsteps on her decks aside from the caretaker crew were those of tourists come to see the surrender plaque in her deck and stand where MacArthur had stood those many years before to declare the war to be over. All the while her interior lay still, dry air circulating through her, halting the passage of time. Richard Nixon narrowly won the presidency over Vice President Humphrey in 1968, negotiated a withdrawal from Vietnam in 1973, and a year later became the first president to resign. The *New Jersey* had long since been returned to mothballs, the *Missouri* had never stirred, and there was talk of scrapping all the remaining battleships. Gerald Ford took over the presidency, the only chief executive not to be elected either to the vice presidency or the presidency. His term was short lived and he was ousted by a public sick of Washington scandal. Ford was replaced by an outsider, Georgia governor Jimmy Carter. Carter's bid for a second term ended with the election of the Great Communicator, Ronald Reagan, a president determined to up the military ante with the Soviet Union until they folded.

While the *Missouri* had lain in hibernation, the Space Age had been born in the late 1950s and early 1960s with *Sputnik,* Yuri Gagarin, Alan Shepard, and John Glenn; it reached its zenith with the first landing on the moon by the *Apollo 11* mission in 1969, and entered the realm of the routine with the launch of the first of the space shuttles in 1981 and the Russian *Salyut* and *Mir* space stations. America fought a long and unpopular war while *Missouri* slept, and in the aftermath the armed forces entered the doldrums, scorned by the public, neglected by those who doled out the taxpayer's money. Still the *Missouri* slept at Bremerton. Tourists did not neglect her. They continued to walk her decks, to stare at her guns, to try and grasp the real meaning of the bronze plaque in her deck alongside the number two turret. But what exactly was the *Missouri?* A stop on a tour? A relic? Or a valuable member of the fleet being kept in storage until just the right time? Belowdecks, even as the tourists gaped and photographed each other near one of the big guns or on the surrender deck, time continued to stand still. The passing years did not exist. It was still 1955 down there. World War II was a recent memory, Korea an even more recent and very bitter one not yet replaced by Vietnam. Americans still believed in government, looked upon their president, Ike, as a fatherly figure. Had he not led them to victory in World War II with that famous grin and ability to get along with everyone from Roosevelt to Churchill to De Gaulle? *I Love Lucy* dominated the early days of television, not in reruns, but with a new episode every week. Disneyland had just opened and kids everywhere were wearing coonskin caps and emulating Davy Crockett. The racial turmoil of the 1960s was still in the future, as were the demonstrations on college campuses against the Vietnam War and the Establishment.

At one time there had been a crew aboard *Missouri,* as she was the accommodation ship, a sort of flagship, for the Bremerton Group. The men who maintained the reserve fleet lived aboard her. Before the *Missouri* had arrived they had been aboard the *Indiana,* but had buttoned her up and filed over to the Mo in 1955. Eventually they left her, too, and the time capsule, driven by the dehumidifiers, hummed on. Outside, ships were dragged from their berths and taken away as the years caught up with them, but inside the big battleship it was still 1955. And it remained 1955 through the 1950s, through the churning, burning 1960s, through the psychedelic 1970s. The Beatles came to America, but belowdecks on the *Missouri* the music was still by Glenn Miller and

Frank Sinatra. Some people, both outside and inside the Defense Department, called for the striking and scrapping of the battleships. The *New Jersey*'s tour off Vietnam had proved nothing, they said. The battleship was still too expensive, still too big a target, still too old to be of any use in a modern war. But the *Iowa* stayed on the navy list.

Then in 1980 there came to Washington a new president. He had been an actor in Hollywood when the *Missouri* had been sealed up and put away. He had become the governor of California and then made several bids for the White House, the last time in 1976 when incumbent Gerald Ford had won the Republican nomination for president. In 1980, Ronald Reagan's time had come. He named young and energetic John Lehman as Secretary of the Navy. Their goal: a six-hundred-ship navy built around fifteen carrier battle groups and four Surface Action Groups. These last were to be built around the recommissioned and modernized *Iowa*s. The *New Jersey* had been the last battleship in service; she was the first to be brought out of mothballs. The *Iowa* followed her as money for rebuilding of the navy poured forth from the Reagan budgets and Congress. The administration also pressed unsuccessfully for the recommissioning of the *Des Moines*-class cruisers at the Philadelphia reserve basin as well. Like the battleships, these were relics from another age when the big gun was still thought to be king. They rivaled the *Iowa*s in the length of time spent in mothballs. The *Salem* was laid up in 1959 and was followed by the *Des Moines* in 1961. Both were stricken three decades later, having never rejoined the fleet.

Finally, in 1984 came the word that the USS *Missouri* would end her long slumber at Bremerton. She would no longer be a time capsule: 1955 would vanish aboard her as she rejoined the fleet of the mid-1980s. The *Missouri* would be recommissioned. Her gangway again felt the tread of footsteps but these were not tourists nor were they sailors come to inspect her. These were men whose job it was to prepare the *Missouri* for a journey. They turned off her dehumidification system. They rigged a massive eight-ton towing chain. On 14 May 1984 tugs eased her back and away from her pier at Bremerton, the pier she had shared with the *New Jersey*, now occupied by the mothballed cruisers *Chicago* and *Oklahoma City*. The tugs pushed her until the slack was taken up on the tow chain by the salvage ship *Beaufort*. Out to sea she went as crowds of onlookers watched and the waters of Puget Sound and the Straits of San Juan de Fuca filled with small pleasure boats seeking a close-up look at this dreadnought about to be brought back to life.

*Fig. 60. The Missouri under tow from Bremerton to Long Beach for reactivation in 1984. U.S. Naval Institute*

There were mixed feelings in the Seattle area. The *Missouri* had been theirs for over a generation. She was a popular tourist attraction. Now she was leaving, proudly to be sure, not to the scrap heap, but back into the United States Navy, her long wait in reserve finally rewarded. Twenty sailors rode aboard the battleship as she was towed slowly for eleven days and twelve hundred miles to the Long Beach Naval Shipyard where workers would prepare the third of the *Iowa* class for duty again (fig. 60).

The *New Jersey* had rejoined the fleet two years earlier. Such was the importance attached to her recommissioning that President Reagan presided over the ceremony and placed the ship back into commission. The *Iowa* was recommissioned a few weeks before the *Missouri* began her tow down the coast. Plans were already under way to bring the *Wisconsin* out of Philadelphia in a few years, and in 1986 she would be towed from the shipyard for nearly two years of modernization. But that was in the future. In 1984, it was the *Missouri's* turn.

It would cost about $475 million to reactivate and modernize her.

Scaffolding soon surrounded her superstructure. A huge mast that sprouted from her after stack was removed. The igloos were lifted off the forty-millimeter mounts that had not seen the open air for three decades. After all this time in preservation they were removed and discarded, no longer needed. The guntubs they sat in went, too. All of her five-inch mounts were removed. Some would not be put back. As was the case with the reactivation of the *New Jersey* in 1969, spare parts would be hard to come by. The museum battleships *North Carolina, Alabama,* and *Massachusetts* were searched for spares that could be used aboard the *Missouri* and other *Iowa*s. The worn-out and weathered teak decking was replaced. (The *Wisconsin,* when she was reactivated a few years later, had nearly 140,000 linear feet of new decking installed.) A Plexiglas dome was fitted over the surrender plaque to protect it when it was reinstalled. A large structure was built around her forward tower superstructure to house electronic warfare equipment. Her main battery turrets were examined and made ready. The *Missouri* began to live again, fitted out for naval life in the last decades of the twentieth century. Four of the ten five-inch mounts were ultimately removed to make room for the cables and wiring for her new Harpoon antiship missiles and Tomahawk cruise missiles. Gone were the scores of antiaircraft weapons that defended the ship against Japanese kamikazes, replaced by just four Phalanx Gatling guns, each capable of hurling a curtain of heavy bullets at one hundred rounds per second into the path of an oncoming missile. The electronic and communication suites were upgraded to 1980s standards.

In early May 1986 the *Missouri* sailed once more under the Golden Gate Bridge and into San Francisco Bay. A large crowd at Pier 30–32 near the Oakland Bay Bridge was on hand as a trio of navy and civilian tugs gently pushed her against the side of the pier where line handlers made her fast to the pier (fig. 61). Overhead, red, white, and blue balloons floated out over the bay and up into the blue California sky. San Francisco was to be her new home port. The mayor, Dianne Feinstein, had lobbied hard for this when she learned that the battleship home ports were to be scattered among several cities, and she had succeeded. So the *Missouri* would be recommissioned there, as well. In 1944 the *Missouri*'s sponsor had been Margaret Truman, who in 1986 was pierside at San Francisco to watch as the ship she had christened rejoined the fleet. Secretary Lehman was there, too, watching as the *Missouri*'s crew, a great many of whom had not been born when she was first com-

*Fig. 61. Tugs push the* Missouri *to her San Francisco pier for recommissioning in 1986. U.S. Naval Institute*

missioned, ran up the twin gangways in their blues, lined the rail, and brought the ship ceremoniously back to life.

By late 1988 all four of the battleships were back in commission and another war awaited two of them in the Persian Gulf. Iraq invaded Kuwait, its neighbor to the south, in August 1990 and set in motion a massive United States and United Nations response. The *Wisconsin* was ordered to sail for the Persian Gulf shortly afterward as part of Operation Desert Shield, the Pentagon's defensive deployment to halt Iraqi leader Saddam Hussein at the Kuwait-Saudi border and prevent him from seizing the Saudi oil fields. In November President George Bush decided to double the American forces in the region, giving himself an option for invading Kuwait and forcing the Iraqis out if diplomatic efforts and economic sanctions failed to do so. Three more carriers were sent along with another battleship to reinforce the *Wisconsin*. The battleship was the *Missouri,* steaming off to a war zone for the first time in forty years.

She was, in fact, the only battleship left to send. The *Iowa* had suffered a turret explosion in her number two turret on 19 April 1989 that killed forty-seven sailors. The cause was never determined, though such turret explosions and accidents were not unheard of. The equipment inside the turret of the *Iowa* was repaired and plans were under way to repair the turret itself when it was announced she would be retired. The Cold War was ending. Mikhail Gorbachev was in power in the Soviet Union, continuing the policy of openness and limited reform begun during the Reagan administration. Reagan had gambled that a military buildup would bankrupt the Soviets if they tried to keep up, and he was right. The Soviet Union was falling apart. Tension between the two countries was at its lowest ebb since the beginning of the Cold War, and the Soviets were cooperating—if not fully, then at least significantly—with United States efforts to isolate and force Iraq out of Kuwait. As always, when the end of a war was on the horizon—in this case the Cold War—the budget cutters went to work trimming the defense budget. As always, one of the most visible targets in the effort to reduce spending was the battleships. The *Iowa,* with only two of three turrets in operating condition at the moment, was first. Back to mothballs she went, this time at Norfolk. The *New Jersey* was next. She had the most sea time of any and during this last commission had been active over eight years. She was in the process of deactivation when the Iraqis invaded Kuwait.

The *Missouri* sailed for the Gulf in December 1990. All diplomatic efforts failed to eject the Iraqi troops from occupied Kuwait and the United Nations imposed a 16 January 1991 deadline for their withdrawal before military measures were authorized. The deadline came and went. As darkness fell in the Gulf the crews aboard the *Wisconsin* and *Missouri* prepared for war. The Allied plan was a massive air and cruise missile strike against Baghdad and other command and control centers on the first few nights of the war to paralyze the Iraqi high command and then destroy their ability to coordinate a response. Then the air forces of the United States, Great Britain, France, and Italy would demolish the integrated air defense system protecting the country and seize air superiority.

The *Wisconsin* was the coordinating ship for the Tomahawk cruise missiles to be fired from the ships at sea, and that night the two battleships joined American cruisers and destroyers in opening fire on Iraq, not with guns, but with missiles. The image of a Tomahawk missile streaking away from the *Wisconsin* made the covers of many newspapers and news magazines around the country. Once again, the battle-ships were making headlines, though in truth it was the destroyers and cruisers that fired the most significant number of missiles. This fact was not lost on those who called the battleships too expensive to operate when the same job (missile firing) could be done, and done more often, by a smaller, less expensive *Spruance*-class destroyer.

Nevertheless, for now, in January 1991, the battleship was back at war. For several days the battleships cruised back and forth, lobbing cruise missiles at strategic targets deep inside heavily defended Iraq. Within a few weeks she approached the coast and began firing her main battery at Iraqi troop positions near the coastal town of Khafji. For the next couple of weeks the two battleships alternated off the gun line, fir-ing at various enemy positions and using a remotely-piloted vehicle (RPV), a small drone aircraft with a television camera for spotting. In mid-February, as the air war continued to isolate Iraqi troops on the battlefield and strike at airfields and nuclear and biological warfare sites in preparation for the ground war, the *Missouri* and the *Wisconsin* moved farther up the Gulf to get into position to fire on coastal posi-tions inside Iraq itself. A huge marine amphibious force was ready to hit the beaches there and outflank the Iraqis on the border. Or so the Iraqi high command was led to believe. The threat to the fleet from the thick-ly sown minefields was making an amphibious operation less and less likely, but the American deception continued. Minesweepers and heli-copters cleared a lane through the field to enable the battlewagons to get close enough to shore to shoot, and on 23 February the *Missouri* opened fire again from a few miles off shore.

The next day nine Allied divisions—one French, one British, five U.S. Army, and two U.S. Marine—backed up by several Arab divisions, jumped off from their starting lines and began the final phase of the war. The *Missouri* was still off the coast, firing as part of the deception Allied planners hoped would keep a substantial portion of the enemy forces pinned to the coast, away from the marines and Arab forces now push-ing their way into Kuwait. In the middle of the following night the *Missouri* came under attack while she methodically pounded the shore-line. Two Iraqi Silkworm missiles were fired at the fleet offshore, at the biggest target out there: the *Missouri*. The first missile fell into the sea but the second bore in and exploded. HMS *Gloucester*, a British destroyer astern of the *Missouri*, had shot it down. Later that day the *Missouri* came under fire again, friendly fire this time, when another missile was thought to be inbound on the fleet. Chaff rockets were fired by some of the ships, including the *Missouri*. The chaff rockets sent up a cloud of aluminum strips for the radar-guided missile to lock onto. Unfortunately, the Phalanx Gatling gun aboard the frigate *Jarret* was in full automatic mode and the *Missouri*'s chaff looked like a target to the Phalanx's radar. It opened fire, spraying the *Missouri* with bullets from just over a half mile away. Fortunately, there was only one minor injury.

The ground war lasted just one hundred hours and completely routed the Iraqi army. A cease-fire was signed and both the *Missouri* and *Wisconsin* came home. By the end of September the *Wisconsin* was back in mothballs, first at Philadelphia, then at Norfolk. For the *Missouri* there was one last ceremonial mission. On 7 December 1991 at Pearl Harbor, a short distance across the water from Battleship Row, the ship hosted President and Mrs. Bush for a brief visit as the United States remembered the attack half a century before. Then the *Missouri* headed one last time for home. Her deactivation proceeded during the winter at Long Beach and she was decommissioned on the last day of March 1992. Once again there were no battleships in the fleet, nor were there likely to be any. The Cold War had ended. Germany had been reunited. The Soviet Union had broken up and Russia was now, if not a friend, at least not an enemy. For half a century the United States had been preparing to fight the Soviets. For half a century she had maintained, at considerable cost, a reserve fleet. But those days were over. The day of the battleship, it appeared, was over. Beautiful ships they were. Symbolic they were. Status symbols they were. But expensive they most certainly were. The fleet was being reduced again. In January 1995, the four *Iowa*s finally joined all the other battleships that had gone before. They were stricken from the Naval Vessel Register. There was no longer a single battleship, that symbol of maritime power and might since the turn of the century, in the United States Navy.

Yet the story still did not end. The fight between battleship supporters and those who felt their day was long gone continued and grew more confused. The Senate tried to force the navy to place at least two of them back on the Naval Vessel Register for their gunfire support capability and demanded to know what the navy had in mind to replace them. The navy refused, not wanting to allocate scarce money on maintaining these ships in reserve. But the Defense Department Authorization Bill of 22 January 1996 required the navy to reinstate two of them and maintain them as reserve assets. The *Iowa* and the *Wisconsin* were originally to be maintained in mothballs. This was later changed to the *New Jersey* and the *Wisconsin,* although the *Iowa*'s damage from the turret explosion had been almost completely repaired and she was in much better material condition than the *New Jersey.* Both were reinstated on the Naval Vessel Register, not in 1996 as the Senate had ordered, but on 12 February 1998.

The Senate directed Secretary Dalton to appear before them no later than March 1999 and explain why it took two years to reinstate the battleships despite the order to do so in 1996, to outline the plan for maintaining a battleship infrastructure (ammunition, spare parts, training facilities, repair equipment), and to deliver a cost estimate for making the battleships seaworthy. Adding to the melee surrounding the dreadnoughts, the senators from New Jersey challenged the decision to reinstate any battleship, then backed off when it was apparent that the Senate Armed Services Committee was intent on having two of the ships reinstated. The senators then challenged the decision to reinstate the *New Jersey,* demanding that she be replaced on the register by the *Iowa,* charging that the *Iowa* was in better condition and, not coincidentally, freeing up the *New Jersey* for transfer to the Battleship *New Jersey* Historical Foundation, which was attempting to raise enough money to have her towed to her home state as a memorial. In 1999, the swap was made, with the *New Jersey* being struck from the NVR a second time and the *Iowa* reinstated. She, along with the stricken *Forrestal* and *Saratoga,* had been towed to a new reserve fleet berthing at Middletown, Rhode Island in September 1998, while the *Wisconsin* remains at the James River reserve fleet anchorage.

The Mighty Mo was donated to the USS *Missouri* Memorial Association in August 1996. On 23 May 1998 she was towed one final time from her Bremerton home of over thirty-seven years to Pearl Harbor. After a brief stay in Astoria, Oregon to allow the fresh water of the Columbia River to kill any saltwater marine organisms on her hull, the *Missouri* resumed her tow astern of a single tug. She arrived at Pearl Harbor on Father's Day to be berthed temporarily at the pier built over the mooring quays that once held the *Maryland* and *Oklahoma.* Still the controversy surrounding her did not die. A group of Kitsap County, Washington citizens (where Bremerton is located) filed suit against Secretary John Dalton and the navy a few days before she began her trip across the Pacific, challenging his authority to donate the battleship and requesting clarification that the *Missouri* was not in fact in better shape than either the *New Jersey* or *Wisconsin* and perhaps should remain in mothballs (in Bremerton, of course). But this was not to be. She will be outfitted as a museum ship in Pearl Harbor and will open to the public in 1999. Her berth will be at the south end of Battleship Row, near where the *California* sank nearly sixty years ago. Not far away from where she will finally come to rest lie the twisted, sunken remains of the battleship *Arizona*, corroding badly now after so many years underwater. Thus, the ship that became symbolic of America's entry into World War II will be joined by the ship that was the scene of final victory, a ship preserved throughout the decades in the mothball navy.

Eight days after the Japanese surrendered, the USS *Midway* was commissioned. A year and a month after the end of the Persian Gulf War, nearly forty-seven years later, she was finally decommissioned and laid up in reserve. She was the first American carrier built with an armored flight deck, a lesson learned as a result of the damage inflicted on the fleet by the kamikaze. When the *Midway* entered the fleet she was the largest aircraft carrier in the U.S. Navy; when she was retired, she was the smallest. She could carry 137 of the most modern aircraft of 1945, but when she was laid up at Bremerton in 1992 her small size prevented her from operating the F-14 Tomcat and the S-3B Viking antisubmarine aircraft. Her planes flew air strikes against North Vietnam in 1965 and against Iraq twenty-six years later. The *Midway* provided a glimpse of the future of seaborne strategic missile power shortly after World War II when captured German V-2 rockets were launched from her deck. She provided a look at the past when she was moored next to the *Missouri* in mothballs almost half a century later, a pair of World War II vessels that served longer than their designers could have dreamed.

It was the mission of the three *Midway*s, should the Soviets attack western Europe, to lay atomic waste to the Soviet heartland. So important was this mission that none of the three was sent to the Korean War. They remained where they were, plying the waters of the Mediterranean, protecting the southern flank of NATO. The *Midway*s were modernized during their careers, just as the *Essex*-class ships were, receiving the angled deck, more powerful catapults, stronger elevators and hurricane bows. The *Midway* was the most heavily modernized of the three. Her flight deck area was greatly increased, giving her a distinctive, extremely angular layout. She made three Vietnam tours in all and over the course of her long career more than two hundred thousand sailors called the *Midway* home.

For eighteen years, between 1973 and 1991, she called Japan home, the first carrier to be based overseas. As she was already forward deployed she greatly reduced the time it would take a U.S.-based carrier to reach the scene of trouble off Korea or in the Indian Ocean. She was based at Yokosuka and ten years after her first combat tour off Vietnam she returned along with the *Coral Sea,* the *Enterprise,* and the old worn-out *Hancock* to cover the withdrawal of American citizens as the North Vietnamese army overran South Vietnam. Time and again the *Midway* was called forth from her Japanese base. In 1980 it was the Iranian hostage crisis that summoned her. In 1990 she was ordered to the Persian Gulf as part of the reinforcement of the naval forces of Operation Desert Shield. She would go to war again when her planes flew strikes throughout the war that lasted from mid-January 1991 through the end of February.

Her air group was much like that in the photograph of her at sea taken shortly before the Gulf War (fig. 62). She may not have flown the biggest aircraft in the fleet but she certainly flew the most advanced—the F-18 Hornet—and the plane with the biggest punch—the A-6E Intruder medium bomber. Two Hornets in low-visibility gray are on each of her two catapults (the *Midway* did not have a "waist" catapult), while the some of the Intruders are parked just forward of her island. When she returned to the United States after her final war cruise in 1991, her place in Japan was taken by the *Independence* and in the fleet by the increasing numbers of *Nimitz*-class nuclear powered behemoths. She was never intended to be laid up for any length of time. Workers at Bremerton installed cathodic protection and dehumidification equipment, but like most ships decommissioned in the last few decades she was not given an inactivation overhaul to keep her machinery in good working order for the next crew to report aboard in five, ten, or twenty years. She was old, younger than the *Missouri* moored next to her, but she had not aged as gracefully. She had not spent more than half of her life in reserve. She had many more nautical miles under her belt. A carrier's existence was a hard one. Her planes were jolted into the air via her catapults, the energy and heat of the launch absorbed by the bulkheads and beams and ribs. Her planes slammed down on the deck in a controlled crash landing, perhaps hundreds of thousands of times. The arresting wires brought the planes to a halt and the carrier's frame absorbed that, too.

No, the *Midway* would not sail again. She lay across Pier F from the

*Fig. 62. The Midway at sea shortly before the Gulf War. U.S. Naval Institute*

*Missouri,* very high in the water. It is somehow strange to see a big flat-top here. The expanse of flight deck is deserted. Yet not so long ago it was the scene of highly intense, highly choreographed, and highly dangerous activity. The only true way to have an understanding of carrier air operations is to see them firsthand, to watch them from Vulture's Row high in the island. No one goes near the flight deck, no one goes near the open air of Vulture's Row without tiny foam rubber inserts ("foamies") for each ear. The noise of a carrier flight deck is almost unfathomable. It is frightening. Never mind the flames from the engine nozzles, missiles, bombs, and rockets slung underneath the aircraft. Just the noise alone is scary. Without the foamies it is quite apparent to the visitor that instant and painful deafness awaits anyone exposed to that noise for even a second or two. The noise surrounds, envelops, pierces one. It is invasive. You can feel it. On the bigger carriers, the ones that fly the Tomcat, the noise, awe, and fear are taken to a new level. A

Tomcat on the catapult screams. It *screams.* The empty flight deck looks huge. Put fifteen or twenty aircraft on it, their engines running, and it is quite small.

There was plenty of noise on that flight deck in the Red Sea on the night of 17 January 1991 as the *Midway* went to war. Four other carriers, the *America, Ranger, Saratoga,* and *John F. Kennedy* were launching planes as well. The *Theodore Roosevelt* was on her way to her assigned station. On the *Midway,* as on the others, the young flight deck crewmen, many just out of high school and yet bearing so much responsibility for safely launching and recovering these multimillion-dollar aircraft, moved with a studied but purposeful calm. An E-2C Hawkeye warmed up beneath the island, a ring of crewmen surrounding it, arms down at their sides moving forward and back, forward and back, for as long as the big props on the Hawkeye spun. They were the safety cordon, to keep away the unknowing or unwary from being minced and carried away by the wind. One by one the jet engines on the planes making up that night's strike were started. The noise level grew and grew and grew until it seemed it could not possibly grow any louder, that every particle of air, every molecule between the planes' engines and the ears of whoever was listening (and everyone was listening), was filled with noise. Men in red shirts pulled the arming pins from the air-to-air missiles on the Hornets and from the noses of the bombs underneath the Hornets and Intruders. Others in purple shirts, the "grapes," fueled the birds. At the forward edge of the landing area a helicopter took off in case a plane went down on takeoff. Astern of the carrier a destroyer or cruiser took up station in the carrier's wake. This was the plane guard ship. The yellow shirts directed the first Hornets to the carrier's only catapults, her bow "cats." Behind the jets, rising from the deck as their nosewheels were fastened to the catapult shuttle, came the jet blast deflectors. One by one the *Midway*'s air group was whisked off the edge of the deck into the darkness, off to war.

The *Midway* is the smallest carrier in the fleet, but still she dwarfs the *Missouri* on the other side of the reserve fleet pier (fig. 63). Her island, once painted black to mask the soot stain from the jet exhaust of her aircraft, has been painted gray again at Bremerton. The markings delineating her landing area are still there but it does not matter. She will not go to sea again, except under tow. When the supercarriers *Ranger* and *America* were decommissioned, even her place in the reserve fleet was

*Fig. 63. The Midway in reserve at Bremerton, alongside the Missouri. Inactive Ship Maintenance Facility, Bremerton*

not needed. She was stricken and donated to the San Diego Aircraft Carrier Museum in the summer of 1998.

While the *Midway* sailed on through the 1980s, the vessels pictured are three of the dwindling reserve fleet that still lay in mothballs as the Cold War came to an end: from left to right they are the Coast Guard icebreaker *Glacier,* the guided-missile cruiser *Oklahoma City,* and the attack carrier *Oriskany* (fig. 64). The *Oriskany* was named for a Revolutionary War battle, as were the *Saratoga, Yorktown, Bunker Hill, Bennington, Lexington, Ticonderoga, Princeton, Valley Forge,* and *Cowpens.* She was one of the four remaining *Essex* carriers still in reserve that were stricken from the navy list in 1989. The others, also at Bremerton, were the *Hornet, Bennington,* and *Bon Homme Richard.* Only the *Lexington* steamed on but her days were numbered as her old machinery continually failed. She, too, was decommissioned and stricken a couple of years later.

*Fig. 64. The Glacier, Oklahoma City, and* Oriskany *in mothballs at Bremerton. U.S. Naval Institute*

The *Oriskany* was launched at the New York Navy Yard in 1944, but it was to be six more years until she was commissioned. Work on her incomplete hull was suspended in 1947 and she became the prototype of the basic *Essex* conversions in the postwar years. It was not until 1950 that the "O-Boat" joined the fleet. She headed for the Mediterranean as the Korean War continued to drain American resources into the western Pacific. In 1952 the *Oriskany* took her turn with Task Force 77 off the Korean coast. From 1965 until the end of American involvement in the Vietnam War eight years later, the *Oriskany* was either on Dixie station off South Vietnam or Yankee station in the Gulf of Tonkin. Enemy action did not damage the warship; fire, that age-old curse of the ship, did.

On 27 October 1966 in Hangar Bay One, a huge fire started on the starboard side of the hangar well forward when a magnesium flare exploded in a flare locker. It quickly spread through five decks and the results were as deadly as any World War II kamikaze strike on one of her sisters. Forty-four men died in the blaze. Many were pilots who had returned safely from dangerous missions over Vietnam just hours before, had successfully landed, then had their young lives snuffed out aboard their own ship. One of them was the commander of the *Oriskany*'s air group. For three hours the men of the *Oriskany* fought the spreading fire, which threatened to explode bombs and fully laden aircraft. Teenage crewmen, like their fathers and uncles aboard the *Ticonderoga* and *Essex* over twenty years before, jettisoned bombs overboard and frantically pushed aircraft out of the way of the flames as others fought to contain and control the fire. Finally, the flames were doused, smoke billowing skyward from the crippled flattop as it had off others at Lingayen Gulf and Okinawa. The *Oriskany* was out of action. Back to the States she steamed to San Francisco where over the winter of 1966–1967 she was repaired. By the summer she was back in combat. Her air wing of Crusaders, Skyhawks, and prop-driven Skyraiders again pounded the Vietcong and North Vietnamese. That summer the men of the *Oriskany* had a look at what their ship had looked like the previous year when the carrier *Forrestal* experienced a similar fire. The *Oriskany* steamed in to help and watched as the *Forrestal* burned and burned, finally being saved by actions no less heroic than those of the crew of the O-Boat.

Many of the surviving *Essex*-class carriers reported for duty off Vietnam. The *Ticonderoga* was in company with the new *Constellation* when North Vietnamese patrol boats attacked two American destroyers in the Gulf of Tonkin in August 1964 and began the full-scale involvement of U.S. forces in the fighting between South Vietnam and the Communists. The antisubmarine carrier *Kearsarge* joined the supercarrier *Ranger* shortly after the incident to provide protection against Red China's submarine fleet, but in general the old carriers like the *Oriskany* were there to aid larger carriers with their huge air wings in launching strikes against the North Vietnamese and Vietcong. Because of their small size, the old carriers could carry only a limited attack wing of F-8 Crusader fighters, A-4 Skyhawk and A-1H Skyraider light attack aircraft and E-1B Tracer early-warning aircraft. The attack carriers *Hancock* and the *Bon Homme Richard* joined the bigger carriers like the new *Enterprise*, nuclear powered, almost three hundred feet longer and displacing over fifty-four thousand tons more than her namesake. Antisubmarine warfare (ASW) carriers like the *Hornet* and the *Kearsarge* were used for search and rescue duty; two other ASW carriers, the

*Intrepid* and the *Shangri-La,* were converted for use as limited attack carriers.

But they were getting old, these World War II veterans, and they could not handle the bigger naval aircraft joining the fleet, such as the F-4 Phantom and the A-6E Intruder. After decommissioning at Alameda, the *Oriskany* was towed up the coast to Bremerton. Mothballing a ship in 1976 was different than mothballing one in 1946. Safe storage was the term now. No longer were the ships afforded a complete inactivation overhaul. Damaged or broken equipment was no longer repaired, its condition was simply noted for members of the reserve fleet caretakers and the future reference of any crew that might come aboard to reactivate the ship. The inactivation of the ship was left to the crew itself, with no help from shipyard personnel. It was nowhere near as complete as that done before. One of the key elements was sealing the ship from the outside so that the low humidity level necessary to prevent deterioration could be maintained. That was not being done with the thoroughness of prior years and the ships that arrived at the Inactive Maintenance Facilities after 1976 began to show signs of deterioration about six months after they arrived. Moisture in piping led to rust and the loosening of connecting joints. Electrical wiring would fail. Bulkheads and machinery would rust. The hulls would have their watertight integrity maintained through cathodic protection, which was still religiously carried out, but the dehumidification procedures began to be less and less effective because of less and less preparation work by ships' crews (Callaghan, *All Hands,* 34–40). Naval and military budgets fell with the end of the Vietnam War and the high level of inflation in the 1970s. Money to properly preserve the ships in the mothball fleets at Bremerton, Philadelphia, and Norfolk was no longer in those budgets.

By the time Ronald Reagan took office in 1981 there were just fifty-six ships at Bremerton, twenty-eight ships and craft at Philadelphia's back basin, and another three at Norfolk. There were few major combatants. To maintain a fifteen-carrier force was considered essential by the Reagan administration. Some of the supercarriers were almost thirty years old and would require extensive overhaul and rebuilding to keep them in the fleet. Like the FRAM modernization of the destroyer forces, this carrier modernization was designed to add a number of years to the life of those carriers that would be reaching the end of their service lives in the 1980s. Thus at least one ship would be in the yard for several years. For the fifteenth carrier, the Reagan administration turned its eyes toward the mothball fleet. Specifically, to the two attack carriers residing at Bremerton, the *Bon Homme Richard,* and the *Oriskany.* The *Bon Homme Richard,* the "Bonnie Dick," had been laid up in 1971 after six combat deployments to Vietnam. Except for her modernization period from 1953 to 1955, she had been in continuous service since she first had been pulled from Bremerton in 1951. The cost estimate for reactivating one of these carriers was high, over a half billion dollars, and Congress said no. Secretary Lehman later wrote that he understood why when he visited the Bremerton Inactive Ship Maintenance Facility. The *Oriskany,* he said, was in bad shape, a "horror." The flight deck had warped and grass was growing two feet high on it (Lehman, *Command of the Sea,* 174). Wooden flight deck preservation long had been a problem in the mothball fleet, and the safe storage practices of the recent past meant that the O-boat had begun badly to go to seed. On top of that, her small size meant small, less capable, and equally old aircraft. The *Oriskany* was not reactivated, nor was the *Bon Homme Richard.* The fifteen-deployable-carrier fleet would have to wait for the completion of the *Theodore Roosevelt* and the refits of the old *Coral Sea* and *Midway.*

So the *Oriskany* and the others stayed in mothballs as the *Theodore Roosevelt* joined the fleet and construction began on the *Abraham Lincoln* and the *George Washington.* The old ships were never recommissioned and in 1989 all four were stricken. The *Hornet* and the *Bennington* had spent nearly two decades in mothballs at Puget Sound. The *Bon Homme Richard* was sold for scrap in 1992. The *Bennington,* too, was sold for breaking up. The *Hornet* time and again staved off the scrappers and was finally donated by the navy as a museum in Alameda. The *Oriskany* stayed in Bremerton for another six years after her striking until sold to a company in Oakland, California for $1.2 million on 29 September 1995. In fact, that California company bought quite a bit of scrap metal in the form of old naval vessels that day: the old landing ships *Monticello, Thomaston,* and *Point Defiance,* the former landing ship (then submarine support vessel) *Point Loma,* and the submarine rescue ship *Pigeon.* All were tied up at the old Mare Island Naval Shipyard to await scrapping and were joined there by the *Oriskany.*

She was towed down from Bremerton, up San Francisco Bay to Vallejo, and she too was tied up at the now defunct naval shipyard (fig. 65). There the *Oriskany* sat. When the contractor defaulted on the sale, the navy took possession of her once again. Parts of her were cut away and taken to the *Hornet* in Alameda, where volunteers were turning CV-12 into a museum. Still the *Oriskany* sat tied to the wharf. She was dark inside, silent, with no hum of engines, no vibration underfoot, no gentle sway as the ship caught the Pacific swell. Her hangar was like an abandoned warehouse piled with pallets and equipment, except that in this warehouse, thirty years before, a horrible fire had raged. Sailors, who had grown up reading about the heroism of other sailors at war a generation before in the last "good" war, were forced to act without thinking, to respond to training. Young men had again died while at war, not the World War II of the history books and fathers' stories, not the Korean War foolishly called a police action. This was a war that grew and fed on itself until no one, it seemed, could figure a way out short of just picking up and leaving. This was an unpopular war where the ships did not come home to cheering crowds and "Well Done" signs and where everyone wanted to know the stories behind the medals and campaign ribbons.

*Fig. 65. The Oriskany awaiting scrapping at Mare Island in 1996. Author's collection*

The *Oriskany*'s mast had been cut down and lay against her superstructure as she was towed down the coast. The faint outline of her number thirty-four could be seen on her island, and her name, now in

Fig. 66. Stern view of the decommissioned and stricken *Tripoli* at Suisun Bay. Author's collection

indistinct gray rather than black, was visible only to the occasional pleasure boat that ventured under her round stern. The green glass of her bridge and pri-fly was visible in Vallejo across the narrow strait. She looked huge there, until one had the chance to stand next to a nuclear carrier and realize just how small the O-boat really was. The rust streaked her sides, the water lapped at her hull, and she sat there tied to the dock month after month. Most people strolling along the Vallejo waterfront or casually looking at the ship from the deck of a ferryboat bringing commuters home could not tell what ship she was. But they talked about her in idle tones, about where she came from, what she had done, about who she was, about who she might have been.

She looks like a carrier, that's for sure, they would say. A big one. An old one. Maybe it's the *Hornet,* the one they saved for a museum. But that's over in Alameda, isn't it? Maybe it's another one. Going to take it out to sea and dump it, some say. Going to cut it up for Japanese cars, others say. Wonder what ship that is over there? Some do know. She's the O-boat. The *Oriskany.* CV-34. CVA-34. Built during the war. The big war, remember? Her planes flew missions in Korea. Went to 'Nam a couple of times. Had a bad fire there, killed a lot of guys. Are their ghosts still aboard her? Some say so. She's been in Bremerton since the bicentennial. Now she's come here to die. The old O-boat. A good ship.

Not far from where the *Oriskany* awaits her fate lies another veteran of a later war. At the stern of the decommissioned and stricken helicopter carrier *Tripoli,* berthed among the ships of the National Defense Reserve Fleet at Suisun Bay in September 1996, a pair of heavy chains secure her in place and more lines bind her to the stricken oiler *Wichita* next to her. Both of her elevators are folded up next to her hull (fig. 66). The *Tripoli* is not mothballed. She is not awaiting another call to service. Like many ships in the fleet of the late 1980s and throughout the 1990s, her time has come. She was one of four of her class, the *Iwo Jima*s, to be stricken. There were seven altogether and only the *Guam* still served in her original role, that of helicopter carrier, into 1998. The *Inchon,* the last to be built, has been converted to a mine warfare ship. She carries helicopters but they are minesweeping helos, not troop carriers. One other, the *New Orleans,* is in reserve. The others—the *Iwo Jima, Guadalcanal,* and *Okinawa*—were victims of age, budget cuts, and the emergence of more capable ships in the role they helped pioneer, that of vertical envelopment, the landing of marines by helicopter instead of landing craft.

With the advent of atomic warfare in 1945, the Marine Corps was forced to examine its role as an amphibious landing force. The hierarchy came to the conclusion that if a marine amphibious group of ships and assault troops were to survive off a beach against an enemy who possessed nuclear weapons, one thing was clear: one bomb could wipe out the entire beachhead and the ships offshore. By necessity, the amphibious ships and landing craft had to be concentrated in order to land an effective assault force. The first few waves of an amphibious assault were extremely vulnerable since the landing was easily disrupted by a determined enemy as the troops waded ashore, reformed into cohesive units, and established contact with units on either flank. The ships needed to be in close proximity to the shore so that the short-ranged and thin-skinned landing craft had the shortest possible distance to go before beaching, minimizing their time under artillery and automatic weapons fire. The assault ships had to be in fairly close formation so that a maximum number of assault troops could concentrate on a fairly small beachhead, establish a toehold, fight off counterattacks, and consolidate and strengthen the beachhead so that reinforcements, supplies, heavy artillery, armor, and combat engineers could land. These requirements meant that the fleet was tied together. There was only one real defense against an atomic attack at sea, and that was fleet dispersal. That option was taken away by the very nature of amphibious operations in World War II.

The development of the helicopter changed this. While heavy equipment would still be landed by sea, most of the assault marines would come by air, from over the horizon if necessary. The plentiful *Casablanca*s had been retained in reserve in part because of the hope that one day they could be used as helicopter decks at sea. One, the *Thetis Bay*, was taken from the reserve fleet in May 1955 after nearly a decade in mothballs and towed to San Francisco where conversion to an experimental helicopter carrier was begun. The forward section of her hangar was converted into troop-berthing spaces and the after elevator enlarged to enable her to operate an air wing of troop-carrying helicopters. She was small and could spot only five helicopters on deck at a time, though she had room for a total of twenty-two as well as over nine hundred marines. As an experiment she was a success, demonstrating the capability of vertical envelopment. Although she also served operationally in her new role for a few years, it was apparent that converted CVEs would be inadequate. Design went forward on a new type of ship, built from the keel up as a helicopter carrier. In the meantime, three fleet carriers, all veterans of the early days of Korea, also were converted to carry helicopters and marines: the *Valley Forge, Princeton,* and *Boxer.* But the conversions were austere, in part because of the limited useful lives left in these vessels and in part because a far more satisfactory ship was under construction at the Puget Sound Naval Shipyard.

These ships would not be christened with aircraft carrier names. They were built for the marines and would carry names rich in Marine Corps legend and lore: *Iwo Jima, Okinawa, Guadalcanal, Guam, Tripoli, New Orleans,* and *Inchon.* The first, the *Iwo Jima*, joined the fleet in 1961; the last, the *Inchon*, was commissioned in 1970. They typically carried an air group of twenty to twenty-four CH-46 Sea Knight medium helicopters, four heavy lift CH-53 Sea Stallions, and a few other, smaller helos for gunship support or for utility use. Soon after her commissioning the *Iwo Jima* was in the Caribbean, loaded with assault troops during the Cuban missile crisis of October 1962 (fig. 67). By the mid-1960s she was off Vietnam, landing marines up and down the coast on search-and-destroy missions against the Vietcong.

In 1970, though, she had a far more fulfilling and happy mission: the recovery of the astronauts of *Apollo 13*. Their craft crippled on the way to the moon by an oxygen tank explosion, the trio of astronauts, sup-

*Fig. 67. The helicopter carrier* Iwo Jima *at sea. United States Navy*

ported by mission control in Houston, fought to survive until they could reenter the earth's atmosphere. Cameras aboard the *Iwo Jima* flashed television pictures around the world of the safely recovered astronauts. In fact, with the decommissioning of the carriers, the *Iwo Jima*s took on more of the recoveries of the *Apollo* command modules. This was in the days before the space shuttle, when returning astronauts floated to earth inside their charred ships beneath three huge parachutes to be plucked from the ocean by the helicopters of a nearby carrier. The *New Orleans* recovered half of the remaining *Apollo* missions and became a veteran at it.

Throughout the 1960s, 1970s, and 1980s the seven ships cruised as the centerpieces for Amphibious Ready Groups, small task forces carrying a reinforced battalion of marine infantry. In any world crisis the first question to be asked at the White House or the Pentagon was likely to be, "Where is the nearest carrier?"; the second question was equally likely to be "Where are the nearest marines?" Time and again these amphibious ready groups (ARGs) carrying their Marine Expeditionary Units (MEUs) were diverted to trouble spots. In August 1990 came the Persian Gulf crisis. From air and by sea, marines began to converge on the Persian Gulf in what would be the largest deployment of the Marine Corps since World War II. Two marine brigades were airlifted to Saudi

Arabia as ground troops, and a third, the Fourth Marine Expeditionary Brigade, set sail from North Carolina to provide an amphibious landing capability to strike the flank of the Iraqis should they decide to advance south along the coast toward the Saudi oil fields. The brigade was carried aboard the ships of Amphibious Squadron Two, twelve ships including the helicopter carriers *Iwo Jima* and *Guam.* At the same time another flotilla with the helicopter carrier *Okinawa* at its core headed for the Gulf from the Philippines. Still another carrier, the *Inchon,* was sailing toward Liberia with a battalion of marines on a normal rotation to relieve another ARG on station there. In November, with the defense of Saudi Arabia assured but with the Iraqis unwilling to leave Kuwait in the face of United Nations demands and sanctions, President Bush decided to double the size of the American force in the region. Another marine brigade was ordered from the East Coast to the Persian Gulf. This included in its thirteen ships the helicopter carriers *New Orleans* and *Tripoli.* Thus, by the end of the year over seventeen thousand marines were aboard more than thirty amphibious ships in the Gulf, including five of the navy's seven *Iwo Jima*-class carriers. The *Iwo Jima,* at almost three decades, was the oldest. All in fact were scheduled to be retired within the next few years, but now they were needed.

Together they formed a mighty force, able to hit the Iraqis on their flank should they attack south and to pin down divisions along the coast away from the planned Allied axis of attack far to the west. Amphibious landings were planned, but a huge threat remained: the extensive minefields laid by the Iraqis in the months leading up to the coalition attack on 16 January 1991.

If there were any hope of an amphibious landing in or near Kuwait City or even hope of an effective feint, lanes would have to be cleared in these fields. For one thing, though the Sea Knights and Sea Stallions would deliver the marine infantry over and beyond the beaches, the tanks, artillery and bulk of the food, ammunition, and engineering equipment would have to come by landing craft or hovercraft. The marines would need fire support from the guns of the battleships *Wisconsin* and *Missouri,* requiring the ships to close to within a few miles of the coast in order for their sixteen-inch rifles to reach out to cover marines as they pushed inland.

To clear the fields the British sent minehunters, as did the Belgians and the Saudis. As was the case in Korea, the mine warfare ships of the United States were short in number and long in years. In fact, of the four dedicated mine craft deployed to the Gulf for Operations Desert Shield and Desert Storm, three of them—the *Adroit, Leader,* and *Impervious*—had been built in the 1950s as a result of the sad experience with mines off the coast of North Korea during the war. In addition, the *Tripoli* transferred her marines of the Fifth Expeditionary Brigade to other ships and was loaded with six MH-53E helicopters of Mine Helicopter Squadron Fourteen as well as four Sea Cobra gunships. She was the coordinating ship of the mine clearing force that began work sixty miles east of the Kuwaiti coastline. The ships swept a lane into the fields for thirty-four miles, then proceeded to sweep a box ten miles long by three and a half miles wide south of Faylaka Island, just enough room for a battlewagon to sail in and pound the Iraqi coastal defenses.

On 18 February 1991, as American, British, French, Saudi, and Kuwaiti aircraft continued into the second month of the air campaign to cripple Iraq and soften up her forces in the field for a ground assault, the *Tripoli* became the only *Iwo Jima*-class carrier to suffer any combat damage over their thirty-year span in the navy. In the darkness of the early morning hours her sailors detected the presence of fire control radar emission of the kind used by Iraqi Silkworm antiship missiles. The *Tripoli* commenced a turn to bring her Phalanx Gatling gun to bear, and at 0436 she struck a floating mine. It blew a hole in her hull twenty by thirty feet, about ten feet below her waterline in her starboard bow. The explosion damaged a paint and fuel storage area and dangerous fumes began to waft through the forward part of the ship. She stopped dead in the water and dropped anchor to avoid hitting any other mines. Within thirty minutes, after her calls for assistance, a Battle Damage Assessment team had departed the World War II repair ship *Jason* for the *Tripoli.* Belowdecks her crew shored up bulkheads surrounding her flooded spaces with timber stored for just that purpose. No one had been seriously injured by the mine hit, and although the helicopter carrier could and did continue her mission, she was later replaced by her sister, the *New Orleans.* She was dry-docked in Bahrain for repair after the war and returned to minesweeping duty when her hole had been patched and the damage belowdecks had been repaired.

The *Iwo Jima*s never did participate in an amphibious right hook against the Iraqi troops entrenched along the Kuwaiti coast. General Schwarzkopf, in overall Allied command, wisely decided the risks did not outweigh the potential gains. But their presence and that of the dozens of amphibious ships in the narrow, shallow waters of the Gulf served their purpose in fixing the attention of the Iraqi high command on this very visible, very well known, and very potent threat posed by the navy and marine team. For most of the *Iwo Jima*s, though, the Gulf War was their last mission. The amphibious forces felt the budget crunch and the effects of old age as much as any other component of the fleet. The buildup of the Reagan years had included amphibious ships as well as carriers and the refurbished battleships, and the newer, bigger, more capable helicopter carriers like the *Wasp*s were part of that, and as they entered the fleet, the *Iwo Jima*s bowed out. The *Okinawa* was first, decommissioning on 17 December 1992, less than two years after the Gulf War. The *Iwo Jima* followed in 1993, the *Guadalcanal* in 1994, and the *Tripoli* a year later. The *Iwo Jima* was scrapped, the last stages of her dismemberment taking place on a beach in Texas where she had been run aground. The *Okinawa* and *Tripoli* were towed to the National Defense Reserve Fleet berthing at Suisun Bay in California. There they joined the merchant ships of the ready reserve fleet and other stricken warships awaiting scrap sale or use as a target. Except for some of the oilers like the *Wichita* and *Andrew J. Higgins* moored nearby, the helicopter carriers were the biggest and most impressive ships in the lonely mothball fleet.

The *Inchon* stayed in the fleet and was converted from an amphibious ship to a permanent mine warfare ship. The *Guam* participated in the fiftieth anniversary of the Normandy landings, but as the twentieth century drew to a close she was decommissioned and stricken. The *New Orleans* was decommissioned in October 1997. Like her two sisters she was towed to Suisun Bay. But she was not immediately stricken. She was kept on the Naval Vessel Register in mobilization category C. Unlike category B assets, ships in category C are maintained "as is," preserved only to minimize deterioration. The *New Orleans* remained in that category until October 1998, when she was stricken. She could have recommissioned to replace or augment the *Inchon* or *Guam*, though now she will be maintained as a spare parts bin for the remaining ship. Like the *Tripoli* and *Okinawa* before her, both of which have since been taken from this Maritime Administration (MarAd) berthing, the *New Orleans* sat almost hidden among rows of reserve merchant shipping, as forgotten here among the gray rows of cargo ships, oilers, and rusting Victory ships as she would be tucked away at Bremerton or Philadelphia. More so, for few visitors come out this way. There are few roads along the shore and the surrounding hills are too far away to provide a good view of the ships at anchor. Signs posted on many of the ships read "Keep Back 500 Feet." Yet it is possible on a late summer afternoon to take a speedboat or a pleasure boat out among the bleak ships that no longer appear on the navy list.

The navy list, or the Naval Vessel Register (NVR) is the "official inventory of ships and service craft in custody or titled by the U.S. Navy." It traces its origins from the Ship's Data Book and the Vessel Register. Once a ship's construction has been authorized and a classification and hull number assigned such as DDG (guided missile destroyer) number eighty-one (named in this case the *Winston Churchill*), the ship is then listed on the NVR. The NVR continues to list the ship and pertinent data about it until the vessel has been disposed of by the navy. Prior to 1987, a vessel that was stricken had its name removed from the NVR. Nowadays the NVR continues to list the ship, wherever it is, until it has been disposed of one way or another, though the ship is still considered to be stricken from the register and the roll of naval ships and craft. In peace and war, the ships of the mothball fleet could be found there. Under "status" would be listed the words "Inactive, Out of Commission, in Reserve," and the maintenance category was usually *B*, indicating they would receive "the highest practicable degree of maintenance within personnel and funding limitations. Dehumidification and cathodic protection equipment and flooding alarms are installed. Ships selected for this category are the most urgently needed to augment the Active Fleet in an emergency" (www.nvr.navy.mil). The NVR was formerly listed in book form but now is kept only as an electronic document, updated weekly and available, as is the case with an ever-increasing number of documents, on the Internet.

The MarAd fleet is even more forgotten than the naval ships in reserve, for they are mainly cargomen, tankers, oilers, container ships, and troop ships, old World War II Victory ships whose paint peels off their hulls in long strips. The ships are usually assigned to either the Ready Reserve Force or the National Defense Reserve Fleet (NDRF). The Ready Reserve Force is theoretically in better shape, able to be activated quicker than the hulks of the NDRF that are berthed at Suisun Bay, James River, Virginia, and Beaumont, Texas. The concept of a merchant fleet in reserve was tested in Vietnam and again during the Gulf War, when several divisions from the continental army forces were moved via ship to Saudi Arabia. In general the ships proved their worth, though the time to activate them had been greatly underestimated and

*Fig. 68. The missile cruiser* England *at sea. United States Navy*

the effort needed to keep them sailing greatly misunderstood. They were old and cranky and broke down often, but in the end they did the job. Occasionally the navy berths its mothballed ships in the MarAd fleet, as in the case of the *New Orleans* and the surveillance ship *Tenacious,* when space is limited at the Inactive Ship Maintenance Facilities. Or the navy will transfer its stricken ships to MarAd for storage until they are sold for scrap or otherwise disposed of. That is what happened with the *Okinawa* and *Tripoli*. The cruiser *Oklahoma City* was stored there, too, in the mid-1990s. So was the old destroyer *Hull* and the repair ship *Jason* as well as others, victims both of old age and changing times.

The first guided-missile ships were conversions, wartime gun cruisers pulled from mothballs to be converted to this new technology that enabled an aircraft to be shot down by a rocket guided to its target by the ship that fired it. But these ships were stopgap measures. What was needed, what was always better in the long run, was a ship designed from the start to carry missiles. The first of them, named the *Long Beach,* was laid down in 1957. She claimed a couple of firsts: the first nuclear-powered surface warship and the first ship built with missiles as her main battery. She was also the first and last of her type. She was very expensive. The *Leahy*s were next, with the lead ship being completed in 1962. They were known then as guided-missile frigates. The ships certainly were smaller than any cruiser, only 8,200 tons at full load and just 533 feet long, with a crew of a little over four hundred officers and men. Because they were built as frigates they carried frigate and destroyer-type names, that is, naval heroes and admirals: *Richmond K. Turner, Dale,* and *England,* which carried on the name of the plucky destroyer escort of the Pacific war (fig. 68). They were armed with missile launchers forward and aft, like the double-ended *Albany* conversions, and fired the Terrier surface-to-air missile. The nine *Leahy*s were joined by nine more frigates of the *Belknap* class beginning in 1964. These differed from the *Leahy*s in that they were only single-ended-missile ships, with a missile battery forward, and a five-inch gun, helicopter landing pad, and hangar aft. Despite having only half the missile battery, they still carried three-quarters of the missile load of the earlier ships in addition to the gun and helicopter. There were also two nuclear-powered half sisters to each class. These frigates, the *Long Beach,* the cruiser conversions, and the new *Farragut*-class missile frigates and *Charles F. Adams*-class missile destroyers, formed the protective surface-to-air missile cordon around the carriers throughout the 1960s and 1970s.

In 1975 most of the frigates were reclassified as cruisers, but the changes were of course in name only. The new cruisers continued to sail on, one or two assigned to each carrier task force. The Standard surface-to-air-missile became the main antiaircraft missile, and all of the ships received the NTU (New Threat Upgrade): new radar and fire control systems that allowed them to continue to fire missiles then under development. Many were veterans of Vietnam cruises. Six sailed as part of the huge U.S. fleet during the Gulf War, but by then their replacements were already on the scene.

The USS *Ticonderoga,* a guided-missile cruiser equipped with the Aegis antiaircraft warfare system, entered the Atlantic Fleet in 1983. Twenty-six more were to follow. These ships carried the names of some of the most famous ships in United States naval legacy: *Vincennes, Antietam,* and *San Jacinto.* Others carried for the first time the names of battles new and old: *Hue City, Chosin, Cape St. George,* and *Chancellorsville.* These were the most capable antiaircraft missile shooters afloat, and they were joined, beginning on Independence Day 1991, by

Fig. 69. *A line of
decommissioned
missile cruisers at
Suisun Bay. Author's
collection*

the destroyer version of the Aegis system, named for the most famous destroyer captain of them all, the USS *Arleigh Burke*. With the end of the Gulf War and the nearly simultaneous end of the Cold War, with the splintering of the Soviet Navy by the Common-wealth of Independent States, and with the expensive new Aegis-equipped ships under construction, it was decided that their missile-armed descendants would go to the breakers.

Moored in *K* row at the National Defense Reserve Fleet in Suisun is a line of these discarded cruisers, from left to right: the *Sterett, William H. Standley, Jouett, Horne, Halsey, England,* and *Gridley* (fig. 69). The water is calm, the air surprisingly warm on this late summer afternoon on the Bay. The ships are absolutely quiet. In fact, they are deserted. The silence is palpable. Approaching close enough by small boat, one can just make out a faint name on a stern. As with the majority of stricken ships, the formerly black letters have now been painted over with gray, as if to hide their identity or strip it away. The ships ride high in the water. All stores, ammunition, missiles, fuel, electronic equipment, and anything else of any use has long since been removed before the lifeless vessels were towed up from San Diego, under the Golden Gate Bridge, and through the Carquinez Straits to this quiet offshoot of San Francisco Bay. The ships that were once the backbone of the United States surface fleet in the Pacific in the 1960s and 1970s now loom above a visitor in stony, unmoving, eerie silence. They are not surrounded by wharves, piers, shipping and the familiar shipyard sights and sounds in which they spent their active careers. There is nothing out here, nothing but the brown California hills overlooking this graveyard of ships. There was no inactivation process for these ships. No overhaul. No careful inventory of machinery and equipment. No tags left on knobs, dials and switches detailing where a spare part might be found, how to activate a switch, what might have been wrong with it when the ship was decommissioned. No one cared what was wrong because these ships were doomed ships.

They were decommissioned and stricken the same day, with no reprieve, no waiting period. Some were stricken in 1993, more in 1994, and the last three—the *Belknap*, the *Horne*, and the *Richmond K. Turner*—in early 1995. They were part of the peace dividend, the savings in money that would result from the end of the Cold War. The carriers no longer needed them for protection. The new *Ticonderoga*s and *Arleigh Burke*s would take care of the flattops now. At any rate, there were fewer carriers to watch over than there had been when they were built and while they served. The *Coral Sea* had finally gone to the breakers in Baltimore. The *Ranger* had gone to reserve at Bremerton, joining the *Midway* there in 1993. The *Saratoga* was decommissioned and stricken in 1994. Now their escorts were going, too. In one seventeen-month period between October 1993 and March 1995, eighteen cruisers—two entire classes—disappeared from the Naval Vessel Register. They were good ships. None of them were offered for sale abroad, none were considered for mothballs, but the navy and the taxpayer certainly got their money's worth. The *Leahy*s served an average of nearly thirty years apiece, the *Belknap*s an average of almost twenty-eight years, and with the commissioning of new and enormously expensive guided-missile ships, these elderly but still viable warships became superfluous to the needs and budget of the post–Cold War navy. Here is where those in the Pacific Fleet ended up.

The *Leahy*s and the *Belknap*s were not the only victims of the striking orders that eliminated whole classes of ships. Pictured is Fleet Week, San Francisco, in the late 1980s (fig. 70). Each year in October a task force from the Pacific Fleet, accompanied sometimes by a Mexican or Chilean or Canadian vessel, sails through the Golden Gate and ties up along the waterfront to celebrate the navy's heritage and link with the city, a link that has now, for the most part, been severed with the clos-

*Fig. 70. The frigates* Kirk *and* Cook *at San Francisco during Fleet Week. Author's collection*

ing of nearly every facility on the Bay. On this sunny, windy autumn day the USS *Kirk* (FF-1087), a *Knox*-class frigate, is tied up at Fisherman's Wharf, inboard of her sister ship, the USS *Cook* (FF-1083). Immediately astern of the *Kirk,* her periscope barely visible, is the World War II submarine *Pampanito* (SS-383), once mothballed up the Bay a few miles, now a museum ship behind Fisherman's Wharf. Signal flags flying, visitors strolling their decks during open house, the frigates are examples of the United States Navy's antisubmarine warfare force that was built to counter the Soviet submarine threat. The forty-six FF-1052 frigates were built between 1969 and 1974 to escort merchant convoys and amphibious task forces, replacing the elderly wartime *Fletcher* and *Gearing* destroyers that were leaving the fleet in ever-increasing numbers and carrying on the tradition of the small (relatively) inexpensive single-purpose escort ship, the destroyer escort . Yet with the collapse of the Soviet Union the *Knox* class was considered just as expendable as the missile cruisers, only two decades after they began entering the fleet.

Aside from the fifty-one ships of the *Oliver Hazard Perry*-class of guided-missile frigates, the *Knox*-class was the most numerous class of surface warship built by the United States, indeed by any of the western allies, since 1945. Small as they were compared to contemporary destroyers and frigates, they were still large ships when examined next to a *Fletcher* or a *Gearing*, over forty-two hundred tons full load and almost 440 feet in length, against the *Gearing*'s twenty-four hundred tons and 390-foot length. They carried a single five-inch gun, an ASROC (Antisubmarine Rocket launched torpedo) launcher that was modified to fire Harpoons, and an eight-tube short-range surface-to-air-missile launcher aft of the helicopter pad and hangar. The helicopter and the ASROC and her sonar suite were the main weapons the ships had against the massive Soviet submarine fleet whose job it would have been to halt the flow of American reinforcements and supplies across the Atlantic.

In 1990 some of these frigates participated in the naval embargo of Iraq during Operation Desert Shield. The United Nations had imposed punitive economic sanctions against Saddam Hussein for his invasion and annexation of Kuwait, and the embargo was part of the effort, coupled with a military buildup, to get him peacefully to withdraw his forces back to the Iraqi frontier. No ship was permitted to leave or enter an Iraqi port with contraband, and the blockade, and Iraqi attempts to circumvent or defy it, provided some of the most tension-filled days of the crisis before the war.

On 11 August 1990, acting on the authority he believed he had under U.N. Resolution 661 (the imposition of the sanctions), President Bush announced that the United States, unilaterally, had the right to enforce those sanctions and would do so, even though the resolution had specified no means of enforcement and delegated no authority to member nations for that enforcement. On Thursday, 16 August, the rules of engagement were sent to U.S. naval forces in the Gulf. The orders were to stop, board, and search vessels suspected of carrying contraband to and from Iraq. In the meantime the United States continued to press for a U.N. stamp of approval to enforce the interdiction by military means. That approval came on 25 August in the form of Resolution 665. There was no explicit mention of the use of force, rather, the language specified "such measures commensurate" to the circumstances. But the meaning was clear. The coalition had U.N. authority to enforce the embargo and the allies intended to do exactly that.

The blockade, for that is what it was, ultimately consisted of warships and support vessels from thirteen nations: the United States, Great Britain, Australia, Argentina, Belgium, Canada, Denmark, France, Greece, Italy, the Netherlands, Norway, and Spain. Ships were deployed to the Red Sea, the Gulf of Aden, inside the Persian Gulf and the Gulf of Oman, while American, British, and French aircraft patrolled the skies. Merchant ships were queried by radio as to their cargo and destination and any ship suspected of carrying contraband was stopped and boarded. If it was indeed carrying contraband it was ordered away from Iraq. Sometimes shots were fired and troops forcibly landed from a helicopter to persuade reluctant shipmasters to acquiesce. Usually these troops were U.S. Marines taken from the brigades aboard the amphibious ships; occasionally they were Navy Seals or British Royal Marine Commandos. They were covered by either marine helicopter gunships or navy antisubmarine helicopters equipped with machine guns. These takedowns, as they were called, happened rarely, but in the uncertain days of Desert Shield, when nations walked the fine line between war and peace in the Gulf, those incidents increased the tension and war of nerves and the *Knox* frigates were in the middle of it.

On 14 September the Iraqi ship *Al Fao* was repeatedly asked to stop and submit to a search by a pair of Allied frigates, the Australian *Darwin* and the American *Brewton*. The *Brewton* shadowed the Iraqi ship throughout the night and at first light the crew went to battle stations, ready for anything that might happen in these new and uncertain circumstances. Still the master of the *Al Fao* refused to stop. The *Brewton*'s commanding officer ordered a hundred rounds of fifty-caliber machine-gun fire across her bow. The machine gun spat, the shells splashing off the surface of the sea in front of the *Al Fao*. Still she sailed on. Now the *Darwin* opened fire as well, and finally the Iraqi captain ordered the engines slowed. The tension was high. Guns had been fired on the high seas by men of war, not quite at somebody, but close enough to deliver a strong message. The war of words was in danger of becoming a shooting war. No one knew quite how Saddam Hussein or even the ship captains involved would react. Both the American and Australian ships sent boarding parties to search her. For two hours they searched the ship under the resentful eyes of the captain while the *Darwin*'s helicopter flew overhead. Finally, the boarding party was satisfied that this ship contained no prohibited cargo and the *Al Fao* was allowed to proceed.

Two weeks later another *Knox*, the *Elmer Montgomery*, in company with a Spanish frigate, fired warning shots ahead of an Iraqi merchantman and forced her to allow an American-Spanish team to board. Her sister, the *Brewton*, fast becoming a veteran of these operations and again in the company of the *Darwin* as well as the Royal Navy frigate *Jupiter*, with marines took down the Iraqi ship *Almutannabbi* on 13 October. Later that month the oil tanker *Amuriyah*, 157,000 dead-weight tons, was sailing from Aden bound for Iraq. The busy Australian ship *Darwin* picked her up on radar and then her lookouts spotted her. Joining the *Darwin* was another *Knox*-class frigate, the *Reasoner*, a British frigate the *Brazen*, and the amphibious ship *Ogden*, carrying marines. The on-scene commander was the *Reasoner's* skipper and he warned the *Amuriyah* that she would be subject to a search. The *Darwin* raced across her bow, attempting to get her to slow down to avoid ramming. Still the *Amuriyah* plowed on. The *Reasoner's* skipper ordered warning shots. The *Darwin's* fifty-caliber machine gun fired across the tanker's bow, then the *Reasoner* opened up with a roar, her lone, five-inch gun barking and sending shells out in front of the Iraqi ship. Hornets and Tomcats from the carrier *Independence* made low-altitude, low-speed passes over the ships in an attempt to further intimidate the Iraqi master, but he refused to comply. Now came an even more dangerous step as a Sea Cobra helicopter gunship and a second helicopter took off from the flight deck of the *Ogden*. While the Sea Cobra orbited overhead, marines of the Thirteenth Marine Expeditionary Unit (Special Operations Capable) came aboard and took control of the bridge and the engine room, slowing the ship, just as they had the *Almutannabbi*, and allowing a team of Australian and American sailors and Coast Guardsmen to board. They searched the ship, found she was innocent of any wrongdoing, and let her go on her way (*Final Report to Congress*, 74–75).

Eight of the *Knoxes* sailed the waters around the Arabian peninsula as part of the immense American naval armada. Eventually this force would total at one time or another eight carriers (two left before the start of hostilities), the only two remaining battleships, nineteen cruisers, nineteen destroyers, twenty frigates, seven helicopter carriers, twenty-seven amphibious ships, and a number of tenders, repair ships, oilers, replenishment ships, and other fleet auxiliaries that permitted the warships to stay at sea half a world away from their home ports. When the war was over many of them came home to an uncertain future in a world far different from that in which they had been built.

The forty-six frigates of the FF-1052 class were not old when the decision was made to decommission them in 1991. The oldest was twenty-three, the youngest, the *Moinester,* but seventeen years old, barely middle-aged for a warship. Yet the decision was made that the frigates were not really needed. The Cold War was a thing of the past; the Red Army was not going to burst through the Fulda Gap in West Germany and head for the French coastline as the Germans had done in 1940. There would be no need for REFORGER (REturn of FORces to GERmany) exercises, in which the United States rehearsed the shipment of its continental reinforcements to the battle zone. The submarine threat could be handled by the *Spruances,* the *Perrys,* and the versatile Aegis ships. Initially six frigates were to be leased abroad; eight were to go to the Naval Reserve Force (NRF) as training ships (thirteen had already gone to the NRF in the 1980s and early 1990s), maintaining a nucleus of experienced personnel for the remaining thirty-two, which were to be decommissioned and mothballed. They would be able to recommission, it was hoped, in six months, with the NRF crews as the cornerstone of the new crews. This plan was short lived. The funds to maintain them, even in reserve in an "as is" condition, were not going to be available. Between September 1991 and July 1994 all forty-six were decommissioned. Many went to foreign navies. Both the *Kirk* and the *Cook* went to Taiwan. The rest were stricken.

One of these, the *Lang,* stripped bare and discarded, rides at anchor and rots in the summer of 1996 (fig. 71). The barrel on her five-inch mount has been sliced away, rendering her incapable of any further duty as a combat ship. Her ASROC launcher sits empty. Radar antenna have been removed from her "mack" (mast and stack assembly) and the entire mack and antenna assembly painted over in gray. Her hull number has been painted over. Compared to the *Kirk* at San Francisco a decade ago, the *Lang* is a dead hulk. Recall how the fleet looks in that bygone time. Nearby are other, almost identical hulks. The *Bagley* is nestled between the *Leahy* and the big transport *General Patrick.* The *Lockwood* is tied up between the *Gridley* and the *Fox.* The *Meyerkord* sways gently next to the *Jason.* She is one of the few ships retaining much of an identity and possessing a paint job other than mottled gray. On her hangar door the blue, white, and gold of her insignia are still vis-

*Fig. 71. The* Lang *alongside the World War II tanker* Mission Santa Inez. *Author's collection*

ible, though fading away. The *Lang* sits at the far end of the mothball fleet, almost alone. Next to her, fittingly, is a merchant ship, not one she would have escorted in the 1960s, for it is too old. Maybe one of the *Lang*'s destroyer escort ancestors did so. The tanker is the *Mission Santa Ynez* and she is no stranger to these waters. She was built not far from here during World War II at Marinship in Sausalito, one of the instant shipyards that sprang up in the days after Pearl Harbor. The *Mission Santa Ynez* was one of those that slid down the ways into Richardson Bay half a century ago. She is one of the few of her generation and type left. Now a ship representing technology that the men aboard the *Mission Santa Ynez* could not have dreamed of has come to rest beside her.

In 1990 the United States Navy had nine nuclear-powered cruisers in commission. By late 1998 the last two, the *South Carolina* and the *California,* were preparing to be stricken. Rather than incur the extraordinary cost of refueling, the navy simply decommissioned them. Also in the early 1990s, large numbers of nuclear submarines began to decommission. Like the nuclear cruisers, the problems inherent in shutting down and securing a nuclear reactor, as well as in dealing with the fuel rods and radioactive waste aboard, precluded them from being placed in reserve and they were stricken as well. Some were old, others relatively young. The *Silversides* was only twenty-two, the *Drum* just twenty-three when stricken. But their targets, Soviet submarines and the large blue water surface fleet, were disappearing. Like their nuclear cruiser cousins, they were tremendously expensive to refuel. As ships became due for refueling they were instead discarded, extending even to the new *Los Angeles*-class boats. Five days before the October 1995 commissioning of the 688-boat *Columbia,* her sister ship *Omaha* was decommissioned and stricken. The *Baton Rouge* and *Cincinnati* had been stricken earlier in the year. None of these ships had yet reached their twentieth birthday and still had at least another decade of useful service ahead of them. More would follow: the *Indianapolis, Baltimore,* and *Phoenix.* These ships had served only about half of the time they had been designed for; nevertheless, decreasing budgets dictated their removal.

These nuclear-powered ships and submarines were towed to the Puget Sound Naval Shipyard to be dismantled through what was euphemistically called the "Nuclear Powered Ship and Submarine Recycling Program." In fact, it was a scrapping program, complicated by the presence of a nuclear reactor. The reactor was removed from the hull as a unit and taken away to Hanford, Washington for burial. The ship was then cut apart for scrap. The difference was that the navy scrapped the vessel rather than selling it to the highest bidder as in conventionally powered warships. When the Puget Sound Naval Shipyard began to overflow, other shipyards took on the six-month job of defueling the sub's nuclear reactor. The *Cincinnati* was defueled at Norfolk, her reactor removed and shipped to Hanford, then the two halves of the *Cincinnati* were welded back together to enable her to be towed to Puget Sound for scrapping. Lines of stricken submarines and a handful of cruisers awaiting this procedure have filled sections of the Puget Sound shipyard since the early 1990s, resembling, at a glance, the lines of moored hibernating ships that dotted the coastlines in the 1940s and 1950s.

The supercarriers, too, began to leave the fleet. Some had undergone the modern equivalent of the FRAM, called the SLEP (Service Life Extension Program). The carriers that underwent this were gutted, with new piping and electrical systems installed, catapult and arresting gear equipment replaced or overhauled, and the hull repaired where needed. Because of the cost, about $1 billion each, only four conventionally powered ships were modernized. The *Enterprise* was refueled and overhauled as well, a controversial move considering the extraordinary cost, about $2.5 billion for the thirty-year-old carrier. There were new carriers entering the fleet now: the *Abraham Lincoln, George Washington, John C. Stennis.* More were on order: the *United States* (to be renamed the *Harry S. Truman*) and another that would be named the *Ronald Reagan.* Thus the older, unmodernized carriers were taken out of service. The *Ranger* went to mothballs in 1993. She was not overhauled, but dehumidifying equipment and cathodic protection were installed at Bremerton. The *Saratoga* followed a year later. No mothball fleet for her, though. She was stricken. Her antennas were cut down and the tugs took the "Super Sara" away, the number sixty still proudly painted on her island as it had been throughout her nearly four decades in the fleet. The *America* was next, in 1996. Though relatively young, her builders had tried to cut construction costs by, among other things, using thinner plates for her hull than that used in other carriers. Her maintenance costs were higher, as was the potential cost of a SLEP overhaul, and she was retired instead (Polmar, *Ships and Aircraft,* 97). To Philadelphia and mothballs she went before being stricken in 1998. Like the battleships and carriers mothballed there in the past she was far too large for the back basin. Though the shipyard had closed, the navy still maintains a small, forgotten fleet there.

In fact, there are several forgotten fleets—or forgotten flotillas. These small groups of ships are still maintained in reserve category B. Still receiving the "highest practicable degree of maintenance." Still dehumidified. Still receiving cathodic protection. But still—perhaps now more than ever—subject to "personnel and funding limitations." They are, however, the ships "most urgently needed to augment the Active Fleet in an emergency." These ships are assigned to and are under the care of a Naval Inactive Ship Maintenance Facility. Currently, there are four remaining: Philadelphia, Pennsylvania; Bremerton, Washington; Portsmouth, Virginia; and Pearl Harbor, Hawaii.

Philadelphia is the home of the *America,* the stricken destroyers *Comte De Grasse, Conolly, John Rodgers,* and *Kidd,* a destroyer tender, a combat store ship, four oilers, a pair of frigates, and two amphibious cargo ships. Portsmouth (Norfolk) is the hibernation place for four more large destroyer tenders: the *Samuel Gompers, Yellowstone, Cape Cod,* and *Shenandoah.* These are highly valuable ships, hence their place in the reserve fleet, but they are crew intensive, each requiring over six hundred men and women. As the size of the combat fleet goes down,

*Fig. 72. The* New Jersey *again in reserve, next to the* Hornet. *Inactive Ship Maintenance Facility, Bremerton*

so too falls the number of auxiliaries. The submarine tender *L. Y. Spear* is there, too, as well as another amphibious cargo ship and two tank landing ships.

At Bremerton one can find a mix of the old and the new. The venerable *New Jersey* still is there and pictured while in mothballs for the fourth time, alongside the stricken *Hornet* (fig. 72). Nearby are the reserve fleet carriers *Ranger, Independence,* and the stricken missile destroyer *Callaghan,* named for Admiral Daniel Callaghan, killed aboard the cruiser *San Francisco* at Guadalcanal more than fifty years ago. At Pearl Harbor, which half a century ago could hardly have been thought of as a quiet retirement berthing for mothballed warships, lies another destroyer tender, the *Acadia,* a combat stores ship, the *Mars,* two amphibious cargo ships, and a half dozen tank landing ships.

There are also a quartet of fairly modern *Spruance*-class destroyers, the *Merrill, Leftwich, Harry W. Hill,* and *Ingersoll,* awaiting a tow to

*Fig. 73. The USS Clamp at Mare Island. Author's collection*

the breakers. Twenty-four of the thirty-one *Spruance*s have been modified with vertical missile launchers embedded in their deck just forward of the bridge. These carry Tomahawk missiles and ASROC, making them among the most powerful surface ships in the world. Certainly in terms of missiles their firepower dwarfs that of the *Iowa*s. The seven that have not been modified have been decommissioned, mothballed for a short time, and then stricken. To have modified them—with the Tomahawk-equipped *Arleigh Burke*s entering the fleet in significant numbers—could not be justified. Neither could they be retained in the active fleet. So these relatively modern, yet suddenly limited, destroyers were retired to scrap or to serve as spare parts bins for the active, remaining *Spruance*s. None of these decommissioned cans were over twenty when they decommissioned. Like many a ship of another era, they have gone while still relatively new, while still extremely capable. Like many a ship they were the victims of a rapidly changing world and rapidly advancing technology.

From the impressive combatants to the mundane auxiliary ships and craft, the mothball fleet contained examples of them all at one time or another. Pictured is an innocuous-looking vessel, appearing more like a fishing smack than a United States Navy ship. It is the *Clamp* (fig. 73). She was berthed at the Mare Island Naval Shipyard in the early 1990s shortly before it closed. How many of the thousands of commuters passing within view on State Route 37 each day know or care about the history behind her and the other relics there? Though the ships have long since been deleted from the rolls of the active and reserve fleets, they serve as poignant reminders of the forgotten fleet. Not all of the ships in the forgotten fleet were combat vessels or even big auxiliaries like tenders and oilers. The *Clamp* was commissioned in 1943 as a salvage vessel. She was built not far away from where she lay in the photograph at Mare Island, at the Basalt Rock Company in Napa. Despite both her noncombatant looks and role as one of the myriad of small, anonymous auxiliary vessels supporting the huge Pacific Fleet, she saw plenty of the war. When the marines waded ashore through a hail of gunfire at Tarawa, the *Clamp* was there, under air attack five different times while part of Mobile Service Squadron Four, a collection of repair ships, survey ships, fleet tugs, subchasers, net tenders, and minesweepers. When the Marshalls were secured, the *Clamp* was there, working in the surrounding waters, investigating some of the sunken Japanese vessels for both salvage and intelligence value. When the marines were fighting on the bloody island of Iwo Jima, the *Clamp* was offshore, ready to lend a hand to any ship in need of repair or salvage work. When the ill-fated cruiser *Indianapolis* became one of the many ships to be smashed by a kamikaze off Okinawa, the *Clamp* came alongside to render emergency aid to the cruiser that had but a few more months to live. When crippled LST-559 caught fire after being hit by a suicide bomber, the *Clamp* was there to put out her fires. After the war she was present at the first of the atomic bomb tests at Bikini Atoll, leading the other ships of the salvage force into the lagoon after the blast to extinguish fires and control damage on the radioactive target ships. But years before she made her contribution to the atomic age, when the fighting still raged and Bikini was an unknown bit of sand in the middle of the Pacific, she helped pull free a warship that had run aground. That warship to which she would be linked, then and later, was the fast minelayer *Tolman,* now rusting a few yards ahead of the *Clamp* after more than forty-five years.

The *Gearing*-class destroyer *Southerland,* as rust encrusted and ster-

*Fig. 74. The* Clamp, Tolman, *and* Southerland *with the destroyers* Stoddard, John
Paul Jones, *and* Richard S. Edwards. *Author's collection*

ile as the *Tolman* a few feet away, was a veteran of three shooting wars and years of Cold War patrol duty (fig. 74). The summer of 1945 saw her bombarding the Japanese mainland; five years later her guns supported the marine amphibious landing at Inchon. Five combat tours off Vietnam followed during the 1960s, alternating gunfire missions with plane-guard duty for the carriers on Yankee station. In all, *Southerland* earned nineteen battle stars, ten of them during Vietnam. She was stricken in 1981 and more than a decade later still lay at her moorings, her exploits long since forgotten by all but a handful of former crewman. World War II, Korea, and Vietnam were now the stuff of television documentaries, books in libraries, movies, and tales told by grandfathers, dads and uncles at family reunions.

The *Tolman*, *Southerland,* and the three destroyers tied up behind the *Clamp*—the *Stoddard, John Paul Jones,* and *Richard S. Edwards*—were of course much more than stricken derelict ships with their names bare-

*Fig. 75. The Tolman at sea in 1944. U.S. Naval Institute*

ly discernible from the highway bridge astern of them. They were alive once, their bows cleaving the waves as in the photograph of the *Tolman* undergoing sea trials off Bath, Maine in 1944 (fig. 75). Her propellers churn the Atlantic waters behind her, her hull, superstructure, and decks display the camouflage paint that marks her as a ship of war in time of war. The wind blows the salt spray back, drenching any crewman on her deck. Below is the hum, rattle, and vibration of her engines. She is in her element, a destroyer at high speed. For she once was a destroyer. She began life as an *Sumner*-class destroyer named for the captain of the *De Haven*, killed when Japanese dive bombers sank the destroyer in the Solomons in 1943. She was converted to a fast minelayer, trading her torpedo tubes and a few antiaircraft guns for the mine tracks on either side of her deck and the capability of carrying over a hundred mines. She was never used as a minelayer and in fact was decommissioned in San Diego in January 1947. For the next twenty-three years she remained buttoned up, preserved and forgotten. She disappeared from the navy list in 1970, yet still she floated a quarter of a century later at Mare Island next to the *Southerland*. Their guns had been removed long ago and the rust very nearly covers their names.

The *Clamp, Tolman,* and *Southerland* are but reminders of the huge mothball fleets that dotted the coastlines following World War II and in the years since in ever decreasing numbers. Similar fleets will, in all likelihood, never be seen again. Times have changed. The fleet itself has changed. By the end of the century there may be no more than 350 active ships in the fleet. Perhaps a tenth of that number will be in reserve. There will be no mass production of warships as there was in the years preceding and during World War II. Warships are too expensive now. Steel for hulls and for superstructures is still relatively inexpensive, but the electronics that are the heart and soul of the ship, indeed that will be the heart and soul of twenty-first century life, are enormously expensive and constantly changing. The world has changed too. The enemy is the terrorist, the emerging nation in what was once called the Third World, the small nation with the buying power to purchase or develop nuclear, biological, and chemical weapons of mass destruction. It is interesting to note, however, that in the Gulf War of 1991 there existed an inexorable push toward war that went on for five months: a classic military buildup; diplomatic intrigue, pressure, and messages that ultimately failed; a deadline that came and went. Merchant ships were taken from reserve, reactivated, and used to transport the huge American expeditionary force from the United States and from Europe to the Gulf. Conceivably, had the need arisen, warships, too, could have been pulled from reserve and sent to reinforce the fleet in the war zone. The destroyer tenders now in reserve would have been among the first to be reactivated. Possibly the battleships as well, or maybe a frigate to augment the war fleet or replace those sent to the Gulf. Perhaps such a situation will arise. One would hope not, of course. One would hope for a world in which a large active fleet, much less a mothball fleet, would be unneeded. But the past suggests that will not be the case any time soon.

Ships, even warships whose purpose is death, are picturesque in their own way. Some more than others. The salvage vessel rarely evokes the same sense of wonder and awe as does the carrier or battlewagon. The ships were majestic looking in war, serene and tranquil in peace, symmetrical in their orderly rows, the gun barrels, masts, and stacks all in a neat line. Only a hull number distinguished one from another. Each was unique, though only a careful examination would reveal that. But the ships, after all, were just ships. Inanimate objects. Welded and riveted steel. Pipes and cables. Wood planking. Oil. Gunpowder. It was the crew who made them come alive, the crew who truly separated those in mothballs from those in the fleet. The ships did not bleed, suffer homesickness, grieve for lost friends, yearn for letters from home, wonder if they would live another day. The sailors did. It was the sailors who came from all parts of the country to take these ships to sea, to take them out to support the fighting fleet, to take them in harm's way. It was the sailors who burned to death when the kamikazes rained down, who drowned when the torpedoes struck home. It was the sailor who made a ship what it was, gave it a personality.

The ships of the mothball fleet evoked a bit of nostalgia, too, a bit of Americana, a bit of the past as the years rolled by, as World War II, "the Big One," faded into memory. World War II was perhaps the defining event of the twentieth century. National boundaries, rivalries, and animosities are still issues resulting from that war. The United Nations, whose influence waxes and wanes, was a result of the alliance against the Axis powers. The United States entered the war as something less than a first-rate military power and was the preeminent global economic and military force when it ended. As the veterans of that war grew older, got on with their lives, they met in reunions and remembered the good old days, choking back tears as they spoke of buddies lost in

France, on Tinian, over Italy, on the *Birmingham,* on the *Hazelwood.* The long gray lines of silent ships at San Diego and Charleston and Boston and Green Cove Springs were a piece of that war, a reflection of the mighty force that had been assembled by the United States in its darkest and finest hour.

Was the mothball fleet a success? Most certainly it was. As an insurance policy alone it was an enormous bargain. Ships in reserve, fleets in ordinary had been an insurance policy through the years. In his first address to a joint session of Congress, President George Washington said, "To be prepared for war is one of the most effectual means of preserving peace." That was what the postwar mothball fleet was all about. About $213 million had been spent in the five years after the war on Operation Zipper. This was a tiny fraction of the replacement cost of those vessels that were then available to be reactivated when yet another war—and there is almost always another war—broke out. By April 1951, $120 million more, about 2.5 percent of the replacement cost, had been spent on reactivating nearly four hundred badly needed ships (Isenberg, *Shield of the Republic,* 223–224). Korea was the watershed, the vindication for the concept. Get the ships reactivated. Get them seaworthy. Put back the equipment that has been removed. Train a new crew. Get the ships to sea.

The fleet that had been recommissioned, that had been pulled from the vast numbers of combat and auxiliary ships in the navy's storehouse of hibernating ships, would have been the envy of any other country in the world in 1951: thirteen carriers, a pair of battleships, two heavy cruisers, almost eighty destroyers and destroyer escorts and more on the way. Those numbers did not come near to exhausting the supply of ships that could have been returned to duty had the need arisen, the cost been acceptable, and time allowed. Waiting in reserve, for instance, were eleven more battleships, sixty-six more cruisers of all types, hundreds of destroyers and destroyer escorts, escort and light carriers, fleet carriers not yet in the yard for modernization, ships that would never stir again: the *San Jacinto,* the *Pasadena,* the *Colorado,* the *Savo Island,* the *Bennion.*

Were there problems? Most certainly. Again shrinking budgets were at the core. Not all of the ships were put in storage as thoroughly prepared as had been intended. There were not enough sailors, was not enough money to do it properly every time. Machinery in need of repair was left as it was. Records were faulty or not kept at all. At one time a fifth of the reserve fleet was to be dry-docked and overhauled each year so that every five years each ship would have had a detailed examination. That did not always happen. Dry-docking and overhaul were expensive and time consuming. And the mothball fleet truly was the forgotten fleet. It was not a priority as the years went on, as the ships grew rustier, as the likelihood of reactivation for some of them grew more and more dim. Shipyard pier space and dry dock space were valuable and needed for ships returning from sea, needed for ships headed back out. The men of the reserve fleets tried their best. They did a magnificent job of maintenance working with what they had. Given enough money, which translated into proper preservation, maintenance, and frequent overhauls, the ships could have been preserved indefinitely. The reality was different, of course. Public opinion always changed. Public purse strings opened when Americans were in danger; when the danger had passed, the purse strings inevitably tightened again. Out of sight, out of mind. The mothball fleet was usually out of sight. Once the Korean War ended it was mostly out of mind. There were exceptions, of course. The battleships were the most notable. The *Salem* and *Des Moines* might have been reactivated after thirty years had Secretary Lehman not been focused on the heavier firepower of the battleships. Had suitable aircraft and enough funds been available, the *Oriskany* might have joined them. Some old cargo ships were pulled from reserve during Vietnam and the Gulf War, but by and large after Korea, ships went to, did not come from, the mothball fleet.

The idea of a mothball fleet was controversial, too. Hard to believe, given the relatively small amount of money expended over the years in maintaining these mobilization assets, but true. It was even controversial within the navy's ranks, where departments competed for scarce resources and budget dollars. Why, some asked, was so much money being spent on what was essentially an obsolete force, on ships that would never be needed again?

To the navy the ships on the NVR listed in category B or category C reserve were the ships in the custody of the Inactive Ships Maintenance Facilities and MarAd. To the public, they were the ships of the mothball fleet. To some, though, they were the other fleet, the fleet that once had a story to tell, as vivid as any of the ships still under way. They were a microcosm of American history, American naval lore. A look at them was a look at Lingayen Gulf, at Wonsan, at Yankee station, at Desert Storm. They were a symbol of readiness for the future, a visible reminder of the ships of the past corroding in the depths of Ironbottom Sound and the waters off the Ryukus. They were tangible evidence of the war-making potential of the United States. They were formidable and impotent at the same time. The mothball fleet was the great equalizer. The *Fall River* looked much the same as the *Pittsburgh,* the unknown *Nehenta Bay* the same as the *Guadalcanal.* The ghostly ships were no less real, no less a part of the story of the navy and of the United States simply because they were in the navy's storage closet. Ships that became part of a line of steel along a lonely pier. Ships that could be found in any book on naval history. Ships that could be found in very few. Or none. They were the ships of the forgotten fleet.

# Bibliography

## Primary Sources

### Archival sources

National Archives, Pacific Sierra Branch
Record Group 181
  General Correspondence 1956–1958, Pacific Reserve Fleet, Mare Island Group Commander.
  Volume II, Twelfth Naval District Command History, 1903–58.
  Boxes 1–33, Ship Files, Mare Island Naval Shipyard.
  Mare Island History Subject Files.
  Box 1058, Commandant Coded Administrative Records, 1835–56.

### Internet resources

Naval Vessel Register, www.nrv.navy.mil
U.S. Navy Homepage, www.navy.mil
The Current Status of the *Iowa*-Class Battleships, www.warships1.com/index3

### Other

Conduct of the Persian Gulf War, Final report to Congress, Title V of the Persian Gulf Conflict Supplemental Authorization and Personnel Benefits Act of 1991 (Public Law 102–25) April 1992.

## Secondary Sources

### Books and articles

Abbazia, Patrick. *Mr. Roosevelt's Navy: The Private War of the U.S. Atlantic Fleet, 1939–1942.* Annapolis, Md.: Naval Institute Press, 1975.
Adamson, Hans Christian, and George Francis Kosco. *Halsey's Typhoons: A First-hand Account of How Two Typhoons, More Powerful than the Japanese, Dealt*

*Death and Destruction to Admiral Halsey's Third Fleet.* New York: Crown, 1967.

Alden, John Doughty. *Flush Decks and Four Pipes.* Annapolis, Md.: U.S. Naval Institute, 1965.

Ballard, Robert D., with Rick Archbold. *The Lost Ships of Guadalcanal.* New York: Warner, 1993.

Bartholomew, C. A. *Mud, Muscles, and Miracles: Marine Salvage in the United States Navy.* Washington D.C.: Government Printing Office, 1990.

Blair, Clay. *Silent Victory: The U.S. Submarine War against Japan.* New York: Lippincott, 1975.

Boylan, Robert J. "Mothball Fleet/The Nation's Naval Attic." *Navy Magazine,* April 1971, 27–30.

Cagle, Malcolm, and Frank Albert Manson. *The Sea War in Korea.* Annapolis, Md.: U.S. Naval Institute, 1957.

Callaghan, P. M. "Bremerton's Mothball Fleet." *All Hands,* October 1981, 34–40.

Cutler, Thomas J. *The Battle of Leyte Gulf, 23–26 October 1944.* New York: Harper Collins, 1994.

Ewing, Steve. *American Cruisers of World War II: A Pictorial Encyclopedia.* Missoula, Mont.: Pictorial Histories, 1984.

———. *Memories and Memorials: The World War II U.S. Navy—Forty Years after Victory.* Missoula, Mont.: Pictorial Histories, 1986.

Fahey, James C. *Pacific War Diary: 1942–1945.* Boston: Houghton Mifflin, 1963.

Fluckey, Eugene. *Thunder Below! The USS* Barb *Revolutionizes Submarine Warfare in World War II.* Urbana: University of Illinois Press, 1992.

Freeden, Mel. "Scrapping Our World War II Navy." U.S. Naval Institute *Proceedings,* February 1979, 63–68.

Friedman, Norman. *U.S. Destroyers: An Illustrated Design History.* Annapolis, Md.: Naval Institute Press, 1982.

———. *U.S. Aircraft Carriers: An Illustrated Design History.* Annapolis, Md.: Naval Institute Press, 1983.

———. *U.S. Cruisers: An Illustrated Design History.* Annapolis, Md.: Naval Institute Press, 1984.

———. *U.S. Battleships: An Illustrated Design History.* Annapolis, Md.: Naval Institute Press, 1985.

Garzke, William H., Jr., and Robert O. Dulin Jr. *Battleships: United States Battleships, 1935–1992.* Annapolis, Md.: Naval Institute Press, 1995.

Goodhart, Philip. *Fifty Ships That Saved the World.* Garden City, N.Y.: Doubleday, 1965.

Grove, Eric. *Vanguard to Trident: British Naval Policy since World War II.* Annapolis, Md.: Naval Institute Press, 1987.

Hoffberg, Howard J. "The Effectiveness of the Inactivation Program." *Journal of the American Society of Naval Engineers* 64 (May 1952): 425–30.

Howarth, Stephen. *To Shining Sea: A History of the United States Navy 1775–1991.* New York: Random House, 1991.

———, ed. *Men of War. Great Naval Captains of World War II.* New York: St. Martin's, 1993.

Inglis, Thomas B. "The Mighty B." *Shipmate,* June 1945 (Fleet Issue).

Isenberg, Michael. *Shield of the Republic: The United States Navy in an Era of Cold War and Violent Peace 1945–1962* New York: St. Martin's, 1993.

Knight, Ralph. "Uncle Sam is Canning Warships." *The Saturday Evening Post*, 20 April 1946, 6.

Lavery, Brian. *Nelson's Navy: The Ships, Men, and Organization 1793–1815*. Annapolis, Md.: Naval Institute Press, 1989.

Lehman, John F. Jr. *Command of the Seas: Building the 600 Ship Navy*. New York: Charles Scribner's Sons, 1988.

Lemmon, Sue, with E. D. Wichels. *Sidewheelers to Nuclear Power: A Pictorial Essay Covering 123 Years at the Mare Island Naval Shipyard*. Annapolis, Md.: Leeward Publications, 1977.

Love, Robert W. Jr. *History of the U.S. Navy*, Vol. 1, *1775–1941*. Harrisburg, Pa.: Stackpole, 1992.

———. *History of the U.S. Navy*, Vol. 2, *1942–1991*. Harrisburg, Pa.: Stackpole, 1992.

Martin, J. M. "We Still Haven't Learned." U.S. Naval Institute *Proceedings*, July 1991, 64–68.

Martin, Tyrone G. *A Most Fortunate Ship: A Narrative History of Old Ironsides*. Annapolis, Md.: Naval Institute Press, 1997.

Miller, John Grider. *The Battle to Save the Houston October 1944 to March 1945*. Annapolis, Md.: Naval Institute Press, 1985.

Monsarrat, John. *Angel on the Yardarm: The Beginnings of Fleet Radar Defense and the Kamikaze Threat*. Newport, R.I.: Naval War College, 1985.

Mooney, James L., ed. *Dictionary of American Naval Fighting Ships*, 8 Vols. Washington, D.C.: Government Printing Office, 1959–91.

Morison, Samuel Eliot. *History of United States Naval Operations in World War II*. 15 Vols., Boston: Little, Brown, and Company, 1947–62.

Morison, Samuel L., and John Rowe. *The Ships and Aircraft of the U.S. Fleet*, 9th ed. Annapolis, Md.: Naval Institute Press, 1972.

Morison, Samuel L., and John Rowe. *The Ships and Aircraft of the U.S. Fleet*, 10th ed. Annapolis, Md.: Naval Institute Press, 1975.

Morse, C. S., and C. C. Bream. "The Activation of the USS New Jersey (BB-62) at the Philadelphia Naval Shipyard." *Naval Engineers Journal*, December 1968, 859–69.

Muir, Malcolm. *The Iowa Class Battleships. Iowa, New Jersey, Missouri, and Wisconsin*. New York: Sterling Press, 1991.

Newell, Gordon, and Allan E. Smith. *Mighty Mo: The USS Missouri—A Biography of the Last Battleship*. Seattle, Wash.: Superior, 1969.

Nichols, David, ed. *Ernie's War: The Best of Ernie Pyle's World War II Dispatches*. New York: Simon & Schuster, 1987.

O'Kane, Richard H. *Wahoo: The Patrols of America's Most Famous World War II Submarine*. Novato, Calif.: Presidio Press, 1987.

Pawlowski, Gareth L. *Flat-tops and Fledglings. A History of American Aircraft Carriers*. New York: Castle Books, 1971.

Phillips, Cabell. *The 1940s: Decade of Triumph and Trouble*. New York: Macmillan, 1975.

*Pictorial History of the Second World War; A Photographic Record of all Theaters of Action Chronologically Arranged*, Vol. 6, *Your Navy in Action*. New York: Wm. H. Wise, 1946.

Polmar, Norman. *The Naval Institute Guide to the Ships and Aircraft of the U.S. Fleet*. 12th ed. Annapolis, Md.: Naval Institute Press, 1981.

———. *The Naval Institute Guide to the Ships and Aircraft of the U.S. Fleet.* 13th ed. Annapolis, Md.: Naval Institute Press, 1984.

———. *The Naval Institute Guide to the Ships and Aircraft of the U.S. Fleet.* 14th ed. Annapolis, Md.: Naval Institute Press, 1987.

———. *The Naval Institute Guide to the Ships and Aircraft of the U.S. Fleet.* 15th ed. Annapolis, Md.: Naval Institute Press, 1993.

———. *The Naval Institute Guide to the Ships and Aircraft of the U.S. Fleet.* 16th ed. Annapolis, Md.: Naval Institute Press, 1997.

Prange, Gordon, with Donald M. Goldstein and Katherine V. Dillon. *December 7, 1941: The Day the Japanese Attacked Pearl Harbor.* New York: McGraw-Hill, 1988.

Preston, Antony. *Destroyers.* New York: Galahad Books, 1982.

Reynolds, Clark G. *The Fast Carriers: The Forging of an Air Navy.* New York: McGraw Hill, 1968.

Roberts, John. *The Aircraft Carrier* Intrepid: *Anatomy of the Ship.* Annapolis, Md.: Naval Institute Press, 1982.

Rodger, N. A. M. *The Safeguard of the Sea. A Naval History of Britain 660–1649.* New York: W. W. Norton, 1998.

Roscoe, Theodore. *United States Submarine Operations in World War II.* Annapolis, Md.: U.S. Naval Institute, 1949.

———. *United States Destroyer Operations in World War II.* Annapolis: U.S. Naval Institute, 1953.

Schofield, William. *Destroyers: Sixty Years.* New York: Bonanza Books, 1962.

Shaw, James C. "Commanding a Mothballer." U.S. Naval Institute *Proceedings,* February 1951, 161–67.

Sheehan, Donald H. ed. *This is America, My Country.* Vol. 2. New York: W. H. Wise, 1952.

Sigel, Clinton. "The Reserve Fleet." U.S. Naval Institute *Proceedings,* July 1951, 681–89.

Silverstone, Paul H. *U.S. Warships of World War II.* Garden City, N.Y.: Doubleday, 1968.

Stafford, Edward Peary. *The Big E: The Story of the USS Enterprise.* New York: Random House, 1962.

Steichen, Edward, ed. *U.S. Navy War Photographs: Pearl Harbor to Tokyo Bay.* New York: Crown, 1956.

Stillwell, Paul. *Air Raid Pearl Harbor: Recollections of a Day of Infamy.* Annapolis, Md.: Naval Institute Press, 1981.

———. *Battleship New Jersey: An Illustrated History.* Annapolis, Md.: Naval Institute Press, 1986.

———. *Battleship Missouri: An Illustrated History.* Annapolis, Md.: Naval Institute Press, 1996.

Sumrall, Robert F. *Sumner-Gearing-Class Destroyers: Their Design, Weapons, and Equipment.* Annapolis, Md.: Naval Institute Press, 1995.

Terzibaschitsch, Stefan. *Battleships of the U.S. Navy in World War II.* New York: Bonanza Books, 1979.

Urdahl, T. H., and E. R. Queer. "Dehumidification and the U.S. Navy 'Inactive Fleets.'" *Pacific Marine Review,* May 1946, 408–11.

van der Vat, Dan, with Christine van der Vat. *The Atlantic Campaign: World War II's Great Struggle at Sea.* New York: Harper & Row, 1988.

Wells, George. "The Importance of Controlled Humidity in Long Time Preservation." *Journal of the American Society of Naval Engineers* 60 (May 1948): 126–38.

Wheeler, Keith. *War Under the Pacific.* Vol. 6, *World War II.* Alexandria, Va.: Time-Life Books, 1980.

Y'Blood, William T. *Hunter-Killer: U.S. Escort Carriers in the Battle of the Atlantic.* Annapolis, Md.: Naval Institute Press, 1983.

———. *The Little Giants: U.S. Escort Carriers Against Japan.* Annapolis, Md.: Naval Institute Press, 1987.

# Index

# About the Author

Daniel Madsen was born just north of San Francisco in Sausalito, California, where Liberty ships and tankers were built during World War II. His interest in the navy was sparked when, at the age of nine, he watched the USS *New Jersey* silently glide beneath the Golden Gate Bridge, home from her Vietnam tour. From that date he collected books and articles about the navy, visited the ships on Fleet Week each year, and photographed the ships of the fleet whenever and wherever possible. He earned a bachelor's degree in communications and history from California State University, Sacramento, in 1983.

His interest and desire to write about the navy has never waned and *Forgotten Fleet* is his first book. He currently is researching and writing a narrative military history of the Persian Gulf War from his home in Kenwood, California.